Jewish
Meditation Practices
for Everyday Life

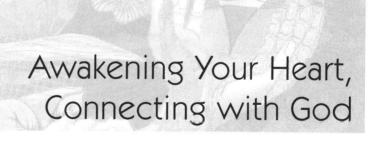

Awakening Your Heart,
Connecting with God

Rabbi Jeff Roth

For People of All Faiths, All Backgrounds

JEWISH LIGHTS Publishing

Woodstock, Vermont

Jewish Meditation Practices for Everyday Life:
Awakening Your Heart, Connecting with God

2009 Quality Paperback Edition, First Printing
© 2009 by Jeff Roth

Vipassana Meditation Guidelines by Sayadaw U-Janaka includes in its Preface the statement that "it was revised again by Bikkhu Pesala ... for free distribution."

Library of Congress Cataloging-in-Publication Data
Roth, Jeff.
 Jewish meditation practices for everyday life : awakening your heart, connecting with God / Jeff Roth.
    p. cm.
 Includes bibliographical references.
 ISBN-13: 978-1-58023-397-2 (quality pbk.)
 ISBN-10: 1-58023-397-X (quality pbk.)
 1. Meditation—Judaism. 2. Spiritual life—Judaism. I. Title.
 BM723.R65 2009
 296.7'2—dc22

                                                            2008055281

10 9 8 7 6 5 4 3 2 1

Manufactured in the United States of America
Cover art: Detail of "A Moment of the Divine," by Anita Rabinoff-Goldman, Pomegranate Judaica; www.pomegranatejudaica.com; (518) 768-2545. From the collection of Dr. Steve and Bonnie Cramer.

For People of All Faiths, All Backgrounds
Published by Jewish Lights Publishing
A Division of Longhill Partners, Inc.
Sunset Farm Offices, Route 4, P.O. Box 237
Woodstock, VT 05091
Tel: (802) 457-4000   Fax: (802) 457-4004
www.jewishlights.com

To my parents,
Alan *z'l* and Eunice Roth
I am blessed to have had parents who loved me
and gave me the space to seek out my own path.

Contents

Acknowledgments   ix
Introduction: Wake Up   1
Are You a Mystic?   3

1. **Waking Up in the Midst of Your Life**   7
   You Have All That You Need   7
   Choosing Your Thoughts   8
   The Beginning of My Own Journey to My Heart   9
   The Heron Who Thought He Was a Chicken   13
   Watch Out What You Wish For   14

2. **Beginning a Practice**   19
   Two Different Forms of Meditation:
      Concentration and Awareness   20
   Setting Your Intention to Experience the Divine   25
   Breathing and the Divine Presence   29
   Chanting the Divine Name   30
   Anchoring the Mind in the Here and Now   32
   The Importance of the Breath   33
   Helpful Exercises and Techniques   36

3. **The Nature of Mind**   41
   Limited Awareness versus Expanded Awareness   42
   Sensations, Feeling Tone, Mental Formations,
      and Perception   43
   The Reality of Pleasant and Unpleasant Sensations   44
   Who Can I Blame for My Problems?   46

Can You Trust Your Perceptions?   47

The Self-Serving Nature of Most Thoughts   48

Don't Believe Everything You Think about Yourself   51

Altered States and Mystical Experiences   57

Warnings for Potential Mystics   61

The Reward of Insights   63

Be Careful When You Speak Your Mind   65

The Annual Forty-Day Program of Purification   68

4. Making the Darkness Conscious   73

The Evil Inclination   75

The Serious and Beautiful Problem of
    Your Childish Consciousness   80

Getting a Handle on Your *Yetzer:*
    The Process of Naming   82

Just Grin and Bear It   86

Learn to Be with Hard Feelings   89

Working with the *Yetzer* by Cultivating Restraint   93

The Debilitating Nature of Doubt   95

5. Embracing the Divine   101

Everything Is God and Nothing but God   101

The Organic Model of the Divine   102

Socialized Meditation Practice   108

The Fourfold Nature of Divine Oneness   111

A Guided Meditation of Peak Experience   130

6. Prayer and Meditation   135

Cultivating Wholesome Mind States   136

Intention in Prayer versus Attachment to Results   138

Starting Your Contemplative Prayer Practice   139

Prayer Is a Ladder That Connects You and God   141

The Prayers   143

7. A Blessing Practice   163

Escaping from Egypt   163

Cultivating a Heart Full of Peace   164

Experience the Power of Giving Blessings   167

Be a Source of Blessing for All Beings   168

Using the Blessing Practice   169

A Guided Meditation for Experiencing Peace (Shalom)   171

A Guided Meditation for Experiencing Joy *(Simcha)*   172

A Guided Meditation for Experiencing
    Lovingkindness *(Chesed)*   173

A Guided Meditation for Experiencing
    Compassion *(Rahamim)*   173

Blessing All Beings   174

Sending Blessings to Difficult People   178

A Note on Keeping the Heart Open   180

Trying Not to Waste Any Blessings   180

Blessings on the Subway and at the Airport   181

A Special Note   182

8. *L'chayyim*—Into Life   185

The Benefits of Regular Meditation Retreats   185

Using the Sabbath as a Day of Deep Practice   187

Creating a Well-Rounded Spiritual Life   188

Torah—Recognizing the Truth as the Path to Acquiring
    Wisdom   188

Practice Awareness All the Time   189

Practicing Eating Meditation   190

As You Walketh by the Way   192

It Is Very Hard to Do This Work Alone   194

Working with Pain   195

Avodah—Cultivating an Open Heart   198

Cultivating Generosity   199

The Result of Practice: Deeds of
Lovingkindness—*Gemilut Hasadim*   201
No End, Just a Journey   202

Appendix A: Psalm 145   205
Appendix B: Resources for Further Learning   207
Notes   209

Acknowledgments

Whatever wisdom and heartfelt sharing I have managed to write down in this book were all the result of some special teachers I have had the merit to encounter. I learned most of the material I refer to in the context of the primary relationships of my life. I am grateful to my partner, Rabbi Joanna Katz, who is on this journey of waking up alongside me. We learn and teach the art of paying attention to life together. My children, Esther, Jesse, and Suri, listened to and inspired many of the stories. It is for them, and for all spouses and children, that I pray we all learn to see our lives more clearly.

I am thankful for my first college roommate, Buddy Glick, who taught me to seek the heart and opened my eyes to the world. Ateret Cohen trained me to be a Jewish camp director. She showed me that Jewish learning could be accessible and exciting. Rabbi Arthur Waskow connected the dots for me between Judaism and social justice. Meeting Rabbi Zalman Schachter-Shalomi helped me reframe my life as a spiritual journey. He opened the doors to the world of prayer and connection to the Divine. This book is filled with his inspiration.

My involvement in meditation began with learning many of these practices from Sylvia Boorstein. She took me on as a special student, inviting me to teach with her regularly. The depth of her insights into daily life as practice and her skills as a teacher warrant my sharing of whatever good comes from this book with her. My colleague Rabbi Sheila Peltz-Weinberg has been a constant support as we apprenticed together and joined an advanced study group in meditation. Norman Fischer has been instrumental in expanding my awareness as a coteacher. I was fortunate to develop the material I share in this book by teaching numerous retreats with others besides Sylvia, Sheila,

Norman, Zalman, and Joanna, including Rabbi David and Shoshana Cooper and Rabbi Alan Lew *z'l*. Other meditation teachers I have worked with directly include Jack Kornfield, Guy Armstrong, Carol Wilson, Joseph Goldstein, Sayadaw U-Janaka, and Ajahn Samedho. It almost goes without saying that the students who have sat on the meditation retreats I have facilitated are my real partners in this work. The intimacy they allow in sharing the deepest yearnings of their souls is what keeps my practice alive.

This book was an idea in my mind with some fragmentary notes until Bert Shaw urged me to begin writing it in earnest. This is only one example of the many ways he has helped me grow. Special thanks go to my editor, Jurgen Mollers. As a fellow student of meditation, he has reflected with me about every idea and every word of this manuscript. His suggestions for additions as well as cuts made a far better book. He brought out the best in me through his careful listening and reflecting on the material I wanted to present. His appreciation for the manuscript was a great gift. He was aided in his editing work by Bill Scheinman and Kristen Burns. Special thanks to Stuart M. Matlins, publisher, Michaela Powell, Emily Wichland, and Kate Treworgy at Jewish Lights Publishing for their help in publishing this book.

A note about translations from the Torah: Except in a few cases where I offer my own translation, most quoted English translations are from Everett Fox's *The Five Books of Moses: Genesis, Exodus, Leviticus, Numbers, and Deuteronomy* (New York: Schocken Books, 1983).

Introduction: Wake Up

Wake up, wake up! Your light, (which you are looking for) is already here. So rise up and shine with it! Awaken, awaken and express it in song. The glory of the Holy (Wholly) One is revealed upon you.

This is a book about waking up. More than that, it is about waking up in order to see clearly our own lives and the world around us. Perhaps most fundamentally, this is a book about our own happiness and the happiness of all other beings. I was twenty-nine years old and living in Portland, Oregon, when I first met Rabbi Zalman Schachter-Shalomi. At the time, I was a member of a small Jewish community that came together to celebrate the Sabbath and Jewish holy days. My interest in Judaism was linked to the prophetic traditions and its pursuit of social justice, and our group promoted progressive causes within the wider Jewish community. By that time in my life I was already yearning for a direct experience of the Divine, an experience of awakening. I wanted to unite my activism with insights grounded in true and vital spiritual experience. But the Jewish prayer services I attended at the time gave me little spiritual insight. There was no sophisticated approach to the meaning or process of the prayers, nor was there a theology that made sense to me about the Being to whom we were praying. One of the organizers of our group had studied with Rabbi Zalman Schachter-Shalomi, and at his suggestion we brought Reb Zalman to Portland to lead a weekend retreat. My contact with Reb Zalman was a key turning point in my life.

On this retreat, Reb Zalman introduced us to techniques and ideas that awakened in me the spiritual side of Judaism for the first time. As an inheritor of the Jewish mystical tradition, he exposed me to ideas about the nature of the soul that were never mentioned in the Reform and Conservative synagogues I had attended while growing up. Reb

Zalman had studied and practiced the mystical teachings of all the major religious traditions. While garbed in Jewish metaphors, his teaching spoke of universal truth from a spiritual perspective that profoundly addressed the nature and purpose of the human experience.

My life's direction changed forever after that retreat. I, too, wanted a vibrant spiritual life with roots in the wisdom of Judaism that didn't ignore the deepest truths of other faiths and secular teachings. I, too, wanted a Judaism that embodied universal values and a concern about the fate of all beings. I met many others on that retreat who also were open to evolving a new Jewish experience that included whatever was truly valuable and helpful in opening the heart and mind and in deepening our commitment to fixing our world.

As Reb Zalman gave us his teachings, it was as if a door had opened in my mind, and through that door was a body of spiritual wisdom I had yet to encounter. I realized that the task of acquiring that wisdom could only be accomplished through contact with teachers who themselves had learned and integrated that wisdom. As a result, I decided to enroll at the Reconstructionist Rabbinical College in Philadelphia, where Reb Zalman and another teacher who had already been tremendously influential for me, Rabbi Arthur Waskow, were on the faculty. Rabbi Waskow was the epitome of someone whose practice of Judaism was seamlessly united to a life of political activism. Zalman and Arthur were both working closely together in renewing Jewish life. After the Holocaust, much of the Jewish experience was focused only on survival, without a broader spiritual vision. But now, meeting teachers like Arthur and Zalman, I found a new vibrancy and relevance to Judaism. I clearly remember the feeling that I was starting a spiritual journey that would take me beyond what I had ever imagined for myself. I had always had a yearning for meaning, but it was only now that I could feel an inkling of where that yearning would lead me.

By a stroke of good luck, when I arrived in Philadelphia I learned that Reb Zalman's B'nai Or Religious Fellowship was looking for an executive director. I applied for the position and, because of my administrative background and personal interest, I got the job. In my years at B'nai Or, I traveled extensively with Reb Zalman. These journeys brought us into contact with various spiritual teachers, including Ram Dass, Jack Kornfield, Jean Houston, Sheikh Muzaffer, Brother David Steindl-Rast, and many others. These contacts offered the opportunity to explore vital spiritual practices from other traditions and to integrate them with the teachings of our Jewish Sages, especially from the mystical and Hasidic traditions. I saw firsthand how this synthesis could be used to enhance and deepen a contemporary approach to Jewish life and spirituality.

When I completed my rabbinical studies, I moved to upstate New York, where my wife, Rabbi Joanna Katz, and I founded the very first Jewish spiritual retreat center, Elat Chayyim. At Elat Chayyim, we were blessed to witness thousands of Jewish seekers experience this new approach to Jewish life and we continued to develop an ongoing synthesis of Jewish practice with the best teachings available in other spiritual traditions. Over the years, we were fortunate enough to have a significant number of teachers share their practices with us—practices that, at the time, were not widely used in Jewish life, such as yoga, tai chi, and meditation. It was in this context that I met Sylvia Boorstein, a Buddhist meditation teacher who also upheld a serious Jewish practice. Sylvia inspired me to attend my first three-day silent meditation retreat (a retreat for rabbis), followed a few months later by an eight-day retreat at Spirit Rock, a mindfulness meditation center in Marin County, California. The practices I learned on these retreats soon became a key element in my spiritual practice.

Are You a Mystic?

Mysticism is generally defined as a direct experience of the Divine. I taught various components of Jewish mysticism for ten years before I was exposed to a serious meditation practice. It was through my experience of mindfulness meditation retreats that I understood, from the inside, what mystics are looking for. I found meditation to be the most direct path to the mystical component of spiritual experience that I had been seeking. It allowed for what Reb Zalman called "domesticating peak experiences." There had been many small moments of awakening in my journey before I began practicing meditation, but working with the practices described in this book allowed me to deepen my own understanding through direct experience of what the Jewish mystics were teaching. The insights they describe are part of our inalienable rights as sentient beings.

When we awaken to our own light, it becomes possible to develop real wisdom about our life. As wisdom allows us to see clearly, our hearts break open with compassion for the struggles of our own lives and the lives of all beings. Awakened with wisdom and compassion, we are impelled to live our lives with kindness, and we are led to do whatever we can to repair the brokenness of our world.

How blessed I have been to have had the privilege of traveling around the world with Reb Zalman! How blessed I have been to meet people with a similar yearning for spiritual awakening as myself! Most likely you are such a person. You may not know exactly what wisdom to seek, but you will recognize it when you encounter pieces of it. Sometimes we can get it just by hearing the sage words of our teachers and friends. And sometimes we have to wait to see it manifest in our own lives. It is an exciting journey, and I invite you to share it with me.

A story Reb Zalman frequently told as we traveled "the circuit" involved his youngest daughter, Shalvi, who was about five years old at the time. One morning, Shalvi woke up and said to him, "*Abba* [father], you know how when you are asleep and dreaming, it seems so real, and then you wake up and realize it was just a dream? When you are awake, can you wake up that much more and realize that *this* is just a dream?"

Initially, this story didn't leave much of an impression on me. Perhaps it was a bit like trying to describe the color red to a blind person. But after I began a serious meditation practice, the story took on importance for me. I think I now understand Shalvi's question, and the answer is a resounding "YES!" Yes, we *can* wake up; we *can* open to a place of awareness that sees and understands life much more clearly than during our normal level of consciousness.

Most of the time, however, it seems that we are sleepwalking. We go through the motions of our lives on a kind of automatic pilot, flying the same route over and over. The problem is that when someone is sleepwalking, serious accidents can occur. It's like the warning they give for certain medications that may cause sleepiness: "Avoid operating heavy machinery while using this product." In our lives, we are indeed operating heavy machinery, and because of our "sleepwalking," we often get seriously hurt by ourselves and others. When we live our lives as sleepwalkers, our fate is as uncontrollable as our dreams. Sometimes we have good days (good dreams) and sometimes we have bad days (bad dreams). But only when we are awake and can see clearly are we able to respond rather than react to life's challenges. Responding from wakefulness means to act with wisdom and compassion. This book is about using contemporary Jewish spiritual practices to bring us to a heart of wisdom. As it says in the Psalms, "Teach us to count [or treasure] each day [moment] that we may be brought to a heart of wisdom" (90:12). I call this heart of wisdom—bathed in compassion, ready to act kindly—the awakened heart.

With this book, I hope to offer a testimony to the idea that all of us are capable of cultivating this heart of wisdom, gradually making it our default way of being. When we see all things with an awakened heart, the world will, in turn, inspire us to love and care for it. Walking a contemporary Jewish spiritual path is a journey toward this awakening.

Let us start the journey.

1
Waking Up in
the Midst of Your Life

A few weeks after I started writing this book, I happened to be in the business offices of my father-in-law, Simon Katz. Pouring myself a cup of water, I noticed a mug on the shelf that had some Hebrew letters on it. They spelled a Yiddish proverb: life is like a dream, but don't wake me up. I was intrigued. Yiddish proverbs often use humor and a somewhat dark perspective to speak about the human condition. Being in the middle of writing a "Jewish" book on waking up, I was wondering what the proverb might mean. Was it claiming that being asleep and dreaming was better than waking up to a world of harsh realities? Was it saying that living a dream was the best possible life? Or was it claiming that life itself was a dream, and if you wanted to stay alive you had to keep dreaming—even if life is like a nightmare. In this book I want to describe another possibility: that of waking up from the dreamlike nature of life into the reality of life, of being fully awake while being in the midst of life.

You Have All That You Need

I believe that each of us has moments in our lives that can lead to this understanding. Our own experiences—whatever they may be—are there for our awakening. You may think that your life is boring or uneventful, but if you know what to look for and how to do that looking, you will find that your life is actually well tailored: it's a perfect fit for you. In fact, the life you are living is the only story that will give you everything you uniquely need in your journey. Everyone enjoys hearing good stories about someone else's life. In the current generation of Jewish seekers, those interested in the spiritual life are often drawn to Hasidic tales, which can offer surprising psychological and spiritual insights. Theologian Rabbi Abraham Joshua Heschel used to say that a Hasidic tale is a story in which the soul surprises the mind. But only by looking into our own lives and into our own story will we find the material for our own awakening.

Reb Zalman wrote a book called *The Hasidic Tales of Reb Zalman*. It contains a number of true stories about incidents that occurred with his actual students and friends. Some people thought it was a bit egotistical for Reb Zalman to write this book because Hasidic tales are usually about the great rebbes (spiritual heads) of the various Hasidic lineages. Reb Zalman's manuscript was eventually reworked by Howard Schwartz and published under the title, *The Dream Assembly: Tales of Rabbi Zalman Schachter-Shalomi*. Schwartz cast the stories as the tales of a rebbe who had lived in Poland in the 1700s. I believe this completely missed one of the points Reb Zalman had in writing the book. Sure, there were some interesting stories in the same genre as other Hasidic tales, but Reb Zalman's bigger point was that these tales didn't just happen to dead rebbes, hundreds of years ago; these stories are happening all the time, and we are all characters in them.

Choosing Your Thoughts

I remember such a moment in my own life that could be its own Hasidic tale. One day as I was driving in my car, I tuned in to National Public Radio (NPR). The voice that was speaking was immediately familiar to me: it was Lionel Aldridge, a linebacker from the championship Green Bay Packer football teams of the 1960s. Growing up in Milwaukee, Wisconsin, I had been an avid Packer fan and knew of Aldridge, so it was interesting to hear him on the radio some twenty-five years later.

I was surprised to learn that during the 1970s Aldridge began suffering from mental illness, gradually becoming more and more delusional, psychotic, and paranoid. His mental state even deteriorated to the point that he lived on the streets, homeless for a number of years. Eventually, friends arranged for him to receive treatment for his illness. On medication, his hallucinations disappeared, and, after some time, he was able to live free of the most distressing symptoms of his illness.

Aldridge told the interviewer that he was able to remain mentally stable on a very low dosage of antipsychotic medications and spoke of his new role as a spokesperson for efforts to help others with similar afflictions. When the NPR interviewer asked him if he still had to deal with delusions and paranoia, his answer simply astounded me. He said that a strange thought would still begin in his mind on occasion, but now he was able to recognize it and simply choose not to think it. He would *choose not to think the thought.* How odd! My jaw dropped in amazement. I had never considered that a person could choose not to think a thought, that we may have that measure of control over our thoughts. Even more important, for the first time in my life, I recognized the possibility that there was a separation between who I am and the contents of my thoughts.

In retrospect, Aldridge's statement does not feel quite as remarkable to me as it did back then; after all, to some degree, we make decisions all the time about whether to think about or ignore certain parts of life. At the time I heard that interview, however, something clicked in me and opened up a whole new understanding.

The Beginning of My Own Journey to My Heart

Every summer since my wife and I founded Elat Chayyim, our retreat center, we have asked for a group of volunteers to help staff our summer program. This internship experience begins with a weeklong training program to develop community and to orient the volunteers to the program they are helping to facilitate. Being an explicitly Jewish spiritual retreat center, we ask individuals—teachers included—to share the course of the spiritual journey that brought them to this place. When I relate the story of my own spiritual journey, I usually begin with my first semester in college.

I grew up in a suburb of Milwaukee. In many ways, my childhood was the best of the suburban dream. I had loving parents, good schools, and a safe neighborhood. My home football team, the Green Bay Packers, was winning the first few Super Bowls. And there were always enough kids to play capture the flag on summer nights. I lived a very sheltered childhood, and I have tremendous appreciation for the love, support, and safety I experienced growing up. Yet, it was necessary for me to move out of that setting to allow another level of growth to occur.

I started college at the University of Wisconsin (UW) in the fall of 1970. The spring of 1970 had been one of tremendous upheaval for the country, and especially for many college campuses. The Vietnam War had driven a wedge into the psyche of the country. Students had been tragically killed at Kent State in Ohio that May. My older sister, Estelle, was a senior at UW during that spring, and the university had been shut down for a few months leading into the summer because of political turmoil. The campus was a hotbed for radical activism. My sister and her classmates never even finished their semester, but they all graduated nonetheless. In August of 1970, the army math research center at UW was blown up in an antiwar protest and a physics researcher was killed. This was one of the most violent protest events of that period.

When I arrived on campus in September, I had very little understanding about the war in Vietnam. My family was not politically active, and I don't remember much about my sense of the war other than it had something to do with a "domino effect" and the need to protect our country from communism. Political protest was a big fact of life at UW that fall, and it was impossible to ignore, but I was experiencing my first extended period away from my home, and my major focus was on how to live on my own and juggle classes and a social life. Perhaps I never would have focused more on the war in Vietnam if not for my roommate, Buddy Glick. Buddy was one of the most wonderful people I had ever met. He was loving, gentle, funny, bright, and artistic, and he knew things about the world I had never considered. In terms of my own growth, the most important thing about Buddy was that he was in touch with his feelings. On more than a few occasions, I would return to my dorm room to find Buddy crying over the war in Vietnam. I was so moved that he could feel this passionately about something happening halfway around the world, when the only thing I could remember ever being that passionate about was basketball. Through my friendship with Buddy, I came to the realization that I wanted to get in touch with my own feelings.

As a kid, I was always drawn to the character of Mr. Spock on the science fiction television show *Star Trek*. One of the cast of adventurers on the Starship Enterprise, Mr. Spock was a science officer who came from the planet Vulcan. Besides having pointed ears, the most important feature about Vulcans was that they were known as being totally logical in their views about life, having eliminated emotions, which they viewed as unwholesome.

Mr. Spock was actually the child of a Vulcan father and a mother from Earth. His character was always evaluating behaviors as either logical or illogical. His counterpoint was the ship's surgeon, Dr. McCoy, called "Bones," who was quite an emotional person, even with his scientific training. The ship's captain, James Kirk, played the balance point for these two poles of human behavior. I don't think I was conscious at the time of why Mr. Spock might have been my favorite character as a child. When, years later, the thought occurred to me that I needed to get in touch with my emotions, I remembered my affinity for Mr. Spock and thought, "I can't believe he was my ideal!" It was a big moment of awakening.

Of course, the really interesting thing about Mr. Spock was his own inner conflict about logic versus feelings—a product of his inter-species heritage. Through its cast of characters, *Star Trek* looked at the conflicts that exist inside all of us —between our desires and our impulses on the one hand, and our rational or logical mind on the other. The Vulcan method of rooting out emotion in order to live more ethically is certainly one way of dealing with the problems of the unruly heart and mind. In retrospect, my affinity for Mr. Spock may have reflected an internal need to harmonize these polarizing forces within myself. The path of awakening that I will describe in this book, however, is a quite different approach to facing some of the same questions.

During college, I began to explore my emotions through a variety of methods, including majoring in psychology and seeking counseling from several psychotherapists. But the real turning point in reaching my goal of getting to know my emotions came over twenty years after the start of my quest, when I began my meditation practice. When I lead retreats, I usually introduce this topic by saying that meditation has helped me in what I call my "remedial emotional education."

Even though I had been working on accessing my emotions for more than two decades by the time I began a serious meditation practice, I still had little sophistication in connecting to and differentiating various emotional states. I believe this was not from a lack of effort but from a defense learned in childhood that helped me avoid painful feelings by staying focused in thinking and analyzing. When my therapist would ask me how I *felt* rather than what I thought about whatever topic we were discussing, the best I could come up with was, "I feel bad," or, "I feel good." However, when I learned to meditate using the techniques I will share with you in this book, I began to pay attention to the sensations within my body. In following these sensations, I was paying attention to how emotions *feel,* not thinking about emotions. Along with this new perspective came some quieting of my mind. In my experience, therapy became far more effective after I started to meditate. Because meditation allowed me to "touch" my emotions, I had something worth talking about in therapy.

Years after I was a psychology major in college, I heard the following funny story on a meditation retreat. A famous Eastern meditation teacher was once lecturing in the United States. The hotel where he was staying happened to be hosting a convention of psychologists. He asked his escorts to tell him what it was that psychologists study. They told him that psychologists study the workings of the mind. The meditation master asked if they meditated. When told that they did not, he replied, "Is that ethical?" In my own experience, it is true that most of what I now understand about the workings of the mind comes from my own meditation practice.

The emotional awakening that began during my first college year also led me to see how interconnected the world is. What was happening in Vietnam was directly connected to life in the United States. This was true not only of the draft but also of the fact that young Americans like me were being sent to fight. The entire basis of the conflict reflected competing world value systems. I also understood for the first time that the privilege I had experienced while growing up was in some way linked to a worldwide system that results in the disadvantage of other people. I am not trying to oversimplify what are no doubt complex causal relationships, but rather wish to emphasize that everything happening in one part of the world affects the entire world. In social work graduate school they called this idea *systems theory*. This interconnectedness is a big part of what I now mean when I talk or think about God. The origin of this understanding started for me during my early college days.

The Heron Who Thought He Was a Chicken

One day I was driving with my daughter Esther, who was eight years old at the time, and told her the following teaching tale. There were once two children who lived on a farm. They loved wandering around in the beautiful country setting and observing the animal life. Having grown up on a farm, they understood a lot about the habits of many different creatures and were always interested in learning new things. One day while they were out playing and exploring, they spotted a great blue heron flying in the sky. They had seen this bird a few times before and decided to follow it. After a few minutes of pursuit, they saw her land on a nest. The two sat down and waited for her to fly away. When she finally did, they carefully went over and discovered an egg in the nest. They were very excited, as they loved watching the process of eggs hatching. Every day they would go back to the nest, anxiously awaiting the arrival of the baby heron.

One morning, however, they noticed that the mother heron was gone longer than usual. She had never left the nest for more than twenty minutes, and now more than an hour had already passed. Finally, they were convinced that the mother was not returning. Out of concern for the unborn heron, they carefully took the egg out of the nest and carried it back to their farm. When they got there, they placed it in the nest of a hen. The hen sat on this egg until it hatched. The baby heron bonded with the hen as though she was its mother and followed her around the barnyard and learned to peck at food like other chickens. It grew up thinking it was a chicken. One day, the now grown heron was in the barnyard when it saw a great shadow sweeping the ground. It looked up in the sky and saw a great blue heron. It was the first time it had seen such a bird, and it felt a slight stirring in its soul. But soon it returned to pecking for food, living its life as if it was a chicken.

I understood the story to be about each one of us. We all come into this life with tremendous potential. Because of the various things we experience, we tend to shut down to much of that potential and live limited lives with a limited point of view. There are many traditional stories in which a child of the king is stolen or somehow lost at birth. The king in these stories is a metaphor for God. The lost child represents each of us and the tragedy of not recognizing our true origin. Each story relates some teaching about this tragedy, sometimes pointing out the way home. But many of us never find a way home. Waking up means realizing our birthright and seeing our true magnificence as beings.

However, when I asked Esther what she thought the story meant, she revealed a very different understanding. She said that the story meant that the young heron was happy being a chicken. I thought this was a great answer, and one in which I took a lot of comfort. It made me feel that she must be happy in her life if that was how she heard this story. In addition, her take on the story pointed to something else: even if we see clearly, we don't necessarily need to change our whole life around. It is possible to be happy right here in the barnyard. Waking up is not necessarily about seeing the world entirely differently. To wake up makes a huge difference in how we respond to what we see, but it doesn't need to mean that we will transform into the most beautiful creature soaring in the heavens. In fact, striving to be unique and special, not to mention rich and famous, can leave us quite unhappy—whether or not we meet our goals. Not understanding the nature of our desires is what ultimately allows them to eat us up, as the next story illustrates.

Watch Out What You Wish For

There was once a man who sought fame and fortune. He specifically decided to make his reputation as a spiritual teacher. He began by traveling from retreat to retreat, from ashrams to monasteries. He checked out all the spiritual traditions, old and new. But as the years went by, he became more and more unhappy. He was no closer to his goal of being a great teacher and had become quite depressed.

One day as he was on his way to a gathering, he found himself in the middle of a beautiful forest. He sat down under a magnificent tree and began to reflect on where his lustful quest had taken him. He knew that he was miserable, and decided right in that moment to give up his pursuit. He saw that his motivation was not a wholesome one. In coming to this realization, he felt a great moment of ease and expansiveness. He began to look around at the beautiful setting in which he found himself. In his drive for fame he had not had the presence of mind to experience the beauty already available to him. Now, he marveled at the magnificence around him. He saw the rich hues of many colors. His heart melted as he saw a chipmunk pop its head out of a hole. Even the fly landing on his hand provided a brilliant tingle through his body.

What he didn't realize was that this was not just any old tree that he had sat down under. It was a magic tree that had the power to make his dreams come true. For hours, he sat peacefully under this tree. Then he thought to himself, "This is a beautiful place. Wouldn't it be great if I could just live here forever?" No sooner had he thought this than a house appeared in a clearing not far from the tree. "Wow!" he thought. "Now I can live here." He sat happily a while longer and then began to get hungry. "Wouldn't it be great to have a bite to eat?" he thought. And instantly a table appeared in front of the house, filled with his favorite foods. His mouth began to water as he thought how nice it would be to have someone to serve him the food. Just then a servant came out of the house and piled a tray with the food and brought it over to him. He expressed his thanks and enjoyed the meal. Once again he was feeling full of pleasure. He thought that this was the perfect situation. "All I need now is a partner to share this life with me." As you might expect, the door of the house opened and out came the perfect gendered person for him, and he instantly fell in love.

The man began thinking to himself that this was a strange set of occurrences. The thought entered his mind that perhaps all of these experiences had to do with the tree he was sitting under. "What if it is a magic tree?" he thought. "What if there is a demon in this tree?" Suddenly, a demon jumped out of the tree and landed in front of him. Frightened beyond belief, he thought, "What if it eats me up?" And it did.

And that is where the story ends.

I think that this is a "true" story, with many layers. Seeing through unwholesome motivations and letting go of them allows for a great sense of ease and peace. Letting go does help us to be in the moment and to appreciate what we have at hand. But this insight alone does not provide for an understanding of the deep connections between our mental states and the reality they create. Sooner or later we get hungry again, and because we live in a physical body, we can't avoid that hunger. New desires arise and, even if they all are magically fulfilled, new doubts, fears, and other negative thoughts fill our minds. Ignorance of the very nature in which our minds work lets these negative thoughts create their own reality—a reality that will ultimately swallow us up. For many people in our consumerist society, if we simply think of something we want, we can probably have it. We are encouraged to want things, and the more we get the more we want. In the end, we get swallowed up by our desires and our fears. Most of us need tools to change this tragic way of thinking.

I remember a two-week silent meditation retreat I took a couple of years ago. I was on my way to the dining room from the meditation hall when I noticed that I started to feel a bit anxious. This surprised me, since there was nothing particularly troubling going on and I was appreciating the way the retreat had gone so far. I immediately thought that I must be doing something wrong. On the retreat, I was taught to pay constant attention to my body, so I started focusing on the physical sensations associated with the anxiety and realized that it originated in the pit of my stomach. It felt purely physical, not emotional. Seeing that clearly, I had a sudden insight into the connection I had made that "when I feel bad, I am bad." I had identified with the physical sensation, taking it to be "me." Without thinking about it, a simple bodily sensation had become a sign of my own inadequacy, summed up by the phrase, "I must be doing something wrong." It was liberating for me to see that unpleasant things can and do arise without us feeling like we are doing anything wrong.

In subsequent years, I found this insight to be helpful in different ways. My father and brother both died at relatively young ages from heart attacks. As a precaution after my brother's death, I began taking a daily aspirin at the advice of my doctor. I did this for about five years. During that time, whenever I went on a meditation retreat, I would notice a bit of a nervous stomach. It did not have a big impact on the retreat experience and was not so prominent in my consciousness. I thought that it might be from trying too hard to maintain constant awareness. I thought that perhaps I was getting anxious because of my striving. It even struck me as humorous that meditating could make me a little stressed out.

After about five years, I went on a longer retreat with a very demanding teacher. On that retreat, the pain in my stomach became much more noticeable than ever before. I assumed it must be related to my changed eating pattern, since I eat very moderately on retreats and sometimes lose three or four pounds per week. After this retreat ended, some of the stomach discomfort continued. It was bothersome enough that I went to see my doctor. Even before the appointment, I was thinking about my stomach and the connection to meditation retreats and I realized that the first time I noticed this sensation came around the time I began taking my daily aspirin. I had always known that there could be a connection between aspirin use and stomach irritation, but I had never realized that my stomach ailment could be a physical and not an emotional symptom. For years, I had been experiencing a very low level of what I assumed was anxiety connected with stress of work, relationship, family, and all the other demanding areas in life. I stopped taking aspirin, started a course of antacid instead, and after a month or so my stomach pain disappeared. In fact, I felt altogether better than I had for quite a while. How often we suffer unnecessarily if we don't pause to take a deep look at our own patterns.

If you work with the practices in this book, I believe you will be able to see for yourself that it is possible to see through your habitual patterns of thinking and behaving and gain instead a deeper understanding of your own life and the lives of those around you. Things are not simply the way they may seem on the surface. Our conditioning, however, often leads us to inaccurate conclusions about the truth of things. One of the deepest facets of this mistaken view is our over-identification with our own thoughts. We become trapped in our smallest sense of self. With only a bit of careful attention, and by using some of the tools offered in this book, I believe we can begin to see for ourselves the nature of our own conditioning. With that seeing, we can learn to work wisely with that nature and, in some ways, become liberated from it.

As we progress in cultivating our moment-to-moment awareness, a very different picture of life starts to emerge. As awareness expands, we become less identified with our conditioning and freer to respond creatively. We come to see the interconnected nature of all things. We see that all things that arise, whether pleasant or unpleasant, do eventually pass away. These realizations, which blossom when we pay attention to our own experience, help us cultivate a sense of calm and clarity in the midst of our lives. They also open in us the heart of compassion as we recognize that these common pitfalls are shared by all human beings. As we begin to integrate these insights, we find ourselves acting more kindly and from the place of the wise heart.

Your own life is the perfect vehicle for this practice. The tools in this book are offered only to allow you to see for yourself. It is this direct seeing from your own experience that is more important than any opinion I might offer. Because you are unique, your own insights will be the most helpful. I have offered personal stories in the hope that you will see that you, too, have the stories you need to wake up. Your own life is the most important life to study. It is perfectly designed for your unique path to waking up. You don't have go to a library or anywhere special to do this work. Right here is the perfect place, and right now is the perfect time. You are your own teacher. Let's get started.

2 Beginning a Practice

Beginning a Jewish contemplative practice starts with learning to use the activity of the mind as a tool to wake up. I will use the terms *contemplation* and *meditation* somewhat interchangeably. Think of contemplative techniques as an inclusive set of practices that have a meditative approach at their core. By "meditative approach," I mean the techniques we can use to develop calmness, clarity, and awareness in the normally scattered mind. By default, our minds are flooded with thoughts and sensory impressions. Generally, the thoughts in the mind tell us stories about what happened in the past or what we intend to do in the future, or they evaluate and judge what we are experiencing. We can call this activity of the mind *discursive thinking*. Everyone's mind is like this. In order to work skillfully with the discursive nature of the mind, it is important to not only avoid being totally captivated by the discursive thinking, but also to not fight it. Instead, we should try to develop a witnessing quality that can recognize what is occurring in the mind at any moment.

When we get caught up and identified with the stories our minds tell us, we are unable to stay present in each moment. But by being aware of the actual process of thinking rather than being caught up in the thinking itself, we can stay present and awake in each moment. An important point to emphasize is that the present moment is the only moment where existence can be directly experienced. The past and future do not exist except as concepts. "Right now" is the only moment where we can fully meet life. When our minds are lost in reflection on the past or planning for the future, which they are most of the time, we are not really present to what is happening now. In that sense, we miss out on the chance to appreciate being alive, since *now* is the only moment in which we can be alive. From a theological perspective, you might say that the only way to experience the Divine Presence is in the "divine present." We can think about the Divine conceptually, but the actual lived experience of the Divine can only be had in the now. When we are lost in thought, we also lose the experience of the Divine Presence.

Two Different Forms of Meditation: Concentration and Awareness

When it comes to teaching meditation as a technique, I will refer to two basic categories of meditation: *concentration practice* and *awareness practice*. Concentration practices establish calmness, stability, and focus, and are a necessary foundation for seeing clearly in a sustained way. That which we see, the truth that underlies each moment of experience, is what we can call awareness practice. The concentration practice is in the service of developing the awareness practice. I am going to repeat this last sentence because I want to emphasize the point: the concentration practice is in the service of developing the awareness practice.

When people hear the term *meditation,* most think of concentration practices, probably because beginning meditation is usually about establishing concentration. Concentration practices are very effective in this regard but may not in and of themselves lead to wisdom and awakening. They can sometimes lead to profound insights, but when concentration practices are not paired with awareness practices, they also can become a trap of self-created pleasurable seclusion and delusion. In order to understand how the two practices can work together, we need to examine both more closely.

The term *concentration practice* refers to a technique in which the attention of the mind is directed to a particular object of focus. We all know this basic meaning of the word *concentration*. In order to read and comprehend the words written here, you need to concentrate on them. If your mind drifts and you think about something else, you stop concentrating on these words. In meditation, the process of directing our attention can be called *aiming* at a particular object of focus. This is the first step in meditation. The second step is *sustaining* the attention on that object. Concentration meditation is simply this process of aiming and sustaining the attention on a particular object of focus. Many meditation practices start with and use concentration practices.

Concentration and awareness practices are oftentimes used in tandem, but for didactic purposes it is helpful to discuss them as two techniques. We can think of concentration as the tool that can help train the mind to focus on and stay in the experience of the present moment. When we do that, we become aware of what is happening right now. This awareness of the present moment is what I am calling awareness practice. It is through this awareness that wisdom can arise. When we are lost in thought, we are not really aware of what we are experiencing in the moment. Concentration, in and of itself, does not necessarily lead to greater wisdom. For example, a cat can stare at a mouse with tremendous concentration, but it is not getting wiser in the process. The development of our ability to concentrate helps us to initiate an awakening of attention, pulling it away from discursive thought. In that state of awakened attention, we can then observe assorted mental and physical phenomena, which allows us to become aware of the nature of mind and its effect on our lives. I will describe this process in greater detail later in this book. As our ability to stay awake grows, so does our understanding of the nature of mind and other phenomena. Encouraging the arising of this understanding is what this book is all about. But in the beginning of our practice, we need a strong emphasis on developing our concentration skills.

Returning to concentration practices, let us consider the object of focus, which can vary tremendously. You probably have heard of many common meditation objects. These include the breath, the body, a word repeated over and over in the mind (mantra), sounds, or sights. For example, the Zohar, a primary book of Jewish mysticism, teaches that we should stare (aim the attention) at a candle flame. The object of focus is not critical in learning the technique of concentration or in developing the skill of concentrating, but the choice of objects does have a huge impact on the results of contemplative practice. This book will work with many different objects, but for now I want to focus on the technique itself.

Most everyone's experience in directing the attention to a particular object of focus is that the attention wanders to another object or gets lost in thought. The basic response to this wandering attention is to return the attention to the chosen object of focus as soon as you notice that you are no longer focused on it. It is fairly common for people to feel frustrated that they cannot sustain the focus for very long without stray thoughts arising. While this frustration is normal, especially in our goal-oriented culture, it is similar to being disappointed that you can't play a piano sonata the first time you ever touch a piano. The ability to sustain attention on an object of focus is a skill that can be acquired over time with practice. Even with increased success, the attention will still wander—although less frequently and for shorter, unnoticed periods. For people who practice long periods of silence in a calm retreat setting, there may be some extended times where stray thoughts do not arise. But having no thoughts is not the goal of concentration practice. The goal is to calm and stabilize the mind. With concentration there can be a diminishment in the volume and frequency of discursive thought. This can help facilitate the deeper insights of awareness practice.

Usually we tend to be "lost" in thought. A great metaphor for describing the effect of concentration practice is the snow globe. When you shake up the globe, the "snow" pervades the water inside it, and as it settles, it looks like it is snowing. If you imagine the globe as being the mind, then the snow represents the thoughts, which are swirling around in the mind. Concentration practice helps the snow of our thoughts to settle. When the snow settles in the globe, you can see the other objects more clearly. Likewise, in the mind, as our thoughts settle, even a little bit, it is possible to see more clearly what the truth of this moment is like. Concentration practice brings calmness and clarity to the mind. It is through this clarity that wisdom can arise. This is the awareness side of meditation practice, which I will discuss in greater detail after our exploration of concentration techniques.

Concentration can be practiced on a fixed object such as the breath or a point of light, or on a moving object, such as random, ambient sounds. Concentrating on a fixed object is called *one-pointed focus*. Concentration on a moving object is called *open awareness* and requires us to direct our attention to whatever sound our ears are hearing, moment-by-moment. Since we can't control the sounds in our environment, the object of concentration changes frequently. We may hear a car going by on the road, then a jet in the sky, then the sound of someone climbing the stairs. Both one-pointed focus and open awareness are very valuable practices. Initially, though, I have found it more useful to employ one-pointed focus for quieting the mind. When trying to pay attention to a moving target, the added input of an open awareness can lead to more discursive thinking as we react to each new sensation. But open awareness is a skill we can use in the more regular experience of our daily lives. I suggest beginning with a fixed object and developing the skill of one-pointed focus in order to develop your ability to sustain attention before moving on to a more challenging open awareness practice.

I often use the imagery of the snow globe when I teach about the value of concentration practice, but here's a story from my own life that illustrates the same point. When I was living on the grounds of Elat Chayyim, the Jewish spiritual retreat center my wife and I founded in the Catskill Mountains of New York, my family decided to make a pond at the site of a natural spring about one hundred yards from our house. When the excavator finished digging the site for the pond, it took about a week for the pond to fill up. The water was very murky, without any of the pristine clarity I was hoping for. When the contractor came by to look, he told me that it would take a few weeks for the finer particles that were stirred up to settle. So I waited for the water to settle and become clear. I would go out each morning with my dog, Malka, to see how the pond was doing. Invariably, Malka would run into the water, stirring up the pond silt. Here I was, engaging in an activity that helped to muddy the pond at the same time as I was wishing that it could be clear.

Meditation can be just like this. When I teach concentration practice during retreats, I point out that there are distracting things we might do that can stir up our minds. If, while trying to stay present in this moment, we pick up a book to read instead, chances are we'll stir up thoughts in our minds. Sometimes internal stimuli can foil our attempts at developing calmness too. A pain in the knee, for example, can lead to discursive thoughts of plans to end our discomfort. Even our thoughts themselves can stir up more thoughts.

I'd like to make a special point about the pond story as opposed to the example of snow globes. What I find important about the pond story is that I found an example from my own life that I could use to illustrate the same points as the snow globe metaphor. When we can take a story from our own lives and turn it into a teaching, it takes on a much richer meaning. As you learn to pay attention to the content of your own life, I am sure you will discover your own examples of the teaching stories I am sharing in this book. It is having the experience for yourself that is the ultimate teacher. Seeing these truths in your own life, moment by moment, is the fruit of the awareness that comes along with practice.

The example of the pond illustrates other valuable teachings. In that example, it is obvious that my desire for the pond to look a certain way caused me some grief. It also made me a little frustrated with my dog, Malka—she was thoroughly enjoying the water while I was try- ing to control both her and the pond. The settling of the mind will occur if certain conditions prevail. We can't force our thoughts to go away any more than I could force the pond to become clear or prevent Malka from jumping into it. After all, as meditation teacher Sylvia Boorstein said when she heard me teach this story, it is the nature of ponds to be murky. Likewise, it is the nature of our minds to be clouded. Being frustrated with the reality of our minds is an example of being frustrated with the way things are. Instead, it is wiser to learn how to work with things "as they are" so that our work may be more effective.

We experience so much sensory input in our daily lives that our thoughts are continually swirling. If we try to focus on a book, the phone rings or the kids call out. And our thoughts themselves become self-propelled engines of more "mind storms" as we worry or judge or desire. Without developing skills in concentration, it is more and more difficult to pay attention to anything. And if we can't pay attention, it is difficult to see our lives clearly, to understand what we see, and to grow as human beings. Concentration is an essential component of mastering certain skills. Athletes, musicians, scholars, and all of us recognize this. Even from a religious perspective, we can see the importance of concentration. Many people, for example, feel that the experience of prayer is not as meaningful as they would like. If you open up the prayer book and your mind wanders to business concerns or relationship problems or what the person next to you is wearing, there is little chance that the words on the page will touch your heart. It is easy to see that the ability to concentrate on the prayers themselves is a precondition for meaningful prayer.

So, the starting point for a Jewish contemplative practice involves learning and practicing some basic skills in concentration. One thing that defines my practice as Jewish is that my object of focus is always God, in one form or another. In chapter 5, I will expand on what I mean when I use the word *God*. For now, it is helpful to work with one particular Jewish teaching that comes to us from the *Baal Shem Tov*, the founder of the Hasidic movement who lived in Poland in the early 1700s. The Besht (an acronym of the name Baal Shem Tov) taught that "everything is God and nothing but God." Everything that exists is a part of the Divine. This is the theological overlay that I brought with me when I first learned the contemplative practices I describe in this book, and it is the core teaching of contemporary Jewish mysticism.

Setting Your Intention to Experience the Divine

Since everything is a part of the Divine, then we can have the intention to see the Divine manifesting wherever we rest our focus. This intention turns concentration practice into something more than just a technique for working with the mind. It adds the possibility of becoming more aware of what the sacred truth of each moment is revealing. This sacred truth is always available in parallel to the ability to concentrate on what is occurring in the moment. Following the intention of seeing the Divine Presence, each moment of awakened attention brings us in touch with how God manifests in that moment. This would be an appropriate time to start practicing the concepts I have introduced thus far. To do so, I offer a meditation that involves bringing your attention to the arising and passing of the breath.

Breathing the Divine Name

For this practice, we will make an explicit link to the most holy name for God in the Jewish tradition, *Yud Hay Vav Hay*, also called the tetragrammaton. These syllables are the names of the four Hebrew letters that comprise this most holy name, יהוה. The letter *yud* has the sound of the English letter *y*. The letter *hay* corresponds to the English *h*. The letter *vav* is like the letter *v* in English. The Jewish mystical tradition gives us a framework for understanding these four letters of God's name. Let's begin with the letter *hay,* or *h*. As you may have noticed, this letter appears twice in this name for God. If you intone the letter out loud, you will immediately recognize that it is the sound of breathing. Try this: breathe out loudly enough for an extended time so that you can hear the sound of the breath with your own ears. Now, if you do the same thing when inhaling, you'll hear that the in-breath also makes the same sound. The perspective that pronouncing the letter *hay* is the same sound as breathing makes an explicit link between the breath and God's name.

It may not come as a surprise that God's name is connected to the breath. Most religious traditions connect breath with life and with God. The English word *spirit* is related to the word *respiration*. In Hebrew, the words for "soul" *(neshamah)* and "breath" *(nesheemah)* have the same root. *Ruach* means "spirit" in Hebrew, but it is also a word for the wind, or the movement of air, which is like the breath. In Genesis 2:7, when God wanted to make human beings, God breathed into the dust of the earth: "And YHVH, God, formed the human, of the dust from the soil, he blew into his nostrils the breath of life and the human became a living being." So when we pay attention to the breath, it is a way of paying attention to the divine animating life force, which is inherent in each breath while we are still alive.

We have looked at two of the letters (the second and fourth) in the divine name, *hay* and *hay*. The other letters of the divine name provide different insights into the nature of God. The first letter is the *yud*. In Hebrew, this is the smallest letter of the alphabet and when written, its essence is the same as a single point. Since a point has no dimensions in time and space (its scientific definition), we need to draw something bigger than a point so that it can be seen. But Jewish mystics have always understood that the *yud* is connected to the concept of nothingness or emptiness. If we make a link to the breath, as we did for the letter *hay,* then we might consider that the *yud* in God's name corresponds to the state of emptiness that occurs before the in-breath begins. At that point, as the lungs have emptied of air, they contract, like a deflating balloon. While they do not disappear into nothingness, they do get to be their smallest size. Similarly, *yud* does not disappear, but is the smallest letter. If *yud* represents the empty place before the start of the in-breath, then the first *hay* in the divine name corresponds to the in-breath itself.

At the end of the in-breath, before the start of the out-breath, the lungs are now in their most expanded state. This can be called the full state. This full state can be linked to the Hebrew letter *vav*. *Vav* is the straightest letter in the Hebrew alphabet, written as simply a single straight line. To again use the image of a balloon, picture the long, skinny balloons used by people who make balloon animals. Before you start blowing it up, it hangs down, out of your mouth. As you blow it up, it straightens into a single straight line. In this way, *vav* can be thought of as fullness. Just as the lungs are full at the end of the in-breath.

We can now see that the whole cycle of breathing is coded within the divine name *Yud Hay Vav Hay,* as follows:

> *Yud*—Empty
>
> *Hay*—In
>
> *Vav*—Full
>
> *Hay*—Out

Breathing the Universe

Before starting the practice of focusing attention on our breath, I would like to share a few more compelling aspects that are implicit in the biblical image of God breathing into the dust of the earth in order to give life to human beings. Ask yourself the following question: when that first breath that created life occurred, was it an in-breath or an out-breath? You may see from the question that it was both an in-breath *and* an out-breath, and that it is only a matter of perspective how it is seen in the moment. From Adam's perspective, it was the first in-breath. From God's perspective (for the moment, seeing God as "other"), it was an out-breath. Taking an even larger perspective on what this whole verse from Torah might be trying to teach, we can see that there is no such thing as an in-breath without an out-breath. They are linked together. When you or I (part of God) take an in-breath, the universe (the rest of God) makes an out-breath. This is true in more than just a metaphorical way. When we breathe out carbon dioxide, the plant kingdom "breathes" it in. And when the plants "breathe" out oxygen, we breathe it in. So, the metaphor of God's name and its connection to the breath teaches us to see the Divine as an unfolding that is cyclical in nature. We also see that everything exists in one interlocking cycle of being.

If we were to draw a picture of the cycle of being using the words *empty, in, full,* and *out,* it might look like the basic drawing of a wave:

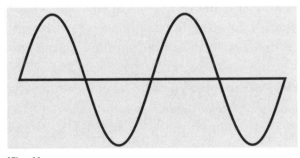

[Fig. 1]

These words describe not only the breath, but also the basic pattern of all existence. What we think of as solid matter really consists of subatomic particles, which are always in motion. And the basic pattern of motion in the universe is the wave. From both Torah and modern physics we learn that the universe began with light, and that light somehow became what we call matter. Quantum physics tells us that light itself is part particle and part wave. While any object could work as our focus in a beginning concentration practice, using the breath calls up the link to the divine name and causes us to pay attention to the underlying architecture of the divine universe at the same time.

Breathing and the Divine Presence

To begin the practice of concentrating on your breath, sit comfortably in a quiet place where you won't be disturbed. Turn off the ringer of your phone. You might begin this and any formal practice session by making the following intention: the act I am about to perform, I do for the sake of waking up to the Divine Presence that pervades all life, in order that I might become an aide in helping all beings to awaken and live in peace and joy.

As you begin to sit quietly, start by noticing whatever thoughts or feelings are present in your mind before you pointedly direct your attention anywhere. After a few moments of this, begin to focus your attention on the arising and passing of each breath. Allow the breath to come and go at its own pace. Don't try to manipulate the breath in any way. See if you can make the primary object of focus the physical sensations that accompany the breath. At the same time, softly begin to connect in your mind the four parts of the breath to the four letters of God's name. When you feel the bodily sensations that are present after the emptying of air from your lungs, silently say to yourself, *"Yud."* As you notice the in-breath arising and the accompanying bodily sensations, say to yourself, *"Hay."* You might extend the inner noting of the word *hay* to cover the whole period of the in-breath. When the in-breath finishes, try to feel the sensations in your body that are present before the out-breath begins, and say to yourself, *"Vav."* As the out-breath begins, say to yourself, *"Hay,"* and extend that noting as long as the out-breath is occurring. Continue to feel the physical sensations in your body as you breathe out.

Repeat this pattern of connecting the letters of the divine name to the parts of your breath for ten minutes. While we begin with the intention to aim and sustain the attention on the object of focus, it is inevitable that your mind will wander. Try not to worry about it or judge yourself. Judging yourself discourages you from practicing because you feel "you're not good at it." It doesn't mean you are a bad meditator; it is just the nature of our minds to be distracted. When you find your attention wandering, simply bring your focus back to your breath and the connection to the divine name. This returning of the attention back to the object of focus is central to concentration practice.

You only need to cultivate the practice of noticing as soon as possible when your attention has wandered. And when you notice that, make a decision to return. This is a skill that can be developed over time. Eventually, you will notice that your ability to sustain your attention on the object of focus will grow. But don't expect your progress to be overly linear in development. Some days your ability to sustain your attention will be better than others. This may be true over periods of weeks or months as well, depending on many other factors that affect your life. For example, you might be less able to sustain your attention during times of life stress than in calm times.

You may find that you continue to judge yourself when your attention wanders. If so, you can work with this in your meditation. When you notice self-criticism, simply file this awareness away for future exploration. This is an example of concentration and awareness coming together. Negative self-judgment is one of the biggest impediments to waking up. For one thing, it makes us feel badly about ourselves, which is not very helpful when it comes to staying in the present moment. Ultimately, cultivating an attitude of self-acceptance is a crucial component of the growth that occurs as you see clearly the challenges you face in trying to be more awake in your life. Indeed, self-acceptance is a precursor to the deep happiness that is possible through this practice.

You might want to undertake this practice daily while working with this book, especially if you are just beginning to explore meditation. But it may be that using the names of the Hebrew letters *yud, hay, vav,* and *hay* is too abstract for you. In that case, consider using the words *empty, in, full,* and *out* instead. English words may resonate for some people more than the Hebrew letters. You might try the practice each way and see which words better help you sustain your attention to the breath.

Chanting the Divine Name

Another meditation practice connected to the divine name can also develop the skill of concentration while making a connection to the entire body. This practice involves chanting the letters of the tetragrammaton with various vowel sounds while imagining that the sound is rooted in different places in the body. It is loosely based on the work of Abraham Abulafia. Abulafia was a Jewish mystic who lived in Spain in the 1200s. His mystical leanings turned primarily to a deep exploration of Hebrew letters and their permutations and combinations. Through working with these practices, he believed it was possible to attain the level of prophecy, which meant a direct communion with the Divine. The following exercise, while not actually created by Abulafia, can introduce you to some of the elements he employed. It is not designed to give you access to prophecy but rather to work with concentration techniques while connecting them to your body and to one of the divine names.

In the chanting you combine the consonant sound of each of the four letters—*y (yud), h (hay), v (vav),* and *h (hay)*—with one vowel sound, working your way through five different vowel sounds, *eh, ee, ah, oh,* and *ooh.* These vowel sounds were chosen because they follow the English vowel order of *a, e, i, o,* and *u.* When the sounds are put together, the chant sounds like *yeh heh veh heh, yee hee vee hee, yah hah vah hah, yoh hoh voh hoh, yooh hooh vooh hooh.* This chanting is done aloud to a single note of your choice, usually a lower note in your own voice's register.

As you chant the first set, *yeh heh veh heh,* try and imagine or actually feel the sound coming from the spot on your forehead directly over the line of your nose and about an inch above the top of the nose. This spot is called the third eye in some traditions. It is close to the pineal gland, which derives its name from the Hebrew words *P'nai El,* or "face of God." It is a spot traditionally connected to "seeing" on levels other than the visual. I include this information about the third eye as a way of illustrating that there are many more layers of experience behind a simple instruction about noticing a particular place in the body. All of the other spots in the body referred to in this exercise are also "special," but rather than delve too deeply into their significance in various traditions, try to notice for yourself, through your own direct experience, whether these particular locations in the body resonate for you in some way. As you chant the second set, *yee hee vee hee,* try to imagine—or actually feel—the sound coming from the center of your throat. This may be the easiest place to notice the vibrations since this is the location of the vocal chords and the vibrations really are coming physically from that place in the body. For the third set, *yah hah vah hah,* imagine the sound as centered in your heart. For the fourth set, *yoh hoh voh hoh,* try to feel the sound as if it is arising from the solar plexus (about five fingers above the belly button). Finally, as you chant the fifth set, *yooh hooh vooh hooh,* try to feel the sound at the base of the spine.

Each of the five sections of the chant should be done on one exhalation of the breath. So the whole cycle of the chant is five breaths long and then repeats from the beginning. For this practice, it is all right to extend the breath so that it is longer than a normal breath. Sometimes, a slower than normal pace is helpful when adding visualizations to a contemplative practice. Imagining the chant coming from a place inside the body is another way of saying that you should direct your attention to that place in the body. By focusing your attention in this way, you remain present in your body even as your mind makes a connection to the divine name. Because this practice uses sound and follows a progressive order, some people find that it is easier to concentrate their attention for longer periods of time than with other exercises. As soon as your attention wanders, you might notice that you forget which syllable to chant. When this happens, start over again from the beginning. Some concentration practices are designed specifically to be complicated in order to engage the mind more fully.

Anchoring the Mind in the Here and Now

So far I have been speaking of concentration practice as being separate from awareness practice, in order to illustrate particular points about the technique. In actual usage, both practices overlap in many ways. Concentration techniques can lead to a great deal of awareness. When thinking aimlessly, we are not usually aware of the content of our thoughts. We may sit and daydream for an hour while driving and not even remember the topics in our daydreams. This is similar to how most of us forget our dreams almost instantly upon awakening. When you decide, however, to direct your attention to a particular place, this tendency of the mind to drift away becomes much more noticeable. In a single hour of concentration practice, your mind may wander hundreds of times. Concentration practices can provide an anchor for the mind as well as a point of reference. Somehow, the anchor of your intention to stay on the chosen object of focus pulls you out of your drift at some point. At that moment of coming back to your object of focus, you can notice where your thoughts took you. This noticing is the awareness benefit of concentration practice. Over time you will become quite familiar with the thoughts that occupy most of your mental time. This can be a humbling experience. You may judge yourself as being petty, obsessive, angry, or full of other undesirable traits. And your self-judgments are themselves thoughts that you'll learn to acknowledge. I'll come back to the topic of what to do with all these judgments later. For now, the point is that concentration practice can lead to great self-awareness, especially if you make that your intention.

During concentration practice, you can return to the object of focus with or without much attention to where your thoughts took you. Both choices are valid. When you really want to develop calm and stillness in the mind, you may choose not to pay attention to the content of your wanderings. But even if you make this choice for the purpose of cultivating temporary clarity of vision, remember that you will later be trained on all of life's experiences, including where your thoughts take you.

The Importance of the Breath

Using the breath as your object of focus has many benefits, making it a particularly useful primary practice. As you work on developing your concentration skills, you might choose other objects of focus to begin with, especially if you find one that more easily sustains your attention. It also can be good to have different objects of focus for different times and for the different results they produce. However, I would like to explain why the breath is such a good object of focus to include in your repertoire and why it is worth the effort to develop the skill of sustaining your attention on the breath.

I have already described the connection of the breath to the divine name, *Yud Hay Vav Hay,* but there is much more. One of the most important aspects of waking up is the ability to stay present with your direct experience in this very moment. As you read these words, you are also breathing. If we were to focus on a mantra, say, the word *Coca-Cola*, we could develop concentration but would miss some valuable lessons. For one thing, unless you happen to be holding a can of Coke in your hand, there is no Coca-Cola in your actual physical experience of the moment. In addition, you had to choose Coca-Cola as your mantra. But when you work with the breath, you don't have to choose to breathe. You only choose to aim your attention to something that is occurring in the moment, in your direct experience. This quality of choosing becomes incredibly important as you try to wake up to the nature of the self, since the choosing implies that there is a chooser. In order to compensate for this effect, it will eventually become important to add practices that are categorized as *choiceless awareness* practices. In those practices, you do not choose a particular object of focus. Rather, you make an intention to be aware of whatever enters your awareness. This practice will be discussed further on in the book.

The breath is also a good object for developing mental calm because it is plain and simple by nature. By contrast, some practices involve focusing on more complicated sensations, such as pain. I will discuss the practice of focusing on pain in chapter 8, and I recommend you use it at times. Initially, though, as you learn the skill of sustaining concentration, choosing a painful sensation will likely not cultivate calmness in your mind. Instead, your mind will probably squirm in the face of the pain and frenetically plan a way to get rid of it. For most of us, breathing is either a neutral or pleasant experience and therefore a much simpler object of focus. However, if you are a person with a breathing disorder, such as asthma, the breath may not be the best object of focus for you. It may remind you of an aspect of your life that you find difficult or disappointing. If this is the case, it might be better to start with chanting or one of the other practices described in this book.

By its nature, our breath is rhythmic. It comes and it goes. One aspect of waking up is the recognition that everything comes and goes. If we look carefully, we see that all things that arise in our lives eventually pass. This is true in all phases of our lives, whether in our childhood, the middle of our lives, or in old age. People and relationships enter our lives and depart. A delicious meal starts and is over. A sensation in the body comes and goes. Resting our attention on the breath provides the opportunity to see this most basic of realities with each breath.

The breath comes and goes without us needing to do anything to make it happen. In the basic breath awareness, we simply notice the arising and passing of each breath without consciously adjusting the pace or controlling the breath in any way. You may find this difficult to do. Many people feel their breath automatically changes when they start paying attention to it. It is common to feel like you can't stop controlling the breath, even if you want to. Breathing is both a voluntary and involuntary function of the body. The lungs are controlled partly by the autonomic nervous system, which is the involuntary system that keeps our organs functioning without any effort. But the somatic system, which controls our voluntary functions (mostly muscles), also allows us to breathe or to hold our breath at will (for a while). It is precisely this dual voluntary and involuntary nature of breathing that makes the breath such a valuable object of focus. One of the central questions we explore in the practice of waking up is, what is the nature of the self? We want to have control over our lives. Working with breath allows us to watch our tendency and desire to control our experience. Yet we can also observe that a part of what we usually think of as our self, our body, is doing its thing without our control. Are you breathing, or are you being breathed? So, while we are practicing concentration techniques with the breath, we are also exploring basic questions of self, the nature of reality, and God's role in the process.

I would like to share a number of techniques I have learned from various teachers to help you as you work at developing the ability to sustain your attention. When using these techniques, it is best to try them by adding them to your practice one at a time. If you develop a daily practice, you might try one of these techniques for a week and see how it affects your overall experience and level of concentration. Over time, you'll learn which ones work the best for you and will be able to call on different ones at different times as needed. I offer these exercises as added instructions to a basic breath awareness practice. In principle, they can be adapted to other core concentration techniques if you are not working with awareness of the breath.

HELPFUL EXERCISES AND TECHNIQUES

Exercise 1

As you practice focusing on the breath, say to yourself on each breath, "Just this breath," and try to sustain your attention through one whole breath. It is helpful to note the beginning of each in-breath, the middle of the in-breath, the end of the in-breath, the fullness before the exhale begins, the beginning of the out-breath, the middle of the out-breath, the end of the out-breath, and the sensation of emptiness before the next in-breath begins. The focus here is to pay attention to just one full in-breath and out-breath at a time. It is exceedingly difficult to maintain an unwavering focus for ten minutes, let alone for forty or more. It is much easier to sustain your focus for the full length of one entire breath. As soon as that breath ends and the next one is about to begin, renew your intention to be present to "just this breath," one at a time.

Exercise 2

As you develop some ability to sustain your attention on the arising and passing of a single breath, you might begin trying to maintain your attention for five or ten breaths at a time. You can do this by softly adding a mental count to each breath. At the end of each breath, simply count, "One, two, three," and so on, all the way up to five or ten. If you get distracted or lose count, simply start over at one. In this practice it is important not to allow the attainment to become a goal in and of itself. There is no goal other than sustaining the attention for longer periods. In that sense, the counting is just a trick to help the mind sustain its attention for slightly longer periods. If you find yourself getting frustrated that you haven't strung together this arbitrary number of breaths, you are probably trying too hard and have gotten too attached to an outcome. If this happens, ease up on the counting. But at the same time, notice how your attachment led to some emotional discomfort.

I have found this practice to be helpful in another way. In my own practice, I often notice that I have made it to five or six breaths without distraction but can't remember ever having gotten to seven. When this happens, I steady my attention as I get to five and then six, and sometimes just this extra attention will pull my focus through this "blind" spot. Learning to become aware of when your attention fades aids the process of sustaining your attention. This leads to the next variation.

Exercise 3

As you rest your attention on the arising and passing of each breath, notice if your mind tends to wander more during the in-breath or the out-breath, or perhaps at the turning point of each in- and out-breath. You might find this difficult to discern because it is hard to be present at the moment you lose your focus. Sometimes you have no choice but to notice this loss of focus in hindsight. However, I have found that because this exercise calls for careful attention, I often catch my loss of focus almost instantly—often early enough to still be on the same part of the breath as I was when I lost focus. As in exercise 2, it is helpful to know that although the attention may wander more at a particular place in the breath cycle, you can strengthen your intention to sustain the attention through that moment. If you find this exercise leads to frustration and agitation, back off and try it another time or perhaps on a meditation retreat.

Exercise 4

All of the exercises above have a common trait that helps sustain the attention: each makes the process of paying attention more interesting. We all know that it is very easy to watch a compelling movie, and not so easy to watch a boring one. When we are interested in something, our ability to sustain our attention increases. In our meditation practice, we can use our creativity to keep things interesting. Ultimately, it is our interest in being awake, happy, and helpful that motivates the entire spiritual life described in this book.

One way of inspiring an interest in the breath is to notice different aspects of it. Try this: during a sitting period, notice five new things about the breath that you never noticed before. For instance, you might become aware of a subtle sensation in the diaphragm, be it at the end of the out-breath or at any other point of the breath cycle, that you hadn't noticed before. On one retreat, as I was aware of the sensations of breathing, I realized that each breath was changed slightly by my heartbeat.

You might try noticing which is longer, your in-breath or your out-breath, and whether the answer changes over time. These are all mundane examples of something interesting you might find in your breath. Sometimes, just looking for these small details provides enough added focus to sustain and deepen your concentration.

Potentially thrilling experiences and insights can arise in your practice. You never know when such a moment might occur, but you can count on the fact that the more attentive you are to the breath, the more often you will uncover something really interesting. I remember once being on a retreat in a center where we did not have a group experience of a daily morning chanting practice (a practice I will describe in chapter 6). Since I like to do that practice, I would chant some of the morning prayers by myself in my room before going to the meditation hall for the first sitting period of the day. However, it was a silent retreat, and so I would chant in silence so as not to disturb anybody. One morning, in the middle of my chanting, I came to a note that was too high for me to reach. This instantly puzzled me, since I was chanting silently in my head! "How can an imaginary note be too high?" I wondered. I began repeating the chant, paying careful attention to the experience. Then it hit me: as I was silently chanting, the muscles in my throat were moving, and when I got to the note I couldn't reach, I could feel my vocal chord trying to contract enough to produce that higher note. This was the first time I was ever conscious of the sensation in my vocal chords. It was an amazing experience for me. When you pay attention, you never know when the next realization will come or how large it might be. The possibilities are infinite.

There is another deeply valuable experience that can arise when you practice concentration. Fixing your attention on an object is also known as one-pointed focus. In one-pointed focus, there is the object that is known and the knower of the object. The knower directs the attention to the object, or to that which is known, and *knowing* arises. It is possible, with practice, and perhaps with grace, that your concentration deepens to a place where the knower and the known disappear as separate entities and all that is left is the knowing, without a knower. In these moments, all self-referencing ceases. In essence, self-referencing is never present in any moment when your attention is fully absorbed in the direct knowing of a sensory experience. But this is usually so fleeting in nature that it is not directly experienced in a conscious fashion. Sometimes, with one-pointed focus, your attention rivets to the object. At that point, no effort is required to sustain the attention, so there is no need for *anyone* to be *making* the experience happen. And in those moments, there is no one *to whom* the experience is happening. This is a valuable experience that can radically change your perspective. It doesn't often happen, and is fleeting when it does. The ceasing of self-referencing can't be successfully sought after because the seeking is counterproductive to having the experience. This is why I call it a moment of grace.

In the following chapters, I will go on to explain how to use the ability to concentrate to become clearer about the nature of being alive. Concentration tools have tremendous potential to change how your mind meets the present moment. As the mind gets more concentrated, some people feel a sense of rapture develop in the body. This rapture can be quite alluring. It can be mistaken as the goal of practice, and when it is, this gets in the way of truly waking up. It is also possible to use concentration techniques to drown out other messages that should be explored for their underlying meaning. When used in this way, meditation can be a hindrance to the clear seeing that this book advocates. But when used properly, these same tools can be just what are needed to begin a deep exploration of life. The clarity and spaciousness of a concentrated mind applied to what arises in each present moment leads us on a path of awakening that provides real clarity and insight. With this insight, the radiant heart/mind can recover its natural luster.

3 The Nature of Mind

Whatis the mind and how does it work? What is a mind composed of? Where is it? How does our sense of identity interface with the working of our minds? The art of waking up in your own life is inextricably connected to understanding the nature of mind in general and the nature of your own mind in particular. It is important to clarify what I mean by the term *mind*. I am not referring specifically to the brain but rather to the complex of mental experiences that include the processors of information that flows into the brain as well as mental concepts that are formed and re-formed as continual input is received. To use an analogy from the computer world, we might say that the mind is both the hardware and the operating system software installed on that hardware.

Mind also refers to *lev,* a biblical term often understood as "heart," but whose meaning can also be defined as "heart/mind." When the Torah uses the word *heart* or *lev,* it is clear from its many contextual uses that it is referring to both heart and mind with the same word. It is quite common to link these two symbols in just this way, since many of us experience feelings as something that occur in both the mind and the heart. Feelings, as well as thoughts, are part of the process of mind.

When speaking about our mind, I am including all the conditioned ways that we perceive reality, some of which are unique to our own particular experience. This conditioned perception includes our sense of identity as individuals as well as the other thought patterns that run through our minds. It is this sense of identity that we usually call "the self." As you will see, this sense of a self is better understood as a flowing aggregate of smaller, transitory phenomena. When grouped together, these phenomena result in a familiar pattern that is automatically perceived as "the self" in which the process of perception is occurring. It is important to explore the accuracy of this perception.

Limited Awareness versus Expanded Awareness

Our normal perception of reality is quite different from reality itself. Even if our perceptions happen to be accurate—most often they are distorted—what we normally experience is, at best, a fragmented view of reality. Realizing this essential difference is key to the process of awakening. Our normal, everyday state of mind can be called "small mind," or *mochin de-katnut,* a term introduced by Jewish mystics to describe our conventional sense of reality. It is the same state of mind described in Reb Zalman's story about his daughter Shalvi that I related in the Introduction—the state that is comparable to a waking dream. This dream-state consciousness is our usual state of mind most of the time. But sometimes, spontaneously or through practice, we can experience a much deeper and richer sense of what is actually occurring in the moment. This heightened state of mind can be called *mochin de-gadlut,* or "expanded awareness." By this designation, Jewish mystics acknowledged that there are states of mind beyond what we normally experience. These states are difficult to describe with words. It is like trying to describe vision to a blind person or the taste of chocolate to someone who has not tried it.

Many of the personal stories I share in this book are about moments in which I had an insight that allowed me to see things in a different way, as if all of a sudden a door in my mind had opened. Some of these moments could best be described as experiences of an awakened state of mind—a state of mind that sees the truth of each moment with greater clarity. Experiences of such expanded awareness are transitory or ephemeral in nature, yet leave us potentially transformed. It is possible to retain the insights that arise during such experiences, so that even when we are in our more habitual mind states, that is, in the *small* mind, we remember that things are not as they always appear and that deep truths are available to us.

Sensations, Feeling Tone, Mental Formations, and Perception

At this point, it may be useful to explore the very nature of thoughts. As I pointed out in the story of former football player Lionel Aldridge, we are not our thoughts. Thoughts can be considered one of the objects of sensory experience. Those of us who grew up in the West were taught that we have five senses: taste, touch, smell, hearing, and sight. The brain collects information from the different sense doorways, and this information becomes a part of the experience of mind. For example, when someone rings a bell, the sound of the bell—that is, the vibrations it sets off—strikes the eardrum, which is the doorway for the sense of hearing. The eardrum relays information through the nervous system to the brain, and what we call the mind *knows* this sensation as sound. In this example, hearing is the sensation and the sound is the sense object that is known by the mind. Likewise, the mind can know tastes, smells, touched objects, and sights through tasting, smelling, touching, and seeing. These represent the traditional five senses. But there is another incredibly important sense doorway: our brain. This is the sense doorway for the mental objects that we call thoughts. Just as the mind can know a sound that enters through the sense doorway of the ear, the mind can know a thought as it enters the sense doorway of the brain. This approach to the nature of thoughts is the basis for everything that follows.

In experiencing the traditional five senses, we can easily recognize the difference between the object that is known in the mind and our identity of self. For example, when I hear a car driving down the street, I don't think of that sound as being me. Neither do I believe that a bird singing in a tree is me. But when we have a thought, we tend to identify with it, to see it as "my thought." Collectively, our thoughts make up the construct that we call "self" or "I." In fact, we tend to think that our mental identity is even more our true self than certain parts of our body. If I lose a foot for some reason, I am still me. But if I forget my identity, who am I? However, when we start cultivating a deeper understanding, we come to realize that our thoughts are just conditioned patterns of mental objects that form in reaction to other sensory stimuli, mental or otherwise. While they are centrally important in our subjective experience of life, they are ultimately no more real than anything else in our experience. Thoughts are not a problem, just as sights and sounds are not problems. But ignorance of the true nature of thoughts can lead us astray.

Let's take a deeper look at the process of thinking. We can label the thoughts that become part of our personal identity as *mental forma-tions*. The word *formations* will help us link this teaching to the language of the four worlds of divine manifestation, which is covered in chapter 5. One of these worlds is called *Olam Yetzirah*, the world of formation, where the process I am about to describe takes place. When I refer to thoughts and memories as mental formations, I am still referring to real things. These mental formations actually exist in the way we usually mean when we say something is real. While it is difficult to refer to them as physical objects, they are no less real. They come into formation through real causes and conditions. It is worth learning about the mechanics of their arising. A mental formation becomes known to the mind by a chain of almost simultaneous events. The first link in this chain is when sensations impact our sensory organs.

Let's use a simple example: the striking of a metal rod that makes a fairly pure tone. This sound is often made to signify the beginning of a meditation period. As the sound waves strike the eardrum in an intact nervous system, one aspect of the mind, called consciousness, knows that the tone is occurring. This raw knowing precedes any classification or recognition of what kind of sound is being made. Right away, we've differentiated two distinct mental events, the hearing itself and the knowing of hearing, or hearing consciousness.

The Reality of Pleasant and Unpleasant Sensations

As this hearing consciousness takes place, the mind simultaneously knows another facet of the experience. The mind recognizes that the sensations are pleasant or unpleasant or neutral—that is, neither pleasant nor unpleasant. This classification of sensations is referred to as the valence or feeling tone of the sensation. The mind is also conscious of knowing this valence, so it is called valence or feeling consciousness.

The practice of paying attention to the valence of experiences as they arise is extremely important to the whole process of waking up because it helps us to see clearly a basic organizing principle of small or everyday mind. I recommend using this lens to watch your daily experiences because of the basic set of reactions that occur in the human mind as a consequence of the experience of valence. When we experience something that is pleasant, the habitual reaction of our mind is, "I like that," "I want more of that," or, "I want to figure out how to keep this happening." The mind proliferates thoughts of this nature following a pleasant sensation as inevitably as gravity on Earth makes an object fall if you drop it from your hand.

Similarly, it will come as no surprise that if the valence is unpleasant, the reaction of the mind is to create thoughts such as, "I can't stand this," "This has got to go," and, "I hate this." One important subset of this reaction to unpleasant experience has to do with thoughts of blame. I frequently undertake longer retreats of my own at Spirit Rock Meditation Center in California, to work with my teacher, Sylvia Boorstein. On my first retreat there, I noticed some pain in the area between my shoulders. I told Sylvia that my back was stiff and sore from the airplane trip. Her response was we often notice places in the body where we are carrying tension when the mind quiets down. The implication was that my pain might be the symptom of a deeper psychological pattern that I hadn't paid attention to, instead of stemming solely from the ride in a cramped airline seat. It is extremely beneficial to watch the mind as it reacts to pain, whether physical or emotional.

Once I worked with a healer who combined kabbalistic teachings with rainbow reflexology. I knew very little about reflexology other than that it involved using pressure points on the bottom of the feet to promote healing. Various spots on the feet correspond to different organ systems in the body. Rainbow reflexology involved diagnosing imbalance in the chakras (energy vortices in the body). Each chakra is associated with a color, and applying colors to the chakras helps balance the system after a diagnosis is made.

The healer made a diagnosis of my imbalance by pushing on a spot on the instep of my foot. I was told that this spot corresponded to the spine. In the kabbalistic version of reflexology, the tree of the *sephirot* (emanations) also corresponds to parts of the body. Each *sephira* is also associated with a color. I laid down on a massage table and had colored felt strips placed over the body parts corresponding to the *sephirot*. To demonstrate that the placing of the colors was significant, the healer pressed on the spot on my foot and asked me to report what it felt like. When he would put the colors in the improper order, I felt more pain as he pressed my foot. When he covered my heart, which corresponds to the *sephira* of *Tiferet* (splender), with a black cloth (a very bad color for people to wear according to this system) and pressed the same spot on my foot, the pain was almost unbearable. I remember thinking at the time that he was just pushing harder. Today, I am much less sure that he was pushing harder.

A year or so after this experience with the healer, I was working with a rolfer. I had suffered serious lower back injuries twice in three years. While I managed to recover both times, I was determined to deal with the underlying muscular imbalances that caused the pain. Rolfing involves deep tissue massage as it attempts to free up motion in the body by loosening connective tissue formations. These formations, which arise out of many past causes, including injuries, tend to freeze the body in postures that are not balanced. This leads to unhealthy stress on other muscles. Rolfing is intense work and can be uncomfortable or even painful. As my rolfer worked on certain areas of my body, he would ask me for feedback on how it felt. One day he was working deeply in a way that caused me a lot more pain than in the past. I asked him if he was applying more pressure than usual. He assured me he wasn't and it dawned on me that the pain I was experiencing had to do with constricted places in my body, and not with something he was doing. My mind's first inclination was to assume that the rolfer was the source of my pain rather than owning up to the fact that *I* was constricted somewhere.

Who Can I Blame for My Problems?

I can't overemphasize what an important moment of awakening this experience with the rolfer was for me. The idea that we immediately look to blame someone else for our unpleasant moments has become a key insight for me in all my relationships. Whenever anything uncomfortable pops up on my inner reality map, my mind's first response is to point the finger of blame somewhere outside myself. My reaction often quickly moves beyond the mind into actual finger pointing, anger, and noncompassionate actions. While it is true that sometimes someone may be pushing on me a little harder and contributing to my discomfort, I usually find that the problem is not "out there," but "in here."

Let's return to the experience of valence. There is a third possibility of feeling consciousness besides pleasant and unpleasant, and that is the experience of a sensation that is neither pleasant nor unpleasant—what we might call neutral. You might be able to guess what the mind does with such an experience. It says, "Boring. Let's change the channel." This mental reaction occurs so quickly that it usually goes by completely unnoticed and our attention immediately moves on to a different sensation. This causes us to pay no attention at all to a huge percentage of experiences, many of which are neutral in their valence. My term for this ignoring of the neutral is *ignore-ance*. It is important to understand these common human reactions to the valence of our experiences because they are the expression of what Buddhists call the root poisons of greed, hatred, and ignorance.

Can You Trust Your Perceptions?

Let's return to our example of sound. A third function arises in the mind following the bare knowing of sound and the consciousness of whether the sound is pleasant, unpleasant, or neutral. This third function can be called perception. In the original example of striking a pure tone on a metal rod, we might perceive that we are hearing the sound of a bell. This perception comes as a thought. As it arises in the mind, this thought can also be known, so we have perceiving consciousness. Up to this point we have mentioned three layers of consciousness: first, the consciousness that hearing was occurring; second, the consciousness of whether the sound was pleasant, unpleasant, or neutral; and third, the consciousness of the concept of the bell, which the mind knows as a thought. This third step in the process of knowing is critical because it is at this point that we can begin to speak of the accuracy of our perceptions. The perception "bell" may or may not be true or accurate. The word *bell* is a common term for a certain class of objects, but the term is not inherently a part of the physical entity in question. In that sense, names are already a function of mind, not of the object, per se. Because of this, there is the possibility that our perception could be erroneous—a bell may not have produced that sound at all.

I am sure you can think of times in your own life where you had erroneous perceptions. I remember one time in my own life, during a drive across the country. I stopped for a night with relatives in Phoenix. My next scheduled stop was to see a friend who was an AmeriCorps VISTA volunteer in Missouri. Being young and impulsive, I set out without the thought in mind of where I might stop along the way. It was about a twenty-six-hour drive. It was not till the first light of dawn that I really began to feel tired. Earlier that morning (around three a.m.), I got a speeding ticket in Texas and had to go into a small town where they actually woke up the judge and held court to determine my fine! It was a scary event, but it kept me awake a while longer. In the early morning light, I decided to stop and pulled into the parking lot of a hotel along the highway. Walking toward the lobby entrance, I had the feeling that it looked expensive and decided to get back in my car. I drove a while further and then began to feel even sleepier. I decided that I would stop at the next available rest area and sleep in my car. I began watching for rest areas, but none appeared. Soon I was praying for one, feeling really exhausted. Finally, I saw a rest area sign off in the distance and felt relieved. But as I neared the sign, I was stunned and disappointed to discover that what I had taken to be a sign for a rest area was merely a scrawny tree by the side of the road. I had perceived what my mind wanted to perceive. These misperceptions can occur all the time—whether we are fatigued or not. Often, they are related to a strong desire for a particular event. The mind creates its own reality.

The Self-Serving Nature of Most Thoughts

The fourth component of mind following the knowing of sensation, the valence of the sensation, and the perception of an object is the creation of thoughts and feelings, which we will call *mental formations*. These are broader mental phenomena than perceptions. They are the mental actions that tend to comment on or make plans to deal with what we are perceiving. The brain is the sense doorway for these mental formations. The mind is organized in such a way that it creates ever more complex formations out of the sensations, valences, and perceptions it has experienced.

In the example of the sounding of what we've perceived to be a bell, the mind may create mental formations such as, "Thank God the bell rang, now I can eat lunch," "Wow, that period ended so soon; I was just getting focused," or, "The teachers on this retreat don't know what they're talking about! This meditation stuff is worthless!" You can see that the way the mind reacts depends on many factors. If you were enjoying the practice, you might have one set of thoughts. If you were feeling discomfort or judging yourself as unskilled at meditating, your thoughts would be different. Also, hearing a bell does not mean you have to stop meditating; that response is just a preconceived meaning applied to the sensation. Who says you can't keep meditating after the bell rings? It is just vibration hitting your eardrum, and any meaning beyond that arises from the conditioning and reactivity of the mind.

Mental formations include what we might call our fears, our desires for particular kinds of sensations, and even our own identity or sense of self. The mind tends to organize data and create mental images, including beliefs and opinions, and then take these beliefs to be reality. These beliefs are not necessarily accurate, however. They are usually a support to the mental phenomena we call the self, and are generally self-serving. The mind tries to fit new data into its existing reality maps, reflecting highly habituated or conditioned patterns of thought. A story from my college days illustrates this point and reveals the danger of human conditioning.

When I was just finishing up at the University of Wisconsin, I worked with the B'nai B'rith Youth Organization. This is a nondenominational program for Jewish teenagers that, among other things, provides educational experiences around cultural issues to promote good community values. I attended a particularly interesting workshop called "The Rumor Clinic" that was developed by the Anti-Defamation League of B'nai B'rith. That workshop had a profound impact on me that I can still feel to this day, almost thirty years later.

The workshop was conducted using a filmstrip projector. Twenty or thirty teens gathered in a classroom. Before turning on the projector, the leader asked a group of five teens to leave the room. They were given an order in which to reenter the room at the appropriate times. The leader then turned on the projector, and the remaining group saw a drawing projected on the wall. The first teen was asked to reenter the room and look at the picture for thirty seconds, trying to remember as much detail as was possible. He then turned to face the audience, with his back toward the picture, which remained on the screen. The second teen was asked to come in and stand next to the first, facing the audience, but without looking at the picture. The first teen then told the second everything he could remember about the scene. As the third teen entered, also without looking at the picture, the first teen sat down in the audience and listened while the second teen told the third teen everything she could remember about the scene. As this was happening, all of us in the audience could continually observe the picture on the screen as the story it told was relayed on to others. This went on until the fifth teen heard the story and then told all of us what was in the scene. The final four versions of the story were all told by people who had never actually seen the projected image. This is a complex version of the game "broken telephone," which many of us played as children, where a message was whispered from person to person until the final child revealed out loud to the group what message he or she had heard—usually an entirely different message than the original, as the words became garbled through all the whispering and individual interpretation.

But compared to "broken telephone," which is enjoyable, the Anti-Defamation League workshop was quite chilling. The projected image was a street scene in what might have been the Lower East Side of Manhattan in the 1930s. The scene was reminiscent of the streets around Little Italy in the movie *The Godfather II*. There were many people on the streets, as well as many street venders selling from carts or wagons. In the center of the scene was a vegetable stand. Two young boys stood on opposite sides of the cart. One child was white and one was black. The white child was apparently stealing a piece of fruit. Even though it was a still picture, motion was conveyed and the white child appeared to be fleeing with the piece of fruit. The owner of the stand looked very upset and was yelling at the young thief. The black child did nothing but witness the commotion.

You can probably guess where this is heading. By the time the fifth teen was telling the story, the black child had become the thief. I found this to be profoundly distressing. The racial bias was so ingrained in all of us that the Anti-Defamation League could virtually count on this switch happening in the retelling. I conducted this workshop twice myself, and both times the same thing occurred. It is a clear demonstration of how the mind distorts perceptions. And this is not just a story of how teenage minds work. In fact, I believe the phenomenon of preconceived notions grows as we age.

To demonstrate this tendency of subjective perception even more simply, picture five dots as arranged in figure 2, below.

If I were to ask you what picture you can make from these dots, you might say an N or an X or a Z, or even an hourglass. The nature of the mind is to fill in the blanks or connect the dots to make meaning or pictures out of fragmentary bits of data. The mind tends to hold on to particular ways of seeing once it gets programmed that way. Joseph Goldstein, cofounder of the Insight Meditation Society in Barre, Massachusetts, is fond of using the example of stars in the sky. When we see the seven stars that make up the Big Dipper, most of us take delight in pointing out the constellation to whomever we might be with at the time. As he correctly points out, there is no big

[Fig. 2]

dipper in the sky. We are simply seeing points of light. Yet it is difficult to look up and see these points of light and not think "Big Dipper."

Don't Believe Everything You Think about Yourself

When I was in sixth grade, my teacher, Mrs. Hildebrandt, wrote on my report card, "Jeff is lazy." I remember being very upset at seeing this comment. I had been a fairly average student up to that point, occasionally getting checkmarks for good work as well. I still remember how taken aback I was at her remark. It felt like the most serious personal critique I had ever received. There was something that stung deeply in this remark, something that reflected a real inner flaw.

At the time, I didn't think the remark was inaccurate. I didn't put much effort into my schoolwork. But Mrs. Hildebrandt's remark became a turning point for me in terms of getting better marks in school. Suddenly, I knew I was a lazy person and I was mortified that others could see this huge character flaw. My self-identity of being "lazy" stayed with me for a very long time. When I was in my mid-forties, I discussed this incident with my therapist during one session. She responded by telling me that the most likely truth behind my "laziness" was the fact that I must not have felt very challenged by school and that I was performing accordingly. I can't describe how deeply this rang true inside. It was a huge moment of awakening for me. Other school experiences came into focus. I still remember a few really good teachers who knew how to challenge me. In those classes, I was inspired and I worked diligently because the effort itself felt good, as did the learning.

The truth is, I am a fairly industrious person in the arenas in which I choose to engage. In a way, Mrs. Hildebrandt challenged me with her label of "lazy," and I did respond, but with the added burden of feeling badly about myself. What a shame it was to carry around such a negative self-image for over thirty years! One of the biggest components of waking up is to transform our self-hatred into self-love. Over many years, my efforts to push myself to overcome what I believed was my flawed lazy nature formed a pattern with tremendous conscious and unconscious power.

Our thoughts are completely conditioned by past experiences and are often highly illusory. When we get distracted by the illusion, it's hard to see clearly the way things are. To illustrate this point, I'll share an example I gave my children to explain this particular idea to them.

My meditation retreat practice began after I already had my three children. As I began to leave home for periods of a week or two for retreats, during which time I refrained from even calling home, I felt a need to explain to my children what I was doing while I was away.

I wanted them to get a basic understanding of the goals of meditation, not just to focus on the oddities of not talking or the body postures that one usually associates with meditators. When I asked them what they knew about meditation, they would mimic a sitting pose with a silly look on their faces, so I made up the following story to describe the conditioned nature of mind, which I think helped my children to understand the goals and benefits of meditation.

Imagine that you are listening to a cassette tape through head-phones on a Walkman. The tape is full of the most beautiful music, but the volume is turned down pretty low. At the same time, you are sitting in a room with a large TV, and the volume on the TV is very loud. In addition, someone other than you has the remote control for the television, and this person is randomly flipping through the channels. That is what your mind is like. Stories and scenes are playing out in our mind, and it seems we have no control over them. Meditation teaches you how to get control so you can turn down the background noise and hear the beautiful music playing on the tape.

This story reflects some wishful thinking that if we could quiet our minds, all that would be left is the beautiful music on the tape. Actually, what we hear on the tape may or may not be beautiful—it may be great wisdom or it may be scratchy, annoying, and grating sounds. But at least we can hear the tape for what it is. The beauty comes not so much from the object of attention but from the calm and peaceful heart/mind of the beholder.

The conditioning of our small mind colors how we perceive and interpret what we experience. I sometimes offer the following scenario to Jewish audiences to drive home the critical importance of conditioning's impact on who we think we are: Suppose you were kidnapped from the hospital at birth. If you were then taken to a Palestinian refugee camp and raised to adulthood, what do you think your worldview would be like? It is important to see this "truth" of our conditioning without rejecting it or labeling it as a bad thing. By staying open to this truth, we can make wise choices about how to work with it. It is similar to a computer's operating system. The machine itself has hardware that defines many of its capabilities, but it also needs operating system software to function. It is the operating system that organizes data and decides how to display it. Without installing an operating system, even the best computer can do nothing. Likewise, we need an identity to function in the world. Identity is a positive aspect of small mind. Without an identity, why would you go to work or school during the day, or come home to any particular family? The importance of waking up is to remember that your identity is "just an operating system." We can then use this information to observe more clearly the ways in which we are conditioned and to make wiser choices from that awareness.

I recently heard an example of the complex realities that affect our identity. I was listening to National Public Radio's show *This American Life*. The focus of the show was testosterone. Among those interviewed was a man whose testosterone level had dropped to zero due to some medical condition. He experienced some big changes in his life and his personality before finally receiving the diagnosis of an absence of testosterone. He described first noticing a severe loss of motivation. He would still participate in his normal activities since he knew what he was "supposed" to be doing, but he could also lie in bed for hours looking at the wall. Or he might suddenly stop while walking and stare at a tree or at the cracks in the sidewalk. The object of his attention made very little difference. And whatever he saw, he was completely fascinated by it and satisfied just to look. He saw the deep beauty and perfection in all things. He didn't need to possess or own anything to be happy—the thought didn't even arise. His personality was profoundly changed through the lack of testosterone. So we see that our "identity" is also chemically determined.

Another story in the same show also reflected how blood chemistry might affect our sense of self. The host of the program interviewed a person who had decided to change gender from female to male. Part of this person's treatment included taking injections of testosterone, which affected his muscle development and provided for the growth of more body hair. But the person reported other things that stunned the normally unflappable interviewer. He said that after taking the testosterone he became more capable of handling math classes and also developed an interest in science fiction books. "You're blowing all my beliefs about nature versus nurture," said the interviewer. These stories point out that the nature of the mind is even more complicated than we might have imagined.

In general, it can be helpful to soften our belief systems and to cultivate an attitude of openness. This next story takes place in a small shtetl, or village, where Jews used to live in Russia. Imagine *Fiddler on the Roof.* The town was laid out with a town square in the middle. On one side of that square was the synagogue. Across the square from the synagogue lived the rabbi of the town. Each morning, the rabbi would get up, prepare himself, and then walk across the square to lead the morning prayers. The sheriff of the town was a Cossack, although he was usually nice enough to the town's Jewish residents. The sheriff's morning rounds usually put him in the square at the same time as the rabbi, and they would say good morning to each other. This scene had been going on for thirty years.

One morning, the sheriff added some words to his greeting, saying, "Good morning, Rabbi. Where are you off to this morning?" The rabbi responded, "I don't know." Now, who knows why the sheriff asked the rabbi where he was going. He certainly thought that the rabbi was off to the synagogue just like every other morning. Perhaps it was a totally innocent attempt at conversation, or just a few words of feigned interest. In any case, the rabbi's response threw the sheriff into a tizzy; he thought he was being disrespected. Furious, he grabbed the rabbi by the collar of his coat, dragged him to the town jail, and shoved him into a cell. As the sheriff was closing the cell door, the rabbi said, "See, you never know." The truth is, we never know what is coming, and we might be wise not to put too much stock in what we think we know.

When we soften our beliefs, our conceptual approach to reality starts to lose its grip on us and we slowly open up to a more direct and intimate way of experiencing reality. The experience of the beauty and perfection of things is at the center of what is possible for the awakened mind. As the ability to witness, rather than be lost in, the workings of our mind grows within us, we begin to be awake to the truth of each moment. Our sense of wonder and amazement for all of existence shines through. Here is where our experience touches the mystical sense of "knowing" God directly, of seeing the Divine in all things. In the state of mind referred to as *mochin de-gadlut,* or "expanded awareness," we see past the experience of the small self. In its place is a large Self, which is undivided from all being. This unity with all being is what the mystics mean by *devekut,* or "being one with the Divine."

The practices of waking up can take us to a similar place as that experienced by the man without testosterone. However, we do not need to change our body chemistry to have his experience. By paying careful attention to each moment that unfolds inside the small mind, we can, in essence, see the effects of "testosterone" and many other factors on our personality or sense of self. Freedom comes through understanding the effects of the conditions we encounter, not through needing them to be different.

I am reminded of a story that I heard the contemporary spiritual teacher Ram Dass tell a number of times. Ram Dass originally gained notoriety under his former name, Richard Alpert. Alpert was a Harvard professor who pioneered the introduction of LSD along with Timothy Leary. His experimentation with altered consciousness eventually led him to India, where he met his spiritual guru, Neem Karoli Baba. In one of his early meetings, Alpert reports giving his teacher a very strong dose of LSD so that Neem Karoli Baba could understand the nature of the LSD experience. The size of the dose was one that would lead most people into a very intense hallucinogenic experience. Neem Karoli sat calmly though the "trip," and his only response was to say, "Interesting." Neem Karoli Baba's ability to know what states the mind can go through without losing his awakened witnessing made the wild visions of an LSD trip just another one of those small mind experiences. There is in each of us a larger expansive state of mind that is not flustered by the normal swings of our everyday, small mind.

In sharing stories like these there is always a danger of setting up desires to have altered experiences. But it is important to understand that the true nature of the mind is characterized by a combination of *mochin de-gadlut* and *mochin de-katnut.* In other words, expanded awareness and small mind are both an intrinsic part of being human. The expanded state is not, per se, the altered state. In fact, because it is an aspect of our innate nature, it is not something we need to strive for. It is already present. Waking up is a practice of clearing our obscurations so that we can recognize this innate expanded state. It is true that many contemporary seekers have turned to drugs or to long meditation retreats to attain these experiences. When these states occur, they are often accompanied by a strong feeling of rapture in the body. But this rapture and beauty is ephemeral and is soon replaced by a return to the more habitual state of *mochin de-katnut*. The yearning for these transitory blissful states is one of the greatest dangers facing spiritual seekers. The careful practice of being awake to what is, as it arises, whether pleasant or unpleasant, moment-by-moment, is a more wholesome approach. Over time, this practice results in the ability to rest more steadily in an awareness of both mind states and leads to that inner state of being that we call peace, or shalom.

Altered States and Mystical Experiences

Altered states of consciousness are not exempt from all the errors of misperception already described. They can, in fact, be very misleading for just those reasons. The feeling of expansiveness can lead to a belief that such an experience is "the whole truth." Since these altered states are different from the normal sense of self as defined by our smaller ego, they can mistakenly be seen as the large Self or God nature. In these states, we can experience voices or visions that may seem like they come from angels, God, or even demons. In most cases, these voices or visions are simply the result of the small mind fitting new experiences into its normal patterns of understanding things. For example, when one of my teachers experienced what she described as God's breath on the back of her neck in a period of intense practice, her teacher told her not to reify the experience. Reification is the ascribing of prior views onto a new experience without accepting the experience on its own simple terms. "God's breath" was really just a sense of tingling on the back of the neck accompanied by sensations of openness and expansiveness. Calling that sensation God added an extra layer of meaning. This is not to imply that what my teacher experienced wasn't God's breath, but only to point out that we tend to want to have exalted experiences.

An extreme example of this phenomenon is described in the life of J. Krishnamurti. Krishnamurti was an early-twentieth-century spiritual teacher who had a great impact on many of his generation. He was originally trained by the leaders of the Theosophical Society to become one of their leaders. The present goals of the Theosophical Society as stated on its website are: "To form a nucleus of the universal brotherhood of humanity, without distinction of race, creed, sex, caste, or color. To encourage the comparative study of religion, philosophy, and science. To investigate unexplained laws of nature and the powers latent in humanity."

The Theosophical Society was founded in the United States in 1875. By 1882, the headquarters had moved to India. In the early 1900s, the society's leaders believed that a new spiritual age was about to dawn, and they were looking for the "new world leader." Krishnamurti, whose father worked for the Theosophical Society, was identified as that leader through so-called clairvoyant methods. He was fifteen years old at the time, and was taken under the wings of the top echelons of the Theosophical Society and given intense training in religious and esoteric teachings. A biography by Pupul Jayakar recounts the many transcendent experiences Krishnamurti had. He often saw the various holy teachers residing in realms other than this one who were "directing" the works of the society. Krishnamurti described one such occurrence in a letter to Annie Bassant, the society's president: "In front of me was my body and over the head I saw the star bright and clear. Then I could feel the vibration of the Lord Buddha; I beheld Lord Maitreya and master K. H. I was so happy, calm and at peace."[1]

Krishnamurti had many years filled with such experiences. Yet, as he grew and matured he began to deeply understand the nature of his own mind. He broke off ties with the Society when he realized that his experiences were the result of the deep conditioning that accompanied his training in the beliefs of the theosophists. He eventually renounced his mystical visions. Later, he said that "all images and manifestations, however profound, were projections of the mind."[2] His visions were all connected to the pictures of the saints he had seen in his training. He emphatically taught that his visions, while actual mental experiences, were all delusions caused by his own mind.

Knowing about the mind's tendency to manufacture perceptions based on our conditioning can be an important aid, especially when practicing intensively. As altered states arise, it is possible to learn from them without reading more into them than we should. A few examples from my own retreat experience will illustrate some points in working with altered states.

Once, on the third night of a silent retreat, with eyes closed, I was paying close attention to my breath as it entered my nostrils. My attention became fairly riveted to the sensations, and I began to feel an energy pattern that was both outside and inside my body. It was as if I could feel the breath coming toward me, starting about one foot in front and to the left of my nose. This energy pattern was in itself an interesting phenomenon that served to heighten my attention to this present experience. I remember taking five breaths in this state, when suddenly a full-blown visual hallucination began. I was now standing on the top of a mountain, looking out at other mountains. It was a fairly bleak landscape, in black and white. There was no vegetation, only rocks and boulders in the foreground and mountains in the background. I was stunned at the onset of this vision. It was the first time I had experienced either an energy pattern or a hallucination while meditating. The feeling in my body was similar to that which occurs when using various psychoactive drugs.

As the visual part of my hallucination began, my first reaction was, "Oh wow!" This was immediately followed by, "Oh no!" I had not expected to have these kinds of experiences while meditating. I sought out meditation as a way of becoming clearer in my life. I suppose I had heard that meditation can lead to altered states, but that was not what my teachers talked about, and it was not what I was seeking. So when I began to hallucinate, I was surprised and thrilled ("Oh wow!"). I was also aware that this thrill was a potential trap ("Oh no!"). I did not come to meditation to get high, but rather to get clear. I think this was all instantly clear to me in the very first moment of the hallucination. I entered that moment with much of the sophisticated understanding of human nature already available to me. My motivation was clear, and the trap (lusting after these states) was also clear and therefore avoidable. That does not mean that the traps can be ignored. It is very helpful to have spiritual partners in this work—teachers and friends who can help guide you through potential difficulties as they arise.

I did not know how long this vision of being on a mountaintop would last, and thought that as long as I was here, I should look around and explore. As I gazed out from my vantage point, I slowly shifted my view to the right and was able to see mountains on the horizon. In reality, I was not turning my body at all since I was sitting still with my eyes closed, and my shift in gaze occurred only within my mind. There was nothing particularly vivid about these mountains, but as I scanned the horizon, their features changed, as would happen when looking at mountains in real life. The most interesting part of the visual experience to me was that as I rotated my gaze, I never came back to my starting point. I had rotated more than 360 degrees!

I haven't thought much about the experience since that night many years ago, though retelling it here has piqued my curiosity to check out some aspects of what occurred. I rarely tell the story since the details are not central to the development of the compassionate heart. Having experiences of altered states is also not necessary, and I usually only share these stories with those who have had such experiences, since it can be helpful for them to hear of my own hallucination and reaction to it. Approximately two-thirds of all those who take on a serious contemplative practice do not have these kinds of experiences, and that lack of experience in no way hinders the development of wisdom and happiness that is possible from this work. It may cause a stirring of lust to have visions, but the pitfall of attachment to altered states is also avoided. These altered states are worth discussing, however, because such experiences can be misconstrued.

For my part, I did not think that I had received a mystic vision when I experienced this mountaintop hallucination, but it is possible for the ego to claim such events as a sign of its uniqueness. I was able to witness my ego doing just that, but there was a transparency to this ego reaction, and I didn't become attached to the experience. Sometimes intensive concentration practice is accompanied by undirected movements or contortions in the body. One Friday night, five days into another retreat, I experienced my lips moving into a puckered "kiss" position. I had the strongest sense that this kiss was being met and reciprocated at the "other end." It felt as if a presence—God—was kissing me back, à la the mystical union described in Song of Songs. Once again, I realized that my mind was interpreting the experience with the conditioning and imagery it had stored. I notice quite frequently that some of my most powerful experiences and insights tend to arise on Shabbat when I am on retreat, as this one did. Is this because of the unique nature of Shabbat, or because I have a Shabbat rhythm to my life? Are those two explanations really any different? I think that together they provide a deeper reality than thinking that God appeared to me because it was Shabbat.

Mystical experiences throughout the ages have been characterized by descriptions of altered consciousness. Jewish mystics of the past rarely described the exact nature of their practices, although they occasionally described their visions. When I read about their mystical experiences, a critique comes to mind. While it reveals a kind of hubris to comment on another person's inner experience—especially if they are noted leaders in their communities—it is reasonable to speculate about the possibility that, like all human beings, any person's small ego and their conditioning might play some role in their altered visions. Not every Jewish mystic saw through the veil of their own experiences as did Krishnamurti. While they undoubtedly used techniques that contributed to the arising of altered states, they may have overvalued or misconstrued the results. Some of their texts are marked by metaphysical musings. As my teacher Reb Zalman used to say, these works are often full of "angelshit," a term he coined to be the spiritual equivalent of "bullshit."

Warnings for Potential Mystics

We might find a further refinement of the difference between genuine mystical experiences and visions arising out of ego conditioning in the rabbinic injunction that kabbalah (Jewish mystical teachings) should only be taught to learned men over the age of forty. At first look, this injunction might seem to be an attempt to restrict religious authority to the powers that be. However, if we assume that teaching kabbalah involves instruction in the actual techniques necessary to attain direct mystical experiences, then this injunction points to something different.

I believe the classical Jewish mystics who were committed to a revealed Torah—a Torah that has already defined God's plan for humanity—were concerned about the impact of mystical experiences in which one has direct access to divine awareness. If you can know God directly, then what need do you have for the Torah, especially if your personal revelations are different than what is written? It is reasonable to assume that if you share kabbalistic practices with a learned man who is already over the age of forty, this person will already be very deeply steeped in the premystical foundations of Torah study, and involved in a highly prescribed set of daily Jewish practices. If such a person, then, has direct mystical experiences, it is much more likely that he will understand his experiences through the prism of his already well-established beliefs.

In contrast to this critique, there are additional reasons for this injunction that I appreciate. Altered states of consciousness are quite powerful experiences. They often do break through the habitual workings of the mind. In people whose mental clarity may already be shaky, this breaking through can be risky. It can become difficult to reorganize your thinking into a coherent personality, which is necessary to function in society. So our Sages rightly emphasized the dangers of such practices. The classical story from the Talmud about the dangers of mystical journeys is the following:

> Our Rabbis taught: Four men entered the Garden namely, Ben Azzai and Ben Zoma, Aher and Rabbi Akiba…. Ben Azzai cast a look and died…. Ben Zoma looked and became demented…. Aher cut the shoots…. Rabbi Akiba entered in peace and departed in peace. (Chagiga 14b)

Many people have commented extensively on these lines. Most scholars believe that the practice used by these four men was one of the earliest Jewish mystical practices and was called *merkavah* (chariot) mysticism. It refers to Ezekiel's vision of a fiery chariot (Ezek. 1). Very little is actually known about the practice of *merkavah* mysticism.

Those who practiced it were referred to as *yorday merkavah,* or those who "descend" into the chariot. Some contemporary teachers have construed the practice to be a guided meditation and the descent as an implication of deep inner work.

In any case, the Talmud seems to be indicating that the practice was perilous. Perhaps these men entered a state of mystical union with the Divine. Ben Azzai never came back from that place, and died. Ben Zoma was not able to reintegrate into everyday consciousness. Rabbi Akiba, who in the Talmudic account seems to be the leader of the others, was able to smoothly enter and return. The fourth person is not referred to by name but by the reference of "Aher" (the other). His real name was Elisha Ben Abuyah. He was called "the other" in the Talmud because he had been a great Jewish Sage up until this experience. The reference that he "cut the shoots" was an aphorism meaning that he became an apostate to the normative Judaism of his day and age. His apostasy put him outside of respectability, but his knowledge and wisdom level was undeniable and so he is quoted in the Talmud but never by his name. Theologian Milton Steinberg presents an alternative view to Ben Abuyah's apostasy in the book *As a Driven Leaf.* Steinberg argues that Ben Abuyah is represented as becoming open to all spiritual traditions, not only Jewish practices, through his mystical experiences. His reintegration after mystical union was to see the Divine Presence in all paths and people, not just Jews. Perhaps this story of the four men is the source of the fear that led to the injunction about who should be allowed access to kabbalah. It is, at least, a warning that practices that affect the basic programming code of the human mind should be treated with respect.

The Reward of Insights

In chapter 8 I will explore the importance of adding periods of daylong, weekendlong, weeklong, and occasionally multiweek periods of intensive meditation practice. These are usually best done in some sort of retreat setting, away from our normal daily haunts. During such periods, it is possible to experience unfamiliar mind states that allow glimpses of reality from a new perspective. In this chapter, I want to introduce some of the insights that may arise from such practice in order to reflect further on the normal workings of small mind. For these practices, it is important to have good teachers who have already traveled these paths and who can guide you out of the mental "sand traps" that can come along the way.

One relevant Jewish story takes place in a synagogue on Yom Kippur. The rabbi and the president of the synagogue are commenting to each other while standing on the bimah, the raised platform where the congregational leaders pray. They have just been praying to God, saying, "Dear God, you are so great and I am so small and flawed. Please accept my prayers of repentance," when the two overhear the man who cleans up the chapel praying, "O God, I am such a nothing. May I be worthy of your love." The president turns to the rabbi and says, "Look who thinks he's a nothing."

Not just anyone is ready to be a *nothing*—that is, a person who recognizes that the small self is illusory. In this story, we get the feeling that the poor clean-up man is the "real" nothing. The rabbi and president are *too* full of themselves to leave *mochin de-katnut* behind. The story makes a point about refined contemplative practice. It is important to have a healthy, relatively flexible ego before working with practices that tend to dissolve the ego. On the other hand, an over-inflated ego can be a barrier and lead us to visions of grandeur rather than to grand visions.

The intensity of long practice periods supported by the silent retreat atmosphere can serve as a great purification practice. My coteachers and I often refer to the purifying of the heart that is occurring as we teach retreats. Sometimes, near the end of a retreat, I like to describe what has happened as a kind of "brainwashing." It usually gets a laugh and I break the word apart to show the benevolent aspect of "washing the brain" by cleaning out patterns of misconceptions. But I also am trying to point out how powerful this kind of practice can be and how we need to be cautious and responsible about "reprogramming" the mind. The ability to watch the workings of our minds in a refined way can, in fact, lead to an opportunity to reformat our programming.

Reb Zalman once said that the mind is like tofu. If you are a tofu eater you know that plain tofu is pretty tasteless. The way you give flavor to tofu is by pickling it in some kind of brine. It is the brine that imparts the flavor to the tofu. Therefore, the final flavor depends on the kind of brine you use. What kind of brine are we using to pickle our minds? It is important to pay close attention to the kind of situations we place ourselves in. For example, if we find like-minded friends who want to work on spiritual practice, we add a certain kind of influence that is different than the influence of business partners whose only desire is to acquire wealth. If we watch nothing but sexist or violent films, we condition the mind to accept such attitudes and behavior as normal. The way we condition our minds has a profound effect on our daily lives and our relationships. So, choose your brine wisely!

Be Careful When You Speak Your Mind

One experience I had after a particularly powerful silent retreat at Spirit Rock in California is an example of the promises and perils of deconditioning the mind. Speech has tremendous ramifications, including how it affects our own conditioning. Working with speech is a central religious practice in Judaism, although one that can be very challenging. Perhaps you have heard of the term *lashon harah*, or "evil speech." It usually refers to the use of speech to say something negative about another person. This can cause the estimation of the person in the mind of the listener to be lessened. Speech is very powerful this way. Speech can also implant images in our own minds, which then are repeated over and over in our thoughts. One way of working with speech is to have rules about what should or should not be said. These rules can be difficult to follow. I once heard that the definition of the word *instantaneous* is the time between the arising of a thought and its expression in words. The contemplative approach to working with speech can result in a deep inner realization of the motivation and effects of speech. Periods of intensive practice that include long periods of refraining from speech can offer insights into these effects.

At the end of this same retreat, my teacher, Sylvia Boorstein, asked me if I would like to meet the other four teachers of the retreat. The teachers had been asked to meet with a reporter at the end of the retreat for an interview about what it was like to teach meditation retreats, and Sylvia, who I knew from the time she had spent teaching at Elat Chayyim, invited me to sit in on the interview. Being a retreat center director myself, I was thrilled with the invitation to get a glimpse behind the scenes. The interview took place in one of the teacher's bedrooms. I had been practicing walking slowly and eating slowly, all of the things you do on these retreats to help you calm the mind. When I entered the interview room, I found what seemed to be a whirlwind of activity. There were multiple conversations going on, as well as packing. The reporter turned on the tape and began firing questions. The packing continued at the same time. In that instant, after spending a week in a simpler, much slower rhythm, multitasking looked extremely odd. It was actually difficult to follow the pace of the reporter's questions and the teachers' responses. My mind was still going in slow motion. In that state of mind, I noticed that I, too, had responses to many of the questions being asked about leading a retreat, but since I was sitting in only as a visitor, I didn't have to say anything. It was easy to see my ego wanting to jump in. I wanted these teachers to recognize me as knowledgeable, not just as one of the retreat participants. It was fascinating to be able to see this urge to speak so clearly rather than to be caught up in the actual speaking.

Besides, I had already made one attempt at reentering the world of speech and was just as happy to remain silent. One of the final practices on the retreat was to break silence. Students were asked to break up into pairs and practice conversation with each other. I found this exercise to be quite informative, as well as a little distressing. Each person was asked to share a little of what the retreat had been like, while the other person silently witnessed. My eight-day retreat had been totally powerful and overwhelming. My longest prior retreat had been three days, and was a retreat just for rabbis, many of whom were my closest friends. It was also a very deep experience, but I did not know through that experience what could happen to the mind on a longer retreat.

I reentered the world of speech by sharing my retreat "peak" experiences with my partner. When I finished speaking, my partner began his sharing. His first comment was about how he wished that he, too, could have had the kind of experiences I had. I immediately felt like it had not been so wise to just blurt out my "peak" experiences. It seemed to me that it added to my partner's disappointment. While it would not be very useful or accurate to take full responsibility for causing his suffering, I realized that I may have subtly been bragging and could have shared some more mundane events or the lessons I had learned rather than my peak experience. I felt terrible that my first act of speech seemed so clumsy and possibly hurtful, yet I also appreciated the lesson of seeing how powerful speech is.

When I left the retreat that day, I continued to have some really important realizations regarding speech. One of the first things I had to do the following morning was to go shopping for clothes. When I knew I was going to be in California for this retreat, I had asked a friend in Los Angeles to try to arrange for me to have a meeting with the staff of the Righteous Person's Foundation—Steven Spielberg's Jewish support foundation dedicated to supporting efforts that build a diverse and vibrant Jewish community in the United States. I was hoping to ask for grant support for Elat Chayyim. I had not heard whether this meeting would happen, and was not optimistic that it could be arranged. When the retreat ended on Sunday, I found out that a meeting had in fact been arranged for Tuesday morning. So, Monday morning I found myself at a fancy men's clothing store.

Shopping for clothes has never been one of my favorite activities. I picked out pants, a vest, and two shirts. Then I remembered that I only had a pair of sneakers with me and would need to buy shoes as well. We went to the back of the same store to look at the shoes. They only had Italian-made dress shoes, none of which would fit my wide foot. The salesperson mentioned that there was a shoe store in the same strip mall that I could try. Noticing some impatience begin inside me, I heard the voice in my head about to say, "I hate shopping. Let's just go next door and get this over with." But I said nothing. I have said the phrase, "I hate shopping" many times, but not since that day.

When the speed of thought slows down on a meditation retreat, it is possible to notice many things about the contents of your thoughts before they manifest as actions or words. My first thought after seeing impatience arising in myself was that I didn't want to use the word *hate*. During the retreat I had gotten in touch with a desire to avoid certain kinds of harsh language. So I didn't want to say the words *I hate* regardless of how the sentence might be finished. This pause in what would have been a normal reaction in speaking out my feelings allowed other wisdom to arise as well. At that moment, I realized that "I hate shopping" was not even an accurate statement of how I was feeling in that moment. The fact is, I was really enjoying shopping in that store! I had just lost thirty pounds in the preceding months, and looking at myself in the mirror with some nice new clothing was a pleasant experience. I could also see that it would have only taken one repetition of the phrase, "I hate shopping" to reinstall that negative program on the hard drive of my mind.

The Annual Forty-Day Program of Purification

What are we to do with these minds whose very nature makes it difficult to see clearly? In the Jewish tradition there are periods where inner work is called for. On Rosh Hashanah, the Jewish New Year, it is the custom to begin ten days of serious work in purifying ourselves that culminates in Yom Kippur, the Day of Atonement. These ten days are called the days of repentance or turning (*aseret y'may teshuvah*). On Yom Kippur, we want to have completed this work of purification in order that we might stand in oneness with the Divine Presence.

Our Sages recognized that ten days might not be adequate for the task of purification. They said that we should begin this work not on Rosh Hashanah, but thirty days earlier, at the beginning of the month of Elul, which precedes Rosh Hashanah. This would add up to a total of forty days. Why forty days? Forty is a number of great spiritual significance as it is used over and over in the Torah. After Noah built the ark, it rained for forty days. Moses, we are told, was forty years old when he left Egypt. He then wandered as a shepherd for the next forty years until he came to the burning bush. He lived another forty years after that until he died. When he went up onto Mount Sinai, after the Exodus from Egypt, in order to receive God's word, he was on the mountain for forty days.

Why is forty so important? I first heard an explanation from Deborah Kruger, a fabric artist who was working with this theme of forty. In biblical times, forty was considered to be the number of weeks between the start of a pregnancy and the subsequent birth. Of course, we now know that a better approximation is thirty-eight weeks, because the fertile period comes about two weeks after the last onset of menses. But before we could look inside bodies to understand ovulation, people counted from the time of the last bleeding. This makes forty a very "pregnant" number. Forty, from this perspective, is no longer seen as a literal teaching but rather as a spiritual truth that the Torah wants us to see. Whenever something needs to go through the radical process of conception to birth, or similarly to die out and start over, the Torah uses forty. So, the evil generation of the flood is wiped out in forty days so that the new can emerge. Moses's life as a prince in Egypt ends or "dies" at age forty. It takes him forty years to be reborn at the burning bush. It takes forty days to hear the new revelation on Sinai. And, it takes forty days for us to be ready for the old patterns of thought and behavior to die on Yom Kippur, and for the new Divine Presence to shine through us.

A standard line appears in the liturgy for that period of purification, telling us how to accomplish the necessary transformation. We are told that on Rosh Hashanah our fate for the coming year is written, and on Yom Kippur it is sealed. That is to say, there are natural consequences that result from how we live our lives. This is always true, not only on Rosh Hashanah. In fact, the Talmud makes exactly this point when discussing this idea. R. Jose comments "that man is judged every day," and R. Nathan says, "Man is judged every moment." So the practices for repentance should be used as much as possible year round. In addition, our tradition teaches that if we spend ten days in a serious practice of purification, it is possible to rewrite what the next year may look like. Perhaps we could use any ten days (or forty days) for this process, but it is much more likely to occur if we have the support of others engaged in the same task. The communal nature of atonement (at-one-ment) fosters the process, just as sitting silently with others enhances meditative experiences.

The repentance necessary for our purification is accomplished as follows, according to the high holy day liturgy: *"Teshuvah u-tefillah u-tsedakah mah-ah-vay-reen et ro-ah ha-g'zayrah,"* or, "But repentance and prayer and righteous deeds nullify the evil decree." This can refer to all the practices I discuss in this book. *Teshuvah,* "turning" or "repentance," refers to the deep inner process of exploring our thoughts and deeds, taking an inner moral inventory. *Teshuvah* can be understood as the process of re-turning the attention to the truth of each moment. It is at the core of the practices discussed in this book. Whenever the mind gets lost in thoughts of greed or anger, *teshuvah* is the process of returning to balance and clarity of vision. Prayer is the process of aligning our attention to the Divine Presence, which includes, but is not limited to, some of the prayer practices discussed in this book. *Tzedakah,* "acting righteously," is often defined as the giving of money to worthy causes, but it also addresses the whole realm of living justly in the world—the need to live and act with an attitude of kindness and compassion.

There is another profound teaching available to us that is related to, yet more expansive than, the threefold practice of repentance, prayer, and charity which comes to us in the liturgy. While the liturgy quotes these three methods, the Talmud mentions four things: "R. Isaac further said: Four things cancel the doom of a man, namely, *charity, prayer, change of name, change of conduct*" (Rosh Hashanah 16b). The idea of name change was left out of the liturgy, perhaps because it seemed too easy compared to the other three.

I first came across this Talmudic teaching in theologian Arthur Waskow's *Seasons of Our Joy,* and witnessed it put into practice on Rosh Hashanah retreats sponsored by B'nai Or in the early 1980s, when Reb Zalman would ask participants to take on new names for the year.

Over the years as I pondered this practice, I began to think that the Talmud was suggesting something even deeper then a mere name change. The practice could be construed as really changing your identity, not just the outer label. This is more difficult than it sounds. Even with the profound purification that is possible through intensive periods of practice, the power of old patterns of behavior and identity is fierce. One of the things I realized from teaching the name change exercise myself at many retreats is that once we go back into our normal lives, even with a new name, others treat us like our old selves, and this forces us back into the molds we were trying to escape.

An interesting thing happened when I was researching the material for this section about the process of change during the High Holy Days. When I checked the Talmudic references, I noticed that a fifth method was also left out of the liturgy: "Some say that change of place (also works)" (Rosh Hashanah 16b). This seems to support my own belief that by occasionally going on retreat and leaving the habitual contexts of our daily lives, we can more easily soften our identifications and encourage ourselves to give birth to inner changes. I believe that even making occasional larger changes, possibly relocating, changing your livelihood, or changing the people you hang out with, can also foster change. This presentation of the Jewish New Year cycle is an example of using ritual to encourage the work of waking up. But besides the inner commitment to wake up and giving ourselves the time to do it, we need additional tools to deal with the nature of the small mind. The following chapter explores contemplative ways of working with the particularly difficult mind states that we all experience.

4 Making the Darkness Conscious

As we begin to pay closer attention to the truth of our moment-by-moment experience—especially to the inner mental reactions that accompany sensations, feelings, and perceptions—most of us will start noticing a variety of challenging patterns. For one, we start seeing that our thoughts are often so loud that we barely notice the sensations in our bodies—we are not in the present moment, but lost in a mind storm about the past or future. Equally common and even more humbling is the awareness of how negative our thoughts tend to be. Our minds are often filled with thoughts of self-criticism, or judgment and anger toward others. When we pay attention to the activity of our mind, we become painfully aware of our compulsions and addictions. Although this confrontation with our own negativity can be quite disheartening, it is a crucial step in the process of developing an awakened heart.

My first silent retreat, an introduction to mindfulness meditation for rabbis, came at a time in my life when I was feeling particularly frustrated about a number of things. I would often break out in tears during this retreat. In the silence and sparseness of the retreat form, you come face-to-face with yourself, just as you are, and there is nowhere to hide from your difficult thoughts and emotions. This is why the practice of noticing the truth of each moment is sometimes called a "naked practice." Difficult as this practice is, it helps make the retreat experience immensely valuable. Swiss psychiatrist Carl Jung once said, "One does not become enlightened by imagining figures of light, but by making the darkness conscious…. The latter procedure, however, is disagreeable and therefore not very popular." This is an idea worth reflecting on.

Over the years, I have talked to many people about their meditation practice, and they often seem to think that their practice is going well when everything is calm or blissful. Conversely, their practice is deemed as going poorly when the mind is filled with anger or sadness or worry. While this assumption is quite understandable, it's nevertheless a wrong conclusion about the state of their meditation practice. The truth is that the deepest value of being awake to the truth of each moment comes when we face our difficulties with openness and honesty. As Jung pointed out, most of us try to avoid that route. But waking up fully is not possible without looking deeply at everything it means to be human, the painful and the pleasant, the dark and the light.

Among the issues I was dealing with on that first silent retreat was my compulsive eating. I believe this pattern of behavior arose as an attempt to avoid dealing with difficult feelings. We all have avoidance behaviors that can be called self-medicating. In my own life, I have used food, television, movies, sexual activity, exercise, work, fantasy, and more to avoid noticing the unpleasant sides of my life. But it is important for me to accept without judgment that I do act in these ways. The practice of waking up helps us to see the underlying conditions, including mental patterns that result in the way we live our lives. When we see these patterns for what they are, we become free to try more effective behaviors. Rather than judging our mental patterns as failures, it is important to cultivate compassion for our own humanity. When our hearts open to our own suffering, we begin to also be more accepting of others and to realize that they too have the same struggles.

With an understanding of the value to be gained, we can face our difficult thoughts, desires, and emotions directly. What may look like garbage is actually the raw material for creating the compost necessary for our growth. As with real garbage, we don't want to leave ours lying around, smelling things up and festering. It needs to be treated properly to become fertilizer.

The Evil Inclination

The Jewish Sages called the energy that leads us astray the *yetzer harah,* or "evil inclination." When I first heard about the *yetzer harah* in various Jewish teachings about human nature, I was very turned off by the idea. My sense of self at the time was not open to the thought that I had an evil inclination. I hadn't thought that much about the nature of evil, and certainly didn't think that there was a force of evil with its own power residing within me and pervading the rest of the universe as well.

It was only years later that I began to develop a different understanding of evil and the evil inclination. A familiar story about Shabbat helped me gain this understanding. We are taught that angels come and visit each home on Shabbat. A special song is sung to welcome them in—after the candle lighting and before the blessing over wine. In this story, we are taught that two angels come to each home, the good angel and the evil angel. If the family is one that does not observe Shabbat, the angels might find that the household looks just like it does on other weeknights. No candles have been lit and there is no other sign of Sabbath observance. The house may be messy, and the parents may be busy rushing to get some dinner together. The family may never even get together for a meal. Perhaps the kids eat in front of the television. If the family does manage to eat together, the meal might be filled with yelling or teasing. In this case, the evil angel says, "May next Shabbat be like this Shabbat."

If, on the other hand, the family is one that honors the Sabbath, then the house may have been cleaned up. The dinner is prepared ahead of time and the Sabbath candles are burning. Everyone has put on festive clothes to honor the holy day. As is the custom, the parents may be giving blessings to their children. In this case, the good angel says, "May next Shabbat be like this Shabbat." When I first heard this story, I loved that the two angels say the same thing. The good angel and the evil angel do not represent external forces pushing us in a particular direction. Rather, they are a reflection of the way that we as human beings are conducting our lives, and they point out the corresponding impact. In our tradition, angels are considered to be messengers. These angels can be seen as bringers of consciousness to the situation they find. Their message is a truth about human behavior and the momentum created by our actions.

I remember thinking about this story one day while I was jogging. I go through phases of regular exercise followed by other periods of months or even years without a daily workout. On this particular run, I was reflecting on the fact that I was now running for the third consecutive day, and the good angel came to my mind, saying, "May tomorrow be like today." Momentum is the force in our lives that tends to push us in the same direction we have been heading. This truth about the power of momentum is critical in recognizing the importance of having a daily practice. It reminds me of a Jewish teaching that when some ritual observance is done three times in a row in a particular way, its practice becomes a *hazakah,* or "binding custom," to be continued from that point forward. *Hazakah* means "strong" in Hebrew. When we do something on a regular basis, its habitual force becomes stronger. We can use this truth about momentum to understand our own thoughts as well as our actions.

After using the story of the good angel and the evil angel many times in my teachings, I told it to a group that included eleven rabbinical students. One of them mentioned that she heard the end of the story somewhat differently. In her version, when the house was a mess it was the good angel that had to say, "May next Shabbat be like this Shabbat," and vice versa. I liked this version because it added another layer of meaning. Even the good angel has to recognize the power of momentum when it is not working in a positive way. It is not "good" enough to wait only for the nice situation to arise to make a comment. Angels have no free will, so the good angel is compelled to speak the truth about the "bad" scene, and the evil angel must acknowledge the "positive" behavior. This ending makes it even more imperative that we look at all our behavior because the momentum it generates has a force beyond our intention to do something different next time.

In thinking about the *yetzer harah,* the Sages mention that we have two *yetzrim,* two inclinations, the evil one and the good one. However, although the story of the angels implies that we have only one *yetzer,* how it affects us is completely dependant on our past deeds.

If we follow the origin of Jewish teachings about the *yetzer* and how the Sages developed this teaching, we find the same conclusion.

The first mention of the word *yetzer* comes in connection to God making human beings, in the book of Genesis. This makes sense, since Genesis (from a psycho-spiritual perspective) is a story about the development of human nature and consciousness. The word *yetzer* means "formation" and is connected to the verb *to form*. According to Aryeh Kaplan, a late-twentieth-century scholar of Jewish mysticism, the verb *y-tz-r* is used when referring to something that is formed out of already extant material.[1] For something created out of nothing, the verb *b-r-a* is used, as in the first story of the Bible, when humans are created on the sixth day, in Genesis 1:27: "God created *(b-r-a)* humankind in his image, in the image of God did he create it, male and female did he create them."[2] In the second story, which begins in chapter 2, God forms humans by breathing into the dust of the earth: "And YHVH, God, formed *(y-tz-r)* the human, of dust from the soil, he blew into his nostrils the breath of life and the human became a living being" (Gen. 2:7).[3]

We have already looked at Genesis 2:7 in connection with the divine breath and its relevance to our practice. The last two words of the verse, *living being,* are in Hebrew, *nefesh chayah. Chayah* is the word for living. The word *nefesh* refers to one of the levels of soul that are aspects of consciousness. Here it serves as a clue to seeing in this verse a commentary on the *yetzer*. The *yetzer* is a force related to a lower, or less encompassing, level of consciousness, the level of *nefesh*. (For more on *nefesh,* see the section on the levels of soul/consciousness in chapter 5.)

The word *yetzer* itself is used as follows in Genesis 2:7:

$$\text{וַיִּיצֶר יְהֹוָה אֱלֹהִים אֶת הָאָדָם} \ldots$$

Vah-yee-tsair YHVH et ha-adam…

And YHVH, God, formed the human…

If you look at the first Hebrew word (that is, the one furthest to the right, remembering to read the letters from right to left), *vah-yee-tsair* (and *God* formed), you will see that the second and third letters are the same, the letter *yud*. This doubling of the letter *yud* turns out to be an extraneous usage of the letter. A single *yud* suffices to produce the same word. Whenever a textual reference in Torah contains an anomalous occurrence, that event must be explained. Our Sages said one reason for the extra *yud* in this case was to refer to a twofold formation, or two *yetzrim* (inclinations)—a *yetzer hatov* (good inclination) and a *yetzer harah* (bad inclination)—that were formed at the same moment. Up to this point in the text, we have yet to see the connection between the *yetzer* and the qualities of good or evil. This makes sense since what we see that is "formed" in this verse is the beginning development of human consciousness, before which the concept of evil is not relevant.

Just two verses later, in Genesis 2:9, we are introduced to two very special trees in the Garden of Eden:

> YHVH, God, planted a garden in Eden/Land of Pleasure, in the east, and there he placed the human whom he had formed. YHVH, God, caused to spring up from the soil every type of tree, desirable to look at and good to eat, and the Tree of Life in the midst of the garden and the Tree of Knowing of Good and Evil.[4]

This is the Torah's introduction of evil. Significantly, the word *evil* comes joined to the word *knowing,* linking evil to human consciousness.

The first reference to a *yetzer harah,* an evil inclination, comes a few chapters later, when we are given what seem to be two very specific verses about our evil nature. The story moves past the first family, Adam and Eve, and jumps to a time when there are already many human beings in the world (and hence much evil). In this story, Noah, who was a righteous person in an "evil" generation, is told by God that the earth is going to be covered by a flood. He is told to build an ark to save his family and two of every living creature, so that after the flood the world can be repopulated. In this story, the flood is the instrument that will clear out the evil in the world. I think it can also be a fitting metaphor for the power of evil itself. It is as if to wipe out something as powerful as the flood of evil, an even bigger flood is necessary.

The flood is an apt metaphor for what the power of our addictions and compulsive behaviors feels like—a flood of energy, hard to resist. We can feel flooded by torrents of desire. The metaphor of a massive flood that can destroy all the life of the world points to the magnitude of the task of dealing with our own greed and anger. In Genesis 6:5 we read:

וְכָל־יֵצֶר מַחְשְׁבֹת לִבּוֹ רַק רַע כָּל־הַיּוֹם

V'khall yetzer mahch-sh'vot lee-bo rock rah kall hayom

And every form of their heart's planning was only evil all the day.[5]

This is the first use of the word *yetzer* connected to the concept of a *yetzer harah*. We might translate this key phrase as follows: "And every inclination of the thoughts of his heart was evil all day." This seems like a very clear indictment of human nature at the time of Noah, and perhaps in our time as well. It seems that no room is left for a good inclination.

The building of the ark follows this verse. Noah collects the pairs of animals and ushers them inside it. The flood destroys the rest of the beings on Earth, and when the waters eventually subside, the inhabitants of the ark go forth to repopulate the earth. To express his feelings, Noah builds an altar to offer sacrifices to YHVH as we read in Genesis 8:21: "Now YHVH smelled the soothing savor and YHVH said in his heart: I will never curse the soil again on humankind's account, since what the human heart forms is evil from its youth."[6] The verse ends with the Hebrew phrase:

כִּי יֵצֶר לֵב הָאָדָם רַע מִנְּעֻרָיו

Kee yetzer lev hah-adam rah me-n'ah-rahv

Since what the human heart forms is evil from its youth.

Another translation of the Hebrew *yetzer lev* could be "the inclination of the heart." Here again is what appears to be a blanket condemnation of human nature. From youth onward, the human heart is only inclined to evil.

The Serious and Beautiful Problem of Your Childish Consciousness

As I worked with these verses, I wondered if there was another way to understand their meaning. A friend and colleague of mine, Rabbi Sheila Peltz-Weinberg, reminded me that the Sages had another opinion on the *yetzer,* one closer to the more neutral view I was searching for. In the commentaries to Genesis, the Midrash, we are taught, "But for the Evil Desire, however, no man would build a house, take a wife, and beget children" (Bereshit Rabbah 9:7).[7] The *yetzer* that pushes us into a monogamous marriage is the same *yetzer* that can also result in harmful sexual infidelities. The *yetzer* that leads us to have children can also impel us to abandon our children when they most need us. We may seek not one house but many houses as our obsession with wealth drives a conspicuous consumption. Some of us seek not just a career, but notoriety and power over others.

Considering the importance of dealing with these primal forces, I kept looking at these Torah verses to see if there were perhaps more hints about the way the *yetzer* manifests as evil. Reviewing the words of Genesis 6:5, "And every inclination of the thoughts of his heart was evil all day," brought my attention to the word *thoughts.* The verse does not say that the heart itself is evil but rather that the thoughts of the heart are evil. The problem, in other words, resides in the nature of the thought process and not in the heart/mind itself. Certain types of thoughts create clouds in the mind, and the heart becomes constricted and fearful. This gives rise to unwise and harmful actions. We need to find a way to dispel these clouds if we want to develop a wise and compassionate heart. In the Psalms, we ask to be brought to a heart of wisdom *(levov chochmah):*"Teach us to count each day [i.e., pay attention to each moment] in order that we acquire a wise heart [or an awakened heart]"; *"Limnot yah-may-nu kayn ho-dah, v'nah-vee levov chochmah"* (Ps. 90:12).

A similar teaching can be derived from the second verse about the evil *yetzer* from Genesis 8:21, "Since what the human heart forms is evil from its youth." Instead of interpreting the inclination of the heart as evil from youth onward, we can understand the last phrase—"from its youth," or *may-n'arahv* in Hebrew—to mean that the heart's inclination is evil because of naiveté. Think of the verse retranslated as, "Since what the human heart forms is evil from childish consciousness." This is not to say that naiveté causes evil. Naiveté is the natural starting place for all beings as they begin to interact with their environment. But in failing to move beyond a childish understanding of our own nature, we allow that nature to run the show.

When our consciousness is childish, we want what we want when we want it, and we holler when we don't get it. This is the nature of small mind. (You may wish to review the section in the previous chapter about the mind's typical response to pleasant and unpleasant sensations.) Of course, we don't always act out our every impulse, and we often suppress our annoyance with the denial for fear of reprisal. As a result, we easily fall into anxiety and depression. But a better option than this sublimation is to become more conscious.

It is crucial for all of us to take responsibility for our own nature. In a famous tale, a student asks his mentor what to do about the *yetzer harah*. The student complains that it is following him wherever he goes. The teacher wisely asks, "Is it chasing you, or are you chasing it?" When we are naïve about the *yetzer,* we project it to be outside of us and in hot pursuit. When we bring wisdom to the *yetzer,* however, we learn to see that it is inside us. The childish consciousness does not see the interconnected web of being. It tends to be self-centered and reacts to emotional challenges according to its habits, looking to flee from unpleasant circumstances and unpleasant thoughts. Similarly, we grasp at and try to keep pleasurable experiences. When we bring our attention to clearly seeing the truth of each moment, allowing ourselves to feel whatever the moment brings, we stop the cycle of instant reactions. Instead, we can develop the possibility of opening to each moment from the place of the wise, compassionate heart, which responds rather than reacts to life.

So, in a paradoxical way, exploring the *yetzer harah* with our awareness turns it into a vehicle to achieve balance and happiness. I heard the following teaching on another retreat: A student once asked a teacher, "How can I be happy?" The teacher replied, "Exercise good judgment." The student liked the answer, but in a moment realized another question was waiting to be asked: "How do I learn good judgment?"

"Through experience." "How do I get experience?" "Through bad judgment!"

This story illustrates a very simple statement about how we learn and grow. Another version of this lesson comes in the story of Rumpelstiltskin, when the baker's daughter must spin straw into gold. The raw material of our own lives (the straw) is what we must each use to achieve awakening (the gold). Sometimes we have dreams so wonderful that we are sorry when we wake up. But it is the bad dreams that can give us both the incentive and the experience we need to wake up.

Before moving on to strategies for working with the *yetzer,* I want to return to the first verse in Genesis where the word first appeared, 2:7: "And YHVH, God, formed the human, of dust from the soil, he blew into his nostrils the breath of life and the human became a living being." As I already said, the story of the forming of man is described at the end of that verse as resulting in a "living *nefesh.*" The use of the word *nefesh,* as well as the literal events in the verse itself, implies that human beings have a level of consciousness shared with the inanimate material of the earth. *Nefesh* is a term that refers to the consciousness inherent in all physical objects. As human beings, we are partly made up of the physical universe, the dust of the earth.

In this same verse in Genesis, we are told that, after forming the man, God breathed into his nostrils the breath of life, or *nishmat chayyim.* The word for this breath, *neshamah,* is the same as one of the Hebrew words for "soul," and it refers to a much more integrative level of consciousness. This verse is telling us then that, while we have a *yetzer* that can lead us into evil, we also have the potential for understanding and transforming it through the *neshamah,* which is another part of human nature. We will explore this idea in more detail in chapter 5.

Getting a Handle on Your *Yetzer:* The Process of Naming

So, what can we actually do in our lives to turn our challenging mental and emotional states into a force for good? In a contemplative practice, we take concrete steps to deal with this aspect of our human nature. We begin by cultivating the witnessing quality of mind and we start to take notice of the *yetzer* as it presents itself in our thoughts, our feelings, and our physical bodies. The first step involves recognizing the force of the *yetzer* as it presents itself. Toward this end, it is a useful practice to name the experience of an "evil" inclination through the process of mental noting.

Mental noting is a formal practice that can go hand in hand with the basic instructions given in chapter 2 for paying attention to what is occurring in each moment. As an example, when you pay attention to the arising and passing of each breath as a physical sensation, you can direct all of your attention to just noting the sensation itself and what it feels like in your body. At the same time, you can add a soft, unvocalized mental note such as, "breathing in," during the in-breath and, "breathing out," during the out-breath. By "soft" I mean that your primary focus is on the bodily sensation, and the mental note is in the background. You will need to experiment with mental noting to develop this sense of softness. If the mental note grows in relative volume, you might find that it has become your primary object of focus and that instead of noting the breath, you are doing a silent mantra of the words *breathing in, breathing out.* In this case, you may have lost all awareness of the physical sensation. That is the possible drawback in using mental noting. You can sometimes recognize that the noting has taken over because you may actually be breathing out while noting, "breathing in."

Mental noting is often helpful in bringing what we are experiencing in the present moment into more conscious awareness. In our context here, mental noting can allow us to see the connection in the energy we might be feeling to the primal force of the *yetzer*. The act of bringing consciousness to these powerful natural forces acts as an antidote to evil, since it is unawareness that allows the force to be channeled into destructive or harmful action. So, when I am feeling anger toward someone, it is helpful for me to note, "anger, anger, anger." This may not be enough to stop me from getting angry, but by recognizing the impulse of anger, I begin to weaken my identification with it, and the emotion often fades on its own. Sometimes, just this much awareness is all that we need to stop a harmful impulse in its tracks.

You may be saying to yourself that there is a problem with taking this first step: "How do I remember to start the noting practice when the flood of emotions is already sweeping me away?" While we eventually want to be able to notice impulses as they arise in our daily lives, we train ourselves to do so in the quiet space of a meditation period. One reason it is so much easier in this quiet space is that meditation already incorporates the practice of restraint. When I sit down with the intention to meditate for the next fifteen minutes, I am accepting the idea of restraining from talking, walking, eating, or any other physical act: from "doing" anything. Then, when my anger arises, it is the restraint practice itself that allows me to notice the emotion. As I observe the arising of anger and name it, I can also try to sense what that anger feels like in my body.

The practice of naming difficult forces is hinted at in the Torah. In Genesis 2:18–19, we read:

> Now YHVH, God, said: It is not good for the human to be alone, I will make him a helper corresponding to him. So YHVH, God, formed [y-tz-r] from the soil every living-thing of the field and every fowl of the heavens and brought each to the human, to see what he would call it; and whatever the human called it as a living-being that became its name.[8]

On one level, this story is the start of the Torah's explanation of the relationship between human beings and other beings, but it also moves into the nature of relationships between people. We see in this story that all the other living beings were formed from the earth, just as the first human was. The Hebrew word *adamah* means "earth," so Adam is the earthling, the being formed from the earth. In order not to feel alone, this sole human earthling, Adam, must have a partner.

On a more metaphorical level, this is also a story about working through our own alienation and loneliness as human beings. The first step in that process is to look at what might be called the opposing forces. The English translation from Genesis 2:18, "A helper corresponding to him," comes from the Hebrew words *ezer k'negdo. Ezer* means "helper," but *neged* can mean "opposing" or "opposite." The translation of the verse could be, "Now YHVH, God, said: It is not good for the human to be alone, I will make him a helping opposing force." Once again, we have the concept that the help we need comes from looking to opposing forces. And we learn that these opposing forces were "formed" by God. They are *yetzrim* (inclinations). Before we can integrate these forces into a single complete identity, we have to first look at them as if, from a dualistic perspective, they are external rather than internal forces. All these "opposing" forces are formed from the same "ground" of being that we are. All things in the world can be the source of the help, growth, or union we seek.

Here we see that when Adam needed help, he looked at all the beasts of the world, and as he looked, he named them. The very process of naming is the way to tame the wild beasts in the work of acquiring helpmates. When we name something, the act itself creates a connection to the object named. This can help make scary forces less fearsome. When I hide from my compulsive desires, they seem more like an outside force that is overpowering me. This is the more childish thinking that looks at the evil inclination as an independent force in the universe. But once I can name the force and honestly acknowledge that it is part of me, I can begin the process of inner work to deal wisely with it. Remember that in the Torah the mate Adam eventually gets comes from within. Eve is formed by the splitting of Adam into two beings. The answer to our own alienation can come from this deep inner work. The name "Eve" comes from the same Hebrew root as the word for "life." All life itself needs to be embraced as the partner we need. As we name all of life's experiences, we can begin to overcome our alienation from life.

In addition to naming, restraint is a useful tool in dealing with the *yetzer* at any time in our daily lives, not just in formal meditation periods. We all know and use restraint in our lives. None of us just blindly act out on every impulse. Once we strengthen our practice of noting impulses, each moment of restraint begins to offer us something positive, rather than feeling like a yoke around our necks. Whether we have a commitment to a food regimen such as keeping kosher or being on a diet, we can work with each moment to name the feelings going on inside us and, through restraint, become more aware.

Just Grin and Bear It

After naming our feelings, the next step is to explore what it feels like to be in the throes of the *yetzer,* rather than avoiding it or acting out its impulses. When a difficult emotion arises, we can pay attention to how the emotion feels in the body, letting it blossom and fade in its own time. As we bring attention to these energies, we develop some real insights into our own nature. The insight into the reality of our own struggles is the source of our compassion as we realize the universal nature of the human condition.

I have a favorite teaching story that points out the value of learning to work with our difficult states of mind. A retired Air Force colonel was standing in the express checkout line of his local supermarket. There were a couple people in front of him, including a woman who had currently reached the front of the line. That woman was holding a baby and was in an animated exchange with the young woman who was working the register. The checkout clerk was cooing over the baby and tickling it while everyone in line waited. The former Air Force colonel was getting angrier by the minute. This was the express line after all! He could feel the self-righteous rage building up in him by the second. Fortunately, he had recently completed a stress management class and was able to recognize the warning signals as they manifested in his body. He felt the heat in his face and knew it was a sign of anger. He reminded himself to direct his attention to his breath, and as he did this, he began to feel calmer. One of the benefits of bringing awareness to difficult emotions is that sometimes you begin to see these powerful compulsive energies subside all by themselves, without your having acted upon them. As the colonel focused on his breathing, his judgment about the two women being inconsiderate began to soften. In just moments, his anger had subsided. By the time he got to the cashier, he was able to remark to the young girl that the baby was very cute. She responded, "Oh, do you really think so? That was my baby. My husband was an Air Force pilot who recently died in a plane crash. I needed to go to work to support myself, and so my mother helps out by watching her for me. A few times a day she stops in to buy something so that I can see my baby."

This is a moving story about the value of learning to be with our own unpleasant experiences. The man in line could easily have exploded at the two women cooing over the baby. His initial perception of the situation, that they were inconsiderate, was only one way to interpret the scene. This interpretation was driven by his own ego need to get through the line quickly. How often do our angry reactions cause harm when we fail to bring awareness to them?

The story of the Air Force colonel is quite well known in meditation teaching circles. But it is also important to recognize the teaching stories in our own lives.

I recently led a daylong workshop in Jewish meditation, during which I told this same story. When we reconvened after lunch, we were sitting in silence when I noticed two women begin a conversation at the back of the room. When I sit in silence with a group of people, I occasionally open my eyes to observe what is happening in the room. While I can't look into someone's mind, I can see who is sleeping, who is fidgeting, and who is looking around the room in distraction. I happened to see these two women just as they began to speak. It is my role as facilitator to consider the needs of the group and to help create the vessel of silence during meditation, and I felt a little annoyed at the two women. I caught the attention of one of them who happened to be looking my way (perhaps guiltily?) and I made a hand gesture that they should leave the room. They quickly fell silent and one of the women actually left the room. The other woman sat down. From that point on, she became a marked person for me.

As the afternoon wore on, I would notice occasionally that this woman rarely had her eyes closed during the meditation periods, lowering her worth as a person in my mind. I assumed that she was not enjoying the workshop, and this felt like an affront to my ego. Most of my judging was happening on a subconscious level, since I was mainly preoccupied with my tasks as workshop facilitator. Toward the end of the afternoon, though, during a question-and-answer session, this woman asked about how to use these practices when her mind was overwhelmed by the horrendous real situation she was facing. She was not more specific, but her question immediately changed my perception of her. Rather than being someone who couldn't meditate and wasn't even serious about trying, she became a person who was suffering tremendously, and my heart went out to her. My earlier perception had been formed on the slightest amount of visual stimulation and was based mostly on my ego's reaction to a perceived slight to my role as facilitator. Now I knew a little more about why she wasn't closing her eyes.

After the formal workshop ended, the woman approached me and asked if there was some way she could work with me on the situation she was facing in her life. Instead of being bored with the workshop, as I had originally assumed, she told me that she had really liked it and felt that I was a person whom she could talk to. Not only had I made judgments based on little data, but they were also not very accurate. Had she not spoken up, I would have left with a very different perception of her and not had the chance to see my own faulty (but very human) process in action. It is crucial that we learn to see how these same states of mind occur in our own lives.

Once again, the first step in working with powerful impulses is to practice restraint and then to name the impulse. After becoming conscious of the impulse's presence, your attention can then be focused on what the experience feels like in the body. It is helpful to bring a sense of acceptance so that you can just "be with" the experience without feeling a need to get rid of it. This acceptance is not a statement of resignation or a permanent acceptance of inaction; it is rather an openness necessary to exploring what there is to be learned from such moments. It is also helpful to avoid analyzing why this feeling is present when using this contemplative approach. Analyzing our feelings can be a tremendously powerful tool and a skill we, as humans, should maximize. However, the contemplative practice of just "being with" strong feelings adds other dimensions that analysis does not always reach.

The practice of "being with" can be described as follows. If you are anxious about something, note it mentally—"anxious, anxious"— and then try feeling the sensation in your body. Where exactly does anxiety manifest in your body? Is it a flutter in your stomach or tension in your neck? What do the sensations feel like? Is it a tightening feeling? Is it painful? Is there a sense of heat associated with it, or a chill? Go through the same process for anger or boredom or lust or sadness. Find the places in the body where these emotions are felt. Practice bringing your attention to the body and try to let go of any narrative about these sensations for another time. You will likely have strong thoughts about the cause of the situation or thoughts about how to handle these impulses. As you practice "being with," you let go of the thinking and gently bring your attention back to the body itself, just as in the beginning meditation instructions you learned to gently bring the attention back to the object of focus. Some people find it difficult to experience emotions in their body. If this is the case for you, you can try observing any physical pain, which is usually a more obvious bodily sensation.

Learn to Be with Hard Feelings

Learning to work with the practice of "being with" can have tremendous benefits. The first of these is a quality of self-love and self-acceptance. The difficult feelings of anger, lust, fear, and the like are simply a part of who we are. If we only see them as things we need to get rid of, we just make ourselves feel bad. The mere act of sitting with these feelings and just noticing them is an act of self-acceptance and self-love, in and of itself. Feelings do arise because of various causes and conditions, and in embracing them, we honor their truth and open ourselves to seeing that truth without judging ourselves.

In addition to learning self-acceptance, the capacity for being really present with feelings in a nonjudgmental and nonanalytical way opens up the possibility for spontaneous insight to arise. This is an intuitive wisdom that comes not from the discursive nature of the mind, but rather from a deeper place that is less cluttered by preconceived notions. It is the wisdom that the mystical tradition in Judaism calls *chochmah*. *Chochmah* is the first emanation out of the Divine Oneness. It is the wisdom that precedes the creation of a physical world as we know it. We might say that the wisdom that arises from directly opening to the energy of powerful emotions comes from the ground of being and opens us to seeing the energy behind what it means to be a human being.

In practice, being with difficult feelings can provide us with practical insights. One example of such an experience in my own life happened while I was on the retreat for rabbis that I mentioned earlier in this chapter. On that retreat, besides being preoccupied with sadness and tears, my mind was mostly filled with thoughts of planning. I would bring my attention back to my breath over and over, but quite frequently I would notice that I was planning again. I became aware that there was a pattern to my thoughts, and that most of them involved planning strategies to fulfill my job as director of Elat Chayyim, our Jewish retreat center. I was planning new programs, planning fund-raising efforts, and planning how to get more guests. One way of dealing with obsessive thought patterns while meditating is to notice what feelings are present. While the thoughts themselves are not about the here and now, the sensations in the body associated with them are happening in the present moment. Without trying to figure out why I was so busy planning, just noticing the planning thoughts appearing over and over led to a big insight *(chochmah)* that came in a flash. The planning thoughts all dealt with ways I could be successful with the retreat center project and thereby receive praise from others. I had always told myself that I was involved in nonprofit work as an act of service and generosity to others. In that moment, it was clear to me that my more unconscious motivation was a desire to please rather than a desire to serve. While this might seem to be a scary realization, I found it to be very liberating. It did not decrease my sense of importance about the work I was doing. I was sure it would help me do the work better if I could see through such an important unconscious pattern.

Over the years, as I continued my meditation practice, another crucial insight developed—this time about my eating patterns. When I started the practice of noting the desire to eat, and consciously used restraint from actually eating, I found it easier to be with the sensations inside my body as the desire to eat arose. Up to that point in my life, if I experienced an uncomfortable bodily sensation anywhere between my breastbone and my belly button, I would tend to label it as "hunger." Rather than investigate the sensation, my usual reaction was to go and get something to eat. This was often sufficient to vanquish the unpleasant sensation. The act of eating was either enough of a diversion or pleasant enough in and of itself to avoid dealing with anything deeper. In a sense, this was the same as the process of blaming some external cause—hunger was just a generic experience that arises in all beings but is not reflective of some internal struggle.

This pattern is an old and deep one in me—one I learned in early childhood. I was encouraged to eat frequently by my mother. I am sure she saw eating as a way to deal with difficult emotions. I was able to see this directly when I had my own children and my mother would come and stay with us. She was a wonderful caregiver to my children, but she had a hard time seeing them unhappy (perhaps a typical parental response) for any reason. If one of them would fall and start crying, she would immediately swoop in and offer them a cookie or candy. This was her solution to tears or arguments. While this frequently worked to distract my children, it was a clear example to me of where I had learned my own eating patterns.

As an adult committed to waking up, I know that eating is not the solution to all of life's problems. Using the practices described here, whether on retreat or in daily life, I am able to control my eating and avoid indulging whenever the urge arises. In the space provided by restraint, I instead try to feel deeply into my body. As a result, I have learned to distinguish a variety of sensations that occur in my midsection. Hunger is one of the possible sensations, but it feels different than stress or anxiety or fear. While some of these sensations are similar in a physical sense, they often occur in slightly different regions of my midsection. Through careful attention and patience, I can become aware of what I am actually feeling in the moment. After I have a better sense of what is actually occurring, I can then decide on the wisest and most compassionate response. That response is frequently different than my first reaction, which is to grab something to eat. I certainly still choose to eat sometimes when the sensation of "hunger" arises, but even then it is not with the same level of mindlessness. The process of waking up is life's work, and I find it unhelpful to judge myself or others based on whether we have completed the task. As the Jewish Sage Hillel used to say, "It is not incumbent upon you to finish the work, but neither are you free to desist from it." All we are called upon to do is to keep working at purifying the heart.

It is not always the case that a sensation is a somaticized emotion. Remember my retreat during which I had stomach irritation that I thought was caused by emotional stress and worry? It turned out to be merely acid, which I could then neutralize with medication. What I thought was some underlying unhappiness in my psyche turned out to be merely physical after all.

Sometimes, the direct practice of being with difficult emotions and mind states can be hard, even when you are motivated and know the practice's value. I learned a teaching phrase from Sylvia Boorstein that summarizes the practice of being in the present moment: "Whatever arises, don't duck." When you practice, you might remember this phrase. But I mention this here to make a counterpoint: sometimes the wisest thing to do is to temporarily "duck." Sometimes, being with unpleasant states is counterproductive. When the mind is tired out or when the energy is strong and challenging, keeping your attention directly on the challenging energy can cause your mind to wilt further or contract. In this state, it becomes more difficult to see clearly, and expending further effort just makes things worse. At such times, it can be helpful to change practices. This might be a break or a switch to a more uplifting contemplative practice, such as chanting or prayer or the phrases of blessing. These practices, discussed in chapters 6 and 7, tend to have the effect of softening and expanding the mind and of cultivating wholesome mind states.

The intention behind our movement away from difficult experiences is of great importance. If we move away in the spirit of aversion, our mind may cultivate the aversive response. If we temporarily leave the difficult mind states for uplifting practices, we need to be honest and aware that we are making this choice. Stating the following intention to ourselves can be extremely helpful and self-accepting: "I am switching my practice right now in the service of being better able to deal with this difficult mind state. When I am ready, I will return to it."

We can gain another invaluable insight through the practice of noting and being with difficult feelings. Occasionally, my wife, Joanna, likes to put an inspiring line on our refrigerator. One year it was the following teaching: "Restraint points to the impermanent nature of desire." Since I have mentioned food a number of times, let me give a simple example of this teaching. If I am sitting in meditation and notice the desire for a cookie arising, practicing restraint leads me away from the temptation. All by itself, my attention moves elsewhere. Whether it is to a new thought or to an itch on my neck or to a sense of boredom, I no longer desire the cookie. Desires fade all by themselves. They are an impermanent welling up of energy, not a continuous one, and when we cease identifying with them, we begin to free ourselves from the habits of our minds.

The insight about impermanence is not limited to working with desire. When any of the powerful mind states—such as anger or fear, or for that matter, joy and pleasure—are met with the practice of "being with," we see that they, too, are ephemeral states. While everyone can understand the concept of impermanence, seeing it in your own experience is invaluable. When you can sit with these energies and not react to them, you begin to realize that you have the freedom to respond with more wisdom and compassion. You also see that sometimes no response other than mindfulness of your *yetzer* is needed. When you see this truth for yourself, it is very empowering, because you are building confidence in your ability to handle whatever comes your way.

The power of awakened attention can transform the *yetzer harah* in another way. When you apply sustained attention to a powerful force, such as anger, it is possible to develop a high degree of concentration if you can focus on the bodily experience of anger rather than the narrative of blame or judgment that accompanies it. A strong emotional sensation is often easier to focus on than the breath, which at times can seem more subtle and repetitive. As your attention is sustained on the physical sensations of the emotion, you can achieve a high degree of concentration. This concentration can lead to a rapturous feeling in the mind and body that dissolves the strong emotion into a greater sense of well-being.

Working with the *Yetzer* by Cultivating Restraint

The practice of restraint is a part of every mature adult life. It is not meant just for periods of meditation. There are many desires that arise in my life. Sometimes I react to fulfill the desire, but just as often, or perhaps more frequently, I don't immediately react but just notice the desire and name it. Waking up does not mean ignoring our desires. In the space offered by restraint, the possibility arises that we can respond rather than react to desire. Restraint creates a gap between sensation and my acting on that sensation. In that gap, I can try to make sure that my response will be made with as much clarity as possible and that my actions will reflect kindness and compassion. This is not always possible, but it is a wholesome intent we can cultivate. Sometimes I still choose to act out on my desire but do so with more understanding and with an acceptance of responsibility for the consequences. Sometimes I don't find the clarity I would like. In those cases, I try to wait before reacting, when I can, or I make the best choice out of possible alternatives, knowing that I am merely human.

Much of Jewish practice can be seen in this light of practicing restraint. On the one hand, it is wise to have practices that we follow because we know that we are asleep. Since we know the harmful consequences of acting out of lust, for example, following a practice like refraining from adultery is one way of weakening lust. Similarly, restraining our anger and refraining from killing is a wise course of action. Following these precepts can protect us from some of the unintended negative consequences. And it is possible that during the period of restraint, the impermanent nature of the desire will become clear and the desire will fade on its own, like a fire going out.

When we not only practice restraint but also bring our attention to powerful emotions such as desire or anger, carefully observing how they manifest in the body, we can gain real insights into our own nature and a deeper understanding of the causes and conditions that lead to these moments. The added level of attention helps us to realize how much we have in common with other human beings. When we are awake, we see in ourselves all the difficulties that can lead to unwise actions. This clarity becomes a source of compassion we can draw upon when we see others acting unskillfully.

The Halakhah, the traditional set of Jewish precepts, offers us the possibility for this depth of clarity. Without restraint, our conduct can lead us into patterns of behavior from which it is even more difficult to wake up and see clearly. But following these precepts does not guarantee a positive outcome. It only provides the space for more practice to occur. Without the practice of looking deeply, the Halakhah, or any set of precepts, can become merely an outer mask that veils the light we need. When we restrain ourselves without looking at the deeper emotional patterns of our lives, we can sometimes become even more compulsive in our actions. One set of desires can be sublimated, resulting in another set of compulsive actions not specifically forbidden, such as overeating. Repressed sexual desire in men can result in powerful negative feelings, such as anger aimed at an inappropriate target. Our ability to see and be with our most painful feelings is a crucial step for our own healing, as well as for healing the deep pain in our world.

The Debilitating Nature of Doubt

In talking about the *yetzer,* I have generally been referring to two main categories of impulses: our lustful nature and our aversive nature. Our lustful nature is our impulsive desire to get and hold on to the pleasurable experiences of life. We also have a natural impulse to avoid all of life's unpleasant experiences. This is our aversive nature, which can manifest as fear, anger, blame, and other negative emotions. Yet another category, which is somewhat more subtle but one we all experience nevertheless, is the doubting mind. Doubt, while not always obvious, can paralyze us into inaction. One reason for its subtlety is that it masquerades as wisdom: "What good is sitting around doing inner work when there is 'real' work to be done in the world to stop the bad things that are happening?" In the right context, this can be a very valuable question, but we must learn to recognize the doubting mind and transform it from cancerous cynicism to healthy skepticism.

The Baal Shem Tov taught about the insidious power of doubt. He used a teaching from Jewish numerology to connect doubt to Amalek. Amalek is the name of the first nation that attacked the Jewish people after they crossed the Red Sea in their Exodus from slavery in Egypt. In the Jewish psyche, the Amalek name has become an archetype referring to those who want to destroy the Jewish people. Haman, the villain in the story of Purim, who tries to have the Jews of Persia killed, is a descendant of Amalek. In Jewish numerology, each letter of the alphabet corresponds to a number—the first letter, *aleph,* equals one, the second letter, *bet,* equals two, and so on. Using this system, any two words with the same numerical value are connected in some way. The numerical value for Amalek is the same as the value for the Hebrew word for "doubt," *safek.* The Baal Shem Tov taught: "Amalek is still alive today. Every time you experience a worry or a doubt about how God is running the world—that's Amalek launching an attack against your soul. We must wipe Amalek out of our hearts whenever and wherever he attacks, so that we can serve God with complete joy."

This idea of wiping out Amalek should not be taken to mean eliminating doubt from our minds entirely. Efforts to prevent thoughts and feelings from arising are futile and not the purpose of practice. Jewish tradition recognizes the subtlety of dealing with doubt and focuses on how to handle it, not prevent it. You might say that the correct practice is to go looking for doubt so that it doesn't blindside you. There are specific references in the Torah that actually tell us to remember Amalek. "Bear in mind what Amalek did to you on the way, at your going out from Egypt" (Deut. 25:17) is understood as a commandment for all time to remember that the event provides us with a commandment not to forget Amalek: "So it shall be; when YHVH your God gives you rest from all your enemies round about in the land that YHVH your God is giving you as an inheritance to possess it, you are to blot out the name of Amalek from under the heavens: you are not to forget" (Deut. 25:19). And the verse also alludes to a third commandment: besides remembering and not forgetting, we are also told to "blot out" the name, which can be understood to mean that we should not let the effects of doubt proliferate. We need to be vigilant about doubt and the role it plays in our lives.

The first step to blotting out doubt is to notice it and remember the effects it can have. It is quite common in contemplative practice to have doubt about the practice itself. Most of us are used to acting and doing in the world without frequent reflection. The change of pace from constant doing to frequent reflection can seem foreign. Sitting still feels like we are not doing anything and can cause us to feel guilty, and cause the mind to slip into thoughts of doubt about the value of the practice. In this way, doubt can serve as a vehicle to justify avoiding unpleasant experiences. When I teach a meditation retreat, it is common for participants who are noticing unpleasant mind states to come in to interviews and announce that they have made a mistake in attending the retreat. "The time was not right," I'm often told. "I should be dealing with an important situation at home." But phrases like these are often just rationalizations of the doubting mind.

Some of my strongest experiences of doubt come at the end of silent retreats. Oftentimes the retreat experience has been sublime and full of clarity of mind. When that clarity begins to fade as I reenter my busy, everyday world, I experience a sense of having lost something. I am filled with a gnawing, unpleasant feeling, and my doubting mind thinks, "What was that experience all about?" It can often feel as if the retreat was a rarified, even exalted, experience, yet one of no lasting value. This kind of doubt usually arises whenever we try holding on to the retreat experience. The truth is that all experiences are ephemeral and we can't hold on to them. What does seem to last is the insight that is gained from the retreat, although even this can be lost over time without continued practice.

When noticing doubts, persevering in the practice of naming unpleasant emotions is a helpful tool. Doubt, like other mind states, often arises and passes away on its own. The step of noticing and labeling the doubt helps us to see it as a passing phenomenon rather than the truth. On the first day of a recent retreat, I found myself filled with doubt about whether I could endure the retreat's eighteen days. Thoughts of my subsequent vacation to Hawaii seemed much more enticing than the thought of paying attention to each breath for an extended period. At the time, I never fully dealt with my underlying feelings. When a "reasonable" excuse for leaving the retreat two days early arose, I had already unconsciously made the decision to go.

It is also important to see the positive potential of doubt. Doubt can help transform the *yetzer* into the good inclination. As Rabbi Zalman Schachter-Shalomi teaches, "Faith needs doubt to scrape off the barnacles of superstition." As he explained these words, he pointed out that sometimes we can have direct experience of the Divine Presence in our lives. These are moments that strengthen our faith. But these experiences are not easily translated into words. What we experience is, in many ways, the ineffable. Nevertheless, we do try using words to share the experience with others. These experiences are then often taken too literally, and, in their retelling, even more layers are added. These extra layers are what Reb Zalman would call "the barnacles of superstition." For example, you may think that if you sit in a particular posture and meditate with certain words, God will appear to you because that is how it worked for someone else. Doubt can then become the tool for scraping off those extraneous layers, thus freeing you to have your own direct experience, which then strengthens your faith.

There is another story of the Baal Shem Tov that illustrates the value of living with doubt as we face the more challenging aspects of life. One time, on his journeys, the Baal Shem Tov came to a village where he decided to spend Shabbat. One of the leaders of the town was given the honor of hosting the Baal Shem Tov. The man and his wife lived with their son, Mendel. Mendel was seventeen years old and was profoundly disabled. He had never learned to walk or talk, and he spent all of his time in a bed in a corner of the house. He was their son, however, and the man and his wife loved him and took great care of him.

During the afternoon, in preparing for a festive dinner in honor of the Baal Shem Tov, the man decided to slaughter a goose. As he opened the body of the goose, he saw a blemish in the flesh. It was possible that it was the type of blemish that could render the goose unfit to eat or not kosher. The man would normally take the goose to the town rabbi, but since the Baal Shem Tov was staying in his house, he took the goose inside to him and asked him to rule on whether the goose was kosher. The Baal Shem Tov turned to Mendel and said, "Mendel, can you tell me if this goose is kosher?" Mendel got up from his bed in the corner of the room and walked, on wobbly legs, over to the Baal Shem Tov, took one look at the goose, said, "Kosher," and then promptly died.

The man and his wife were completely beside themselves. After all, this was the first time they had ever seen Mendel walk and talk. And then he had dropped dead. "Don't worry," said the Baal Shem Tov. "Let me explain. Your son was a very famous rabbi in his last life. He was highly respected and very learned. One Friday afternoon, he was studying some sacred texts when a poor woman came to him with a chicken she had slaughtered. The chicken had a blemish and she wanted to know if it was kosher. He was absorbed in his studies but briefly looked at the chicken. He had a doubt based on the look of the blemish so he said the chicken was not kosher. The woman left, and that Shabbat she had no chicken since she was a poor woman and could not afford another chicken. This was a very grave sin the rabbi had committed. When there is a doubt about a ruling and the person involved is poor and will suffer hardship if a strict decision is rendered, then in that case the ruling should be lenient. In his distraction of studying, he failed to take in the full situation of this woman. When he died, he was shown the gravity of this error. It was his only sin in that lifetime. He was reborn as your son and figured he only had one thing to fix up. If Mendel lived a normal life, there was the possibility he could once again be distracted and make other mistakes he would need to repair, so he bided his time waiting to fix up this one error of his last life. When he ruled that this goose was kosher, he was finished with what he needed to accomplish in this life and so he died. Also, the goose was a reincarnation of that chicken and now its soul is being raised up as our Shabbat dinner."

I think this is a beautiful story about the big doubts we may have in our lives. Who could possibly know all the workings of the universe that result in the lives we each lead? Some of us have to face equally difficult situations as the couple in the story. What could be taken as a burden too great to bear can cause some people to doubt the very purpose of life. Yet, we can also rest in our doubt, accepting that not all is known, and accepting that we must live with doubt. And as the story within the story suggests, when doubt is present, it is sometimes important to act on the side of leniency, opening the heart of compassion.

The practice of working with greed, anger, and doubt—those forces that might be called the *yetzer harah*—is at the very core of waking up fully in our lives. I'll close this section by calling your attention to some signs that you can use to recognize when the *yetzer harah* is functioning. Watch out for the arising of self-righteousness, self-deprecation, and self-serving actions. Each of these reminders points to an inflated, egotistical sense of self. When the lion of self rears its head and roars, pay close attention and look deeply inside. Rather than indulging in recriminations when you notice this egoism in yourself, remember that this very imperfect human nature, which all of us share, can be transformed into the perfect compost that you need to awaken. This is the process of domesticating and integrating the wild beast, until both it and you become partners in the oneness of all.

5 Embracing the Divine

As I have mentioned previously, the object of focus in Jewish meditation is always God. Since this is such an essential part of what I am sharing in this book, it may be useful for me to define what I mean by the word *God*. This is easier said than done, since the term *God* is such a loaded concept and many of us have a lot of unlearning to do before we can begin to relate to it. As my coteacher Norman Fischer once said, "God is a three-letter word in the English dictionary."

Everything Is God and Nothing but God

I believe that the main experience of waking up and seeing life and existence clearly is realizing that everything is God and nothing but God. This is the teaching of the Baal Shem Tov I discussed in chapter 2. However, our preconceived and limiting notions about God often come out of a childish consciousness. We can observe this in the development of both an individual's personality and that of the human species. But we can also see a growing understanding of the Divine—individually and collectively—and that, in turn, has an impact on the Divine.

In this chapter, I will share the synthesis I developed for the purpose of recognizing the divine nature of the universe. The synthesis draws on early Jewish thought and texts as well as on later kabbalistic and Hasidic ideas. It also is a product of my exposure to secular life and to ideas that may have originated in other spiritual traditions or in scientific explorations of the nature of the universe.

One day I was listening to a call-in radio program with a local astronomer, Bob Berman. It is a monthly feature of the public radio station that serves the Hudson Valley and the Berkshires. I love listening to the show and am happy when I happen to find myself in the car at the time it is broadcast. Many of the questions often turn to cosmology or the origin of the universe. During this particular show, a caller asked about the expanding nature of the universe, which most scientists think is measurably true. What we consider to be time and space is a part of the existing universe. The questioner wanted to know what the universe was expanding into. In other words, what is beyond time and space?

Bob Berman said that he once heard someone express the belief that after death, "you are nothing." He pointed out that the verb *to be* expressed in the phrase, "You are nothing" is meaningless. Nothing is a state of nonbeing; it is impossible to be nothing. Likewise, we can't meaningfully say what is outside of time and space because "being" only exists within time and space. And, Berman added, while it is worth noting that our minds may be drawn to this question, that does not mean we should keep thinking about it. I might agree that it is pointless to think about the answer to that question, but I do think it is worth noting the yearning that underlies this question, since many of us do, in fact, think about what is beyond time and space. The yearning for the answer is itself instructive. I often find myself pondering the origin of the universe, and when I am in dualistic thought (which is most of the time), I wonder why God created it. Focusing on the answer to the question, "Why?" might send us in the wrong direction and into greater ignorance. But if we focus on the yearning itself, it may help us to understand our own nature—and, paradoxically, bring us closer to the Divine.

The Organic Model of the Divine

One way to frame a discussion about God that I have found helpful and accessible starts with a particular understanding of the theology of the period when Judaism came into being, and then proceeds to recognize the evolution in that theology up to the present day. It includes a visual representation that I first learned from Rabbi Lawrence Kushner, presented in the following diagrams, figures 3–6:

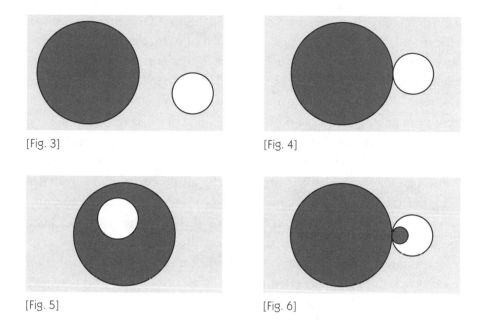

[Fig. 3]

[Fig. 4]

[Fig. 5]

[Fig. 6]

In each one, you will see that there are two circles, a large one and a small one. Let's assume the large circle is meant to call our attention to thinking about God, and the small circle represents each one of us, or for that matter, anything in creation. I certainly would not want to make the idolatrous statement that the large circle is God. But the circles do point to a metaphorical way of visualizing the relationship between God and creation. Focusing on the first set of circles (fig. 3), we see that God is the big picture and creation is a small, little thing. Of course the larger circle should be infinitely big, not really a circle at all. It represents the quality of *Ein Sof* ("without limit") that Jewish mystics use to refer to the Infinite One. This first diagram might be thought of as a version of Jewish theology that originates in the time of Abraham, the patriarch of Judaism who introduced the idea of one God. In that version, God, that which transcends time and space, is the creator of the universe and all that is in it. The universe is represented by the smaller circle.

In this earliest theology, God is utterly transcendent. God is not of this world but rather is the creator of this world. This absolutely transcendent nature was a core belief of Judaism until later mystical teachings began to see the Divine somewhat differently. Keep in mind that

I have already used the verb *to be* in saying that God *is* the creator of this world. But this language can subtly fool us into conceiving of God as existing in a way that is not correct. Perhaps if I said, "God—the creator of this world," the point would become more evident without the word *is*. One reason for making the larger circle black is to represent it as an absence or as nothingness since black is technically not a color but rather the absence of color. The gulf between the circles represents a "totally other" sense of God. Coupled with this totally other sense of the Divine was the image of the all-powerful King. Judaism adopted the metaphorical notion that God was the King of the universe, *melech ha-olam*. It was with this theology that early Judaism grew and developed its spiritual practices. Because of the gulf between creator and creation, as represented by the separate circles, in order for us to know God, God needed to send "a transmission" to this world. Moses and the Prophets were the receivers of this revelation. In the case of Mount Sinai, all people received this transmission, but I'll say more about that shortly. In this understanding, the transmission, or Torah, gives us instructions for living a life as intended by God.

In the second diagram (fig. 4), we see that the two circles are touching. This depicts the spiritual purpose of life. It reflects the religious or mystical desire to be as close to God as possible. In the language of Jewish mysticism, we might use the term *devekut*, which means "to cleave to God," when describing this diagram. The Jewish mystical seeker desires that all his or her life be one that reflects the divine will. The goal of mystical practice is to get as close as possible to God, and then to try to stay there. The whole body of Jewish law, Halakhah, might be seen in this light. Of course, following God's law will also result in ethical action, since God's plan includes God's desire that this creation should become one of peace and love between human beings, and for that matter, between all beings. This period, usually called *olam habah*, "the time to come," is hastened by our actions: "And the voice of weeping shall be no more heard in her, nor the voice of crying.... The wolf and the lamb shall feed together.... They shall not hurt nor destroy in all My holy mountain" (Isa. 65:19, 25).

Before I discuss the third diagram (fig. 5), I should explain the presence of the fourth (fig. 6), which I created to express a transition in Jewish thought that can be traced to the time of the publication of the Zohar (radiance), perhaps the most well-known (though not the most understood) text of Jewish mysticism. The Zohar was written down by Moses de Leon in Spain in the thirteenth century. He claimed to have psychic access to an ancient text that he merely transcribed. Some scholars suggest that parts were written through automatic writing. Moses de Leon said that the real author of the text was Shimon Bar Yohai, who lived in Palestine in the third century. There is a great deal of fascinating scholarly material about the authorship of the Zohar but the theology of the book is what is of interest to us in this chapter. This theology helped catalyze the mystical branches of Jewish spirituality.

The Zohar transformed the concept of the Shekhinah, which in earlier usage in Jewish texts was a general reference to God's presence that might be sensed in sacred moments and places in this world. The Zohar takes the idea farther by stating that part of God's actual essence is in the created universe. Rather than seeing God only as utterly transcendent, the Zohar says that part of God's self is here in this universe, in exile so to speak, from the rest of God. In figure 6, I have added a smaller black circle inside the small white circle to represent the part of God (the large black circle) that is in exile in the created universe. When the circles come together it is possible to reunite that part of God that has left the larger circle. The black dot in the small circle is returned to its (black) source when the two circles come together. *Devekut*, or the cleaving to God, has even more meaning since in this later model it now is a *tikkun,* or repair, of a rift within the Godhead. The black dot also reflects the later kabbalistic notion that within the created universe there are sparks of the Divine Presence.

The Zohar uses gender to describe or represent God's exile. God's feminine side is what we might call the immanent part of God. Somehow, when God created the world, the feminine side of God broke away from the masculine side. Perhaps this is akin to Eve splitting away from Adam. This feminine side, the Zohar's definition of the Shekhinah, resides within the created universe, while the masculine side of God is transcendent. According to the Zohar, the task of humanity is to reunite these two sides of God. For the Jewish mystic, this reunification is the purpose of the commandments or the Halakhah. Before fulfilling them, mystics would say, "I am performing this commandment in order to unify the Holy One, blessed be he, with his Shekhinah." These teachings elevate the status of human beings by allowing them to have a major impact on God. In figure 4, the bringing together of the two circles might be seen as an act of "cosmic copulation"; the language of the Zohar is rich with this sexual metaphor of union.

It is not until the Baal Shem Tov began to teach in the eighteenth century that the next major shift in Jewish mystical theology occurred. Here, we begin to see the teaching that there is nothing but God. In figure 5, the little circle is inside the big circle. The essential oneness of God is now to be understood in a way that does not allow for anything to be outside of God. It furthers the mystic's quest for radical monism and the eventual dropping of all notions of any ultimate duality. This model calls for a reworking of the concept of *devekut,* or "cleaving to God." Because of our divine nature, we as human beings cannot get closer to God. We are already inside the divine nature of everything. We just don't know it. In this model, our spiritual task is to wake up to the reality of interconnected Divine Oneness.

I learned the following story from my friend Max Samson. Two waves, a big wave and a little wave, were floating in the ocean. The little wave looked up and saw that the big wave was weeping. "Why are you crying?" he asked his friend.

"Oh, you are such a small wave that you can't see what I see. I can see over the heads of our brother and sister waves all the way into the shore. All of us are dying as we hit the shore."

"Oh," said the little wave. "You don't have to cry about that."

The big wave said, "If you were able to see what I see, you would cry too."

"No, really," said the little wave. "If you want, I can teach you something that will allay your fears."

"How much will it cost?" asked the big wave.

"Why, nothing!" said the little wave with genuine surprise in his voice.

"Oh, I know," said the big wave. "You're going to tell me that I have to stand on my head for thirty years, or sit with my legs crossed and not move for a week."

"Why would you do that?" asked the little wave. "That would be ridiculous."

"You mean it won't cost anything and I don't have to do all those strange practices? All right, what's the catch?"

The little wave thought for a moment and said, "Well, there is only one small catch. You have to be quiet long enough for me to say six words."

"That's all?" said the big wave. He thought to himself that whatever the little wave told him would be free and he wouldn't have to do many lifetimes of esoteric practice, so he finally said, "I can be quiet that long. Go ahead."

The little wave then told the big wave, "You're not a wave, you're water."

Most of the time, because we are merely human, we do not live with this perspective. In our small sense of who we are, we see things as separate from one another, disconnected, isolated. Our fears make us shore up the walls of personality rather than making them more transparent. In this contracted state of mind, we need rules and guidelines so that we don't harm ourselves and others with our unskillful actions. When we see the interconnected nature of the world, we naturally act out of love and compassion. No one needs to tell your right hand not to light a fire under your left hand. However, since it is hard to stay in such a state of awareness, it is necessary to have practices and ethical guidelines that will keep us from straying too far during moments of less-than-clear seeing. These practices are essential tools for us to do the work of waking up.

One way I like to explain figure 5 is by using what I call the "organic model of the Divine." As a metaphor for this model, imagine your own body. As you know, it is composed of cells, and those cells are part of what we call organ systems. Now, imagine a liver cell in your body. In certain ways, this cell has a separate identity. It has a cell membrane so you can distinguish it from any other cell. Yet, you might also say it is a part of what you refer to as yourself, a bigger level of reality. It is not independent of you, and you are not independent of it. Wherever you go, it goes with you. And if it goes haywire by becoming cancerous, it affects all of you, and all the other cells in your body. It needs to be a liver cell and not a heart cell for *you* to function properly. It is both an individual entity and yet it is a part of the greater implicate order you think of as *You*. The liver cell does not necessarily know (although we can't be sure) what plans you have in mind for it today. And you might not be very aware of how it is functioning or what it is doing or feeling today, although sometimes it might manage to send you a message that becomes conscious.

In a similar way, we can think of everything that exists as being part of the greater implicate order we call "God." In that sense, everything God does affects us, and vice versa. Each of us has our own unique role to play in this divine being. And each of us belongs to groups of larger entities that need to fulfill their function in serving the whole. These might include our family, our species, our tribe, our religion, our country ... you get the picture. And as God evolves, some of these "cells" may become unnecessary, or evolve as well.

Both the organic model of the Divine and the wave model are ways of contrasting the relative with the absolute nature of reality. They both deal with the nondual, which is absolute or ultimate reality, and yet both acknowledge that each individual "wave" has its purpose. I think the commonly used phrase, "Think globally, act locally," applies to our relationship to the absolute. We think, feel, and act primarily in the relative world as embodied beings, or temporary waves. Yet, through our practice, we can learn that there is a bigger picture— that we are not waves, but water.

Socialized Meditation Practice

We can use special meditation practices to illustrate the relational model of the Divine, which reveals our individual uniqueness and our connection to God. One way to do this involves meditating in an interactive way with another person. I'd like to share a formal practice developed by Reb Zalman, which he called "socialized meditation." This practice is done in dyads and makes use of the Psalms as text for mutual exploration. The practice is also called "praying by heart." Usually, when we say that we are doing something "by heart," we mean that we have memorized a text and are reciting it by rote. In "praying by heart," we don't memorize anything but rather share the feelings that are in our hearts as they arise. In Appendix A you will find the entire translation of Psalm 145, which we'll be using in this exercise, but you could use any Psalm or other piece of liturgy, or for that matter, other writings as well. This practice requires you to find a partner to practice with. Both of you can read these instructions and each of you should have a copy of the words of Psalm 145.

To "pray by heart," you and your partner decide who will go first. You will be praying by using the words of the Psalm as a reference point—taking turns speaking—two lines at a time, as laid out in Appendix A. Before speaking, the person who will go first looks at the first two lines of Psalm 145 included here:

I exalt You God and Guide.
I bless your name for all time.

Daily I'll declare your fame,
Till the very end of my life.

Before speaking, read and reflect on each line, trying to take in the content. If there are concepts that you can't relate to, transform those concepts into something close that is true for you. When you are ready, look up from the words and make eye contact with your partner. Then utter the words that you can recite "by heart"—that is, in your own words—that are meaningful to you. Try to imagine that the Divine within you is speaking to the Divine within your partner. I suggest trying to address your partner as the Divine Presence by saying the word "you" to them, while simultaneously imagining or feeling that you are addressing the Divine as "You."

Here is a version of what I might choose to say to my partner after looking at those first four lines of the psalm: "I love singing praises to You, the source of my direction in life. I love to give You blessings in all the forms in which You appear, and I hope I always will. Every day I want to speak of Your wondrous nature. I hope I can remember to do this for my whole life."

As you try this practice you may be amazed at how wonderful it feels—both to offer the words to someone, and to be addressed by another from this perspective. The person who listens does not look at any words but rather sits patiently, waiting to hear from the speaker. When working with a prayer like the one in Appendix A, I advise the listeners to put their finger on the stanza that they will be looking at when it is their turn to speak. This is helpful because the words spoken by their partners may be too altered to recognize which verse was the origin.

When you try to speak from the divine place inside, you may notice the small self, the ego, reacting in its habitual competitive way. It can feel puffed up, taking the credit so to speak, when being addressed as the Divine. Or it can feel inadequate in the face of hearing a beautiful rendering of prayer from your partner. You may hear yourself saying, "How can I possibly top that?" If this happens, as in all the other practices discussed in this book, just try to take note of the experience without judging yourself and return your attention to the meditative exercise.

The sum of what is created by meditating in this interactive way is greater than what either person alone could have created. As an aid to understanding that each individual is a necessary part of the greater whole, it is helpful to hear the Divine yearning in another person and also to see that, together, your mutual yearning creates something greater. It is one of the reasons that singing in a choir can be such a powerful prayer experience.

The organic model of the Divine allows us to use the language of divine immanence as well as divine transcendence without talking about God as outside the universe. Any particular piece of creation is part of a transcendent reality that is larger than that piece. As I have said, it is somewhat nonsensical to talk about what there is outside of existence, since the verb for "being" is by definition tied to existing. This is true about classical Jewish thought as well. Maimonides, the great Jewish scholar, physician, and philosopher who lived at the end of the twelfth century, said that God cannot be described in any way. Only the *via negativa,* describing what God is *not,* is adequate. The radically transcendent aspect of the Divine is unutterable. In contemplative Jewish practice, the goal is not to explain the Divine. Our explanations are merely products of the small mind, which defines things in concrete terms and keeps us trapped by our conceptualizations. That is far different than the direct experience of knowing the transcendence that comes in the realization of expanded awareness, or *mochin de-gadlut*—an experience that leaves us transformed and committed to the greater good.

The Fourfold Nature of Divine Oneness

There is another model for speaking about the Divine that grew out of Jewish mystical teachings. It is usually referred to as the four worlds model. This model originates with the most holy name for God in the Jewish tradition, the four-letter name *Yud Hay Vav Hay*. Jewish mystics need to explain the apparent paradox of whether everything is actually one or whether there are multiple things in existence. To understand God, Jewish mystics look at the traditional name for the Divine. They see language, and Hebrew in particular, as one of the core building blocks of the universe. In more secular terms, you might say that words and language play a critical role in shaping consciousness, and human consciousness shapes the world in which we live.

The name *Yud Hay Vav Hay,* sometimes referred to as the tetragrammaton, is the most holy name for God in Jewish teaching. It is a name that, traditionally, is never spoken aloud. In fact, since Hebrew is a language consisting only of consonants, the only way one could know the proper vocalization of that name was to learn it from another who already knew it. That pronunciation was kept secret within the priesthood. But there was a time, when the Temple was still standing in Jerusalem, that this name was uttered aloud. The Temple was the unique center of worship in pre-rabbinic Judaism. It was destroyed in 70 CE by the Romans in the course of quelling a rebellion by the Jewish inhabitants of Judea. While the Temple was still standing, there was a custom that the high priest would pronounce the four-letter name one time per year, on the holy day of Yom Kippur, the Day of Atonement. He would go inside the holy of holies (the central room within the temple that was the site of the ark, which held the stone tablets on which the Ten Commandments were engraved) and recite the name. This was the high point of the day. Since the destruction of the Temple, the four-letter name of God has not been officially spoken, and since there is no longer an unbroken lineage for the priesthood, the oral tradition of how to properly pronounce it was also lost. Many contemporary Jews believe that refraining from speaking God's name is a beautiful way of handling the problem of how any name, in its finiteness, could be used to represent the Infinite. And even when it was spoken, it was only the high priest (the highest position in ancient Judaism) who could say it, and only on the most holy day, in the most holy place. In that recitation, the high priest was essentially to have transcended his finitude as a human being, so that it was really the Infinite calling out its own name.

Jewish mystics, looking at that name, held that if God's name had four letters, then there must be some fourfold way of understanding the one God of everything. They described four different "worlds" in which God can be understood in different ways. Through this model, they were able to offer a rich and complex system that captures the way in which multiplicity and oneness can be held together. It sees the divine process as a spectrum, with at one end the world we all recognize, full of disparate objects, and at the other, no world of creation at all, where all multiplicity is meaningless. At the same time, the fourfold nature can be thought of as a divine process in which the nature of God moves between the empty ground of being and appearing simultaneously as the physical world we know. And each world itself is a process with a different divine essence. This divine essence is represented by using gerunds, words ending in *ing,* imparting an acting quality to the Divine. This language reemphasizes the notion that God is a process, rather than a subject or a noun.

The fourfold model of understanding God developed by Jewish mystics parallels similar fourfold models for life in other spiritual traditions. I think it is helpful to keep in mind that models are just models. They reflect the normal ways that human consciousness perceives reality. Remember, I spoke about perception and its conditioned nature in chapter 3. While these models are helpful in broadening our understanding, they are only models, not the Divine itself. For example, Jewish mystics also have a tenfold model for describing God's creation. I believe this tenfold understanding of the universe comes out of the basic human experience of having ten fingers, making us organically predisposed to see the world in units of ten. Our entire numerical system is based on the number ten.

Similarly, it might be possible to explain the fourfold system as a basic way human beings classify reality (which is different than reality itself). Since each hand has five fingers, we might imagine that there would be fivefold systems that explain reality. Indeed, there are many fivefold approaches—for example, the five spiritual laws in Christianity. However, a major aspect of human experience, from an evolutionary point of view, is the opposable thumb. Scientists believe that human evolution developed as it did because of the opposable thumb, which is often seen as both related to the four fingers and different at the same time. I can imagine the opposable thumb as a model for seeing the universe as both unitary and fourfold at the same time. It is like the saying, "Two sides of the same coin," only in this example, one side is fourfold in nature and the other side is singular. Try holding up one hand at eye level and imagine it grasping an imaginary sphere with your thumb facing you. The one thumb is in the foreground and the four fingers are in the background. Now, if you rotate your hand so the palm is no longer visible, the four fingers come in to the foreground and thumb recedes from view. The fourfold model I am about to explain is like that—not exactly a unitive God, and not exactly a fourfold God.

As a way of presenting the fourfold model of the Divine, I would like to use a contemplative chant written by my teacher, Rabbi Zalman Schachter-Shalomi. The chart below shows this teaching in a somewhat more graphic form:

Letter Name	World	Sound	Hebrew Letter	Divine Attribute	Words of Chant
Yud	*Atzilut*	*y* in English	י	Being	I Am Holy
Hay	*Beriyah*	*h* in English	ה	Knowing	All Is Clear
Vav	*Yetsirah*	*v* in English	ו	Feeling	You Are Loved
Hay	*Assiyah*	*h* in English	ה	Acting	It Is Perfect

The column on the left gives the Hebrew name of the letter. The third column shows the sound in English made by the letter. The fourth column shows the Hebrew letter itself. The fifth column describes the primary nature of how the divine manifestation presents itself in that world. The second column is the Hebrew name for the world. The sixth column contains the words of a chant that is recited by beginning at the bottom and going upward.

An interesting teaching becomes apparent when we look at the Hebrew letters of the divine name, *yud, hay, vav,* and *hay,* when they are written from top to bottom.

Normally, Hebrew is written from right to left. However, when these letters are written one on top of the other, the resulting picture looks like a stick figure of a human being. This is one way of depicting the idea that human beings are created in God's image. The *yud* on top is like the head. The upper *hay* has the shape of shoulders and arms hanging down. The *vav* is the trunk or spine. And the lower *hay* is like the pelvis and legs. This metaphor need not be taken literally, but rather as a teaching to remind us that we can find the Divine here in creation, and that every person we encounter in our lives, whether friend or foe, is an embodiment of the divine process.

The contemplative chant itself proceeds as follows:

It is perfect
You are loved
All is clear and
I am holy

Taken as a whole, this chant presents a fourfold understanding of how we would perceive our universe if we were fully awake and able to see it from the perspective of expanded awareness. We would experience in each moment the perfect way things are unfolding for us, and how nothing could be different. We would feel connected to all things and be pervaded with a sense of being loved. We would see clearly why things are as they are, and we would understand the interconnected nature of all things. Our recognition would be suffused with a sense of holiness, absent the illusion of a separate person to whom this was happening.

It is important not to become fixed on the idea that you need to see the world this way—such goal setting often only makes us feel smaller, trapped, or unhappy. Rather, use this teaching as a way of orienting yourself to developing a comprehensive spiritual practice that helps you wake up in your life. The chant can be used by itself as a meditative device through repetition and with melody. You might start periods of sitting practice by chanting these words for a few minutes. Doing so can be a concentration practice in itself, but at the same time, the meaning of the words helps set the intention in the heart and mind to awaken to these underlying realities. A detailed explanation of the meaning of the words of the chant will help you utilize them effectively in your own practice.

"It Is Perfect": The Physical Universe as God

This phrase refers to the Divine Presence as something manifesting in the physical world—the world of our bodies and all other physical objects. This includes electrons and atoms and molecules and stars. One way of seeing how the Divine manifests in the physical realm is by acknowledging that the world of matter is governed by inalterable physical laws that unfold in perfect order. This can be described as cause and effect, which includes the laws of physics. In this perfect order, every time you drop something out of your hand, it falls. Two physical bodies attract each other and we call it gravity. The word *perfect* is not meant to be a value judgment. Rather, it means that things unfold as they must. There is a lawfulness and order to things in this realm. Things are as they are.

The language of the first phrase is crafted to work in tandem with the second phrase, "You are loved." The words *it* and *you* are meant to correspond to the teachings of Martin Buber, a famous Jewish philosopher and theologian who was born in 1878 in Vienna. Buber's most famous work was a book on the philosophy and theology of dialogue called *I and Thou,* published in 1923. It contains Buber's beliefs on experiencing the Divine Presence. It is a work that demands deep study, and in these brief words, I hope only to introduce my understanding as it relates to the phrases of the chant under discussion.

Buber says that there are two primary attitudes through which we encounter the world around us—I-it, and I and Thou. The "I" in I-it refers to the basic human preconception that each of us has a separate self. As I mentioned in chapter 3, this is the small sense of self. The "I" of this self encounters the world as consisting of objects that make contact with the "I" through the various sense doorways of the body. In relation to the small self, each of these objects is experienced as an "it." As I walk around, I see things. These things are all examples of it, and I relate to them as objects. The keyboard I am touching is an it. The computer screen is an it. The dog at my feet is an it. The person in the next room is an it. And I generally relate to all of them as objects that generate some reaction. In the I-it mode, I am not in dialogue with these objects. Buber would characterize this primary attitude as the world of alienation, isolation, and separation.

Occasionally, the "I" leaves the world of I-it and makes contact with an object in a new way that changes the experience of the "I." Buber would say that the object—the "it" of the I-It mode—becomes a "You." When I share this teaching in front of a group of people, I deliberately make eye contact with someone who I notice is nodding at my words. At that moment of contact, they have become something different than the object sitting in the room, listening to me teach. In the nodding and the power it has to draw my attention, this person has become a "You." In that moment I have entered into a relationship with that person. They move out of the faceless crowd and into the spotlight of a "You" with whom I have a connection. Buber referred to this moment with the phrase, "I and Thou." When the "and" manifests, it brings the "I" and the "it" into the world of dialogue, transforming the "it" into a "Thou," or a "You." For Buber, this moment of relationship is also a moment of Divine Presence. In German, Buber's theology was called *das Zwischen,* the theology of the "and."

It may help to clarify the title *I and Thou* for those unfamiliar with German. In German and in many other languages, two different words are used to connote the difference between a familiar or intimate *you* and a *you* that refers to a stranger or a person with whom you have a more formal relationship. In German, the familiar form is *du* and the formal version is *sie.* The title of Buber's book in German is *Ich und Du,* and Buber is using the informal version of *you* to connote a person who is your friend. The translators wanted to emphasize that there are two different ways to say "you," so they chose the English word *thou* to call attention to the word. Of course, to our modern ears, *thou* sounds like a more formal way to say "you," but just the opposite is meant.

So, the word *you* in the second phrase of the contemplative chant, "You are loved," implies a transformation, where each one of us is no longer completely separate from the Divine Presence. You are not just some separate "it" but rather in a living "and" relationship with the Divine. Coming back to the first phrase, "It is perfect," you can begin to get a sense of how the Divine manifests in this realm. It is the realm of discrete objects. The four worlds reflect a continuum of ways to see the Divine. The fourth world will be the other end of the spectrum to this world of I-it. It is the end where nothing separate exists from anything else—that is, there is no duality. The I-it world, on the other hand, is characterized by the complete absence of *non*duality. This is a world where things act, one upon the other. Hence, the name for this world in Hebrew is *Assiyah,* which means "doing."

I want to introduce the idea of using all four phrases (and worlds) as an overall framework for a daily meditation practice. This is a separate practice from prayer or chanting or any form of mantra meditation. As I mentioned previously, Jewish meditation always focuses on some aspect of the Divine as it manifests. The fourfold model offers four separate arenas for paying attention to the Divine that, taken together, present a clearer picture than any one of the worlds alone. An example from life may be helpful in this connection. Imagine the following situation: A man is late to an appointed restaurant rendezvous with his fiancée. When he arrives, a huge fight occurs as the woman hurls accusations at him. I'm sure you can think of similar situations in your own life. But how can the four worlds model help in viewing this situation?

There is more than one possible way to understand the scene. For example, the waiting woman may not have eaten for a long time, dropping her blood sugar to the point where it affected her mood. Or, perhaps she has a history from early childhood of feeling abandoned because her parents were often not present either physically or emotionally. This may have left an emotional wound, which is easily triggered by her partner's late arrival. In either case, his actions aren't the only cause of the argument. Without knowing the particulars of such a situation, it is obvious that an array of factors such as body chemistry, emotional wounding, and habitual thought processes are interacting below the surface appearance of any event. When you look at the event through only one lens, you don't see the complexity of the truths of this situation. In order to wake up to the divine reality inherent in each moment, it is likewise necessary to have a fourfold base from which to observe carefully and act wisely. The meditation practices in this section outline an approach based on these four phrases and the four realms of divine manifestation to which they point.

You can use the first phrase of the chant, "It is perfect," as a lens for paying attention to the Divine Presence as it manifests in the physical world. Your object of focus will be the bare noticing of bodily experience. As your attention shifts to thoughts or feelings, gently remind yourself to return your attention to the simple experience of just noticing sensations of body. I'll give two sets of instructions for this practice. It is helpful to choose one of them and use it for a number of days or weeks. At some point in your practice you might choose to switch and use the other set, also for a few days or weeks.

Paying Attention to the Most Prominent Bodily Sensation

Sit in a quiet place and begin by allowing your attention to rest on the arising and passing of the breath. After a few minutes of this, make an intention to broaden out your focus to include whatever is the most prominent bodily sensation that you notice. This sensation then becomes the primary object of your focus. As long as it feels like the most prominent sensation, simply continue to aim and sustain your attention on this object. At some point, you will notice that another sensation has risen to prominence. You can generally know that something else is a more prominent sensation because your attention will already have shifted there without any effort on your part. If the mind begins commenting about the sensation and what to do about it, gently return your attention to simply noticing the sensation itself. If no particular sensation seems prominent, allow your attention to rest on the arising and passing of the breath.

Sometimes when I pay attention to prominent bodily sensations, a strong sensation will grab my attention and remain the most noticeable sensation for quite a while. Other times, especially if there is no major pain in my body and no large story grabbing my mind, the most prominent sensation can change fairly rapidly. It might be more difficult to sustain your attention on shifting sensations. If this is the case, you can always go back to the sensation of the breath when you find yourself lost. Once when I was doing this practice I noticed that my attention was shifting quite rapidly to various places in my body. The various sensations were changing rapidly and I was trying to keep up with them. Although this is a frequent occurrence, I remember this particular time because it triggered an association to a story I once heard on National Public Radio.

It was a theatrical review of a play about Ginger Rogers called *Backwards and in High Heels*. Ginger Rogers was part of a famous dancing partnership with Fred Astaire. In my memory, Fred Astaire was the more famous of the two. The title of the play captures the essential point regarding their relative skills as dancers. In the style of dancing they did, the male is the lead dancer and the female has to follow that lead. So whatever Fred did, Ginger needed to follow. There are disputes about the authorship of the following quote, but someone once said that "she did everything Fred did, and did it backwards and in high heels."

I think this is an apt metaphor for the kind of attention we need in practicing with whatever sensation is prominent. Choosing your own object of attention is more like being the lead dancer. It carries with it a sense of being in control of the situation. But the practice of paying attention to whatever sensation is most prominent as it occurs is like being the dancer who follows the lead—in this case, the lead of the body. This kind of choiceless awareness more closely resembles what life is like in many ways. Most of what happens around us is outside of our immediate control. But rather than be lost in the reactive stories that can occupy the mind from moment to moment, we can be awake to life as it is unfolding and changing. And clearly seeing life unfold is a prerequisite to seeing the divine aspect of this unfolding. But remember: this clear seeing needs to be balanced with appropriate responses to life. Letting go of a sense that we control life is not the same as living a life out of control or passively.

As you become accustomed to practicing in this way, you can work with the added sensibility brought by the phrase, "It is perfect." This is best done by reflecting on the phrase at the beginning of the meditation period. Consider its meaning and reread the explanation if necessary. Make the connection that you are about to pay attention to your physical body, which is one of four places you can become aware of the Divine Presence. Make the additional intention to see each moment of bodily awareness with the sense that "it is perfect," in and of itself, even when you notice a painful or unpleasant sensation. Remember, the phrase, "It is perfect" is not intended to mean that you enjoy your experience. It is more a statement of appreciation that we have a nervous system that can send out warning signals when some physically threatening experience is occurring. After beginning with this mental reflection, try to shift your attention from thinking about the phrase to paying attention to the bodily experience arising in each moment.

Sweeping the Body

Instead of allowing the attention to move and rest on various prominent sensations as they arise, the second method for this practice directs the attention to particular parts of the body in a prescribed order. The practice is sometimes called "sweeping the body with attention." To begin this practice, find a comfortable position to sit in. At the beginning, allow your attention to rest with the arising and passing of each breath. When you have cultivated some degree of presence in the moment (or, at most, after a minute or two), direct your attention to the sensations happening at the bottom of your feet. Depending on how you are sitting, you might feel pressure on the bottom of your feet or on the outside edge, wherever they are making contact with the floor. Try to simply notice the sensation without intentionally making any mental comment on it. As soon as you can feel the sensations in your feet, allow your attention to slowly move upward, focusing on different parts of the body and noticing the sensations in them as you do so.

There is no correct speed for undertaking this practice. If your attention moves quickly up the body, you will gloss over many sensations. If you move your attention too slowly, you may find yourself more easily distracted. Experiment to find a pace that works for you. By this, I mean a pace that allows you to most easily stay present with the whole body with minimal distraction. One purpose of practicing in this way is to be able to notice the whole body. In the previous practice of noticing prominent sensations, only those parts of the body that are compelling ever get noticed. But this ignores many places in the body. Perhaps you can see why both of these practices, taken together, make for a good balance. We want to be able to gain some control over our wandering attention so that, when needed, we can focus it on a particular object. We also want to develop the ability to sustain awakened attention even as our focus shifts from place to place, as it does most of the time.

As you have probably noticed, your attention is usually grabbed by thoughts and experiences other than those suggested in the instructions. Try not to be discouraged by this. It is a normal part of the process of learning how the mind works. Over time you may gain some facility in aiming and sustaining your attention to a particular object of focus. This is a useful skill in life, but like any skill, you will have your own proclivity in being able to develop it, and it might take considerable effort to make it a strong skill. However, regardless of how strong your concentration skill is, the wisdom you gain about the nature of the mind becomes evident as soon as you notice what is actually happening, moment by moment. As we practice paying attention during meditation, we become wiser about the way our mind works, about our habits, and fixations.

"You Are Loved": The Divine Presence in Emotional Connections

Let's return to the second of the four phrases, "You are loved." In the first phrase, our focus was solely on experiencing the physical world on its own terms. It corresponds to the knowing of sensations as described in chapter 3, on the nature of the mind. The phrase, "You are loved" can direct us into understanding another aspect of divine manifestation. It is linked to the letter *vav* in the divine name *Yud Hay Vav Hay*. The names of the Hebrew letters are themselves Hebrew words. The Hebrew word *vav* means "hook." The letter itself is also used in Hebrew the same way as the English conjunction *and*. A hook is something that takes separate objects and links them together; so does the word *and*. *Vav* is the aspect of the Divine that manifests as the process of connecting. As mentioned in discussing Buber, when connectedness is present in our lives, we enter the world of I and Thou. The "other" stops being an object as long as the connection—the "and"—is manifest. In this world, God can be conceived of as the force that brings disparate objects together. When that happens in our own experience, the other people in our lives transform from "it" objects to "You," and the isolation we normally feel is replaced by the feeling of connection with others. That feeling can be called love. The phrase "You are loved" no longer has the word *it* as the subject. According to Buber, the word *You* can only be spoken in connection to another since *You* implies the phrase, "I and You." In saying and hearing these words, I imagine that I am connected with a speaker whom I hear as God addressing me.

As the phrase implies, the focus of "You are loved" is on the feelings that manifest in parallel to the world of physical sensation. Obviously, love is not the only emotion we experience, but it can be seen as the ultimate or divine feeling that best describes the experience of a moment of clear seeing, when the perfection of the physical universe is accepted and when connection rather than isolation is perceived. Perhaps, in another way, love is the only real feeling. There is a teaching in *A Course in Miracles,* a channeled spiritual path, that every human action is either an offering of love or a request for love. For example, even anger is only an emotional reaction to a deeper feeling that love is missing and so is really just a request for that love.

The instructions for practicing meditation with this phrase expand upon the instructions for paying attention to bodily experience. The overall objective in this fourfold set of practices is integrative, so consider these instructions as additions rather than replacements for the prior instructions. This time, you will be adding the practice of focusing your attention on the world of feelings, while continuing to be aware of the bodily experiences of the present moment.

Begin by resting your attention on the sensations of the breath arising and passing. From there, when ready, allow either body sweeping or noticing of prominent sensations to become the object of attention. When your attention feels relatively stable, start to notice any emotional reaction that might be occurring in the mind as the sensations occur. Initially, this practice should be kept at the simplest level, just noticing whether the present sensation is pleasant, unpleasant, or neutral. Seeing the truth that this simple level of emotional reaction is always occurring in the mind is the foundation for understanding the complex mental phenomena that subsequently occur.

The divine world referred to in this second set of experiences is called *Olam Yetzirah*, or the world of formation. As I mentioned previously, it is in this world that the process of the construction of mental formations begins. As the knowing of sensation comes together with an emotional reaction, something composite is formed. These compositions are experienced in the realm of the mind, hence the term *mental formations*. It is in the coming together of physical sensation with valence or feeling tone (pleasant, unpleasant, or neutral) that the small sense of self creates other smaller temporary mental formations we call feelings or emotions.

As I discussed in chapter 3, this process gives rise to thoughts of greed and aversion, two mind states characterized by an incomplete understanding of the moment. That is why the practice of noting the feeling tone of an experience is so important; it gives us insight into what is really happening inside us at this very moment. When you notice that a sensation is unpleasant, what does your mind do? Does it try avoiding the pain by daydreaming, getting angry, blaming someone? What happens when you experience a neutral sensation? Does the mind wander, get bored, fall asleep? By noticing how we habitually respond to pleasant, unpleasant, or neutral sensations, we learn about where we're stuck, about our resistance to staying present and being awake. Gradually, as we practice, we train the mind to be awake and alive in each moment.

After working with the practice of noticing both physical sensations and the feeling tones that accompany them, we can work on noticing the plans of action our mind undertakes when faced with certain feeling tones. For example, if you taste a spoonful of ice cream, you will probably find that the taste is pleasant. Along with this pleasant feeling tone comes an emotion of craving more and more ice cream. As you indulge your desire, you may also have thoughts about the effects of eating the ice cream on your heath or appearance. These can be referred to as mental formations or patterns of volitional fabricating, and they include what we usually call feelings, as well as moods, thoughts, attitudes, plans for action, and even our sense of identity.

Allow your attention to rest primarily with bodily sensations. As they arise, note whether they are pleasant, unpleasant, or neutral, while keeping your primary attention on the sensation itself. You can also intentionally open up your attention to wider vistas. As sensations arise in your awareness, you might ask yourself if you are feeling content or anxious or unhappy about them. For example, if you are sitting and trying to notice bodily sensations and nothing too exciting is happening, nothing painful or particularly pleasant, you might notice that you are having difficulty sustaining your attention on the body. You may be thinking, "This is boring," or, "I think I'll go have breakfast." As soon as you recognize that your attention has shifted from directly noticing bodily sensations, let your attention rest on the fact that thinking has arisen. Or that boredom has arisen. At this stage of practice, try to simply notice what is being sensed. As much as possible, it is helpful to sense these moods, thoughts, and feelings in the body itself. So, if you are feeling bored, which is a mental construction, notice that your boredom also has a bodily aspect as well. Try to locate where in your body you notice these feelings.

As you practice with this second phrase, try to cultivate a sense of appreciation for being able to see things just the way they are. If you notice you are bored, for example, see if you can accept the value in seeing the boredom, even if you simultaneously wish it wasn't so. Just as these practice instructions build on the prior instructions, the phrases also build on each other. So, "It is perfect" is still a good lens for exploring feelings and thoughts. It is good that the sensation of boredom exists. It is there to catch our attention. And as you work with "You are loved" in this part of the practice, try to imagine that these things are not happening to the object you refer to as "me"; your direct experience of these sensations and the "knower" of the sensations are part of one larger reality. In impersonal language, you can realize that a pain in your knee is really a gift from the universe, a loving reminder to wake up.

"All Is Clear": The World of Divine Wisdom

In chapter 3, "The Nature of Mind," and again here in the description of the four divine worlds, I have been pointing out parallel versions of an integrative process that results in what we call "the mind," which includes our sense of self. I have mentioned sensations, feelings, perceptions, and thoughts. According to Jewish mystics, the third world of the divine, *Olam Habriyah*, is the world of wisdom. Wisdom arises through the combination of paying attention, developing skills in concentration, and being aware of the Divine Presence that is manifest in each moment. Wisdom is what results from the clarity of mind that is implied in the phrase, "All is clear." The word *all* refers to the integrative nature of seeing how individual moments of experience can be woven together into a reality map that encompasses the whole. Scientists call this concept the unified field theory. It is the necessary kind of wisdom that points us beyond the boundary of the small sense of self, or *mochin de-katnut*.

The word *all* implies that our practice at this point is designed to focus on seeing how the individual moments of awareness are part of a flowing process where causes and conditions are linked to the nature of the unfolding mind. Up to this point, thoughts, feelings, and perceptions were all considered to be mental formations, and each one could be experienced without explicitly looking at their linkages.

In chapter 3, I pointed out the concept that an unpleasant sensation results in thoughts of aversion. Wisdom, the third foundation for practice, goes beyond the conceptual to help you cultivate insights into what conditions your aversion. In understanding how your own anger or frustration arises, you gain key insights that can lead to the opening of your heart in lovingkindness.

In formal practice, you can still primarily pay attention to your body's experience of each moment. But now you are also watching out of the corner of your eye to see what precipitated a thought. For example, if you think, "Ten minutes instead of twenty will be enough for today's sit," maybe you were having more trouble than usual staying with the breath, leading to a momentary feeling of incompetence. You can recognize this as an unpleasant thought, and you can see for yourself that an aversive feeling can result in an aversive thought: "Ten minutes instead of twenty will be enough." If you are awake in the moment when the aversive thought begins, you can recognize it as ordinary impatience, which is just the truth of that moment. Because you have developed some clarity and objectivity in recognizing the origin of the thought, you know that you don't have to act on it by stopping early. You also know that the next moment might bring you the most exquisite focus you have ever experienced.

But if you miss this moment through mindlessness, you begin to believe that you are not such a good meditator. That thought may slip in and out but not be seen as a thought without much merit. Without realizing it, your mood slips into an aversive state, or doubt arises. Then the thought of quitting early flies in to the rescue. On most days, you give in and stop early. But more and more often, you might begin to catch the whole train of events and see that your thought to quit was not so innocent. You begin to see through the preconceived notion that the number of breaths you can take without a distracting thought is the sign of a good meditator. You realize you are being self-judgmental. As soon as you see this, you know you have the choice to laugh and not take the judgment as the truth. You can awaken to the realization that grasping at a preconceived notion of what it means to be a good meditator leads to self-judgment. Seeing this directly for yourself is the meditative work of "All is clear."

"I Am Holy": The Divine as Radical Monism

Receiving the Ten Commandments at Mount Sinai can be considered the peak mystical experience of the Jewish people. Why is this called the peak experience? The term is itself drawn from what many people consider a great mystical experience, spending time in the mountains. When people are asked where they most experience God, a common reply is being in nature, and being in the mountains is frequently at the top of that list. Many astronauts who have seen the earth from space report a feeling of deep spiritual connection. I can still remember my first backpacking trip, in Bighorn National Forest, and what an awe-inspiring experience it was for me. The opportunity to go camping is like being on retreat. We leave the normal pace of life behind, with its cars, computers, and cell phones. In unplugging, our minds have a chance to settle down, even without formal contemplative practice. We open up to the experience of whatever is arising because we have left our comforts as well as our distractions behind. Up in the mountains we can look out into the valleys and see the world from an enlarged perspective, allowing us to feel a connection to our creator.

For the Jewish people, receiving the Ten Commandments is a peak experience in another way, beside the fact that it occurred on a mountain. Unlike other meetings in Jewish history that took place between God and only select individuals, this meeting was experienced by the entire Jewish nation as a whole. We are taught in the Torah that there were six hundred thousand men over the age of twenty at Sinai, which translates into over two million men, women, and children. All of them had the direct experience of receiving the Ten Commandments, of perceiving God's voice as it is written, "And God spoke all these words, saying …" (Exod. 20:1).

What was this experience like? We are taught, "And all the people saw the thunderings … and when the people saw it, they trembled and stood afar off. And they said unto Moses: 'Speak thou with us and we will hear; but let not God speak with us, lest we die'" (Exod. 20:18–19). From these lines, an interesting set of teachings have arisen about the giving of the Ten Commandments. As Rashi, the most noted medieval Jewish biblical commentator, points out: the people saw, rather than heard, what is normally an auditory experience. In science this is called synesthesia, when sensory input is perceived by other than the appropriate sense organ—for example, seeing a sound or hearing a smell. What this biblical language seems to be telling us is that when

God spoke the Ten Commandments, they were not heard or perceived in the normal sensory way.

These verses also indicate that when the experience occurred, the
people were afraid and retreated. Here we have a moment when the
Jewish people were exposed to a direct connection to the will of
the universe, and it was an instinctive moment of fear. The people
seem to have responded to a major sensory overload and decided they
would rather rely on Moses to be the intercessor. As we explore what
this experience might have been like, we can understand what might
have caused this recoil. There is a radical nature to really waking up.
The actual universe may not look like what our conditioned notions
tell us about the nature of reality. This is sometimes referred to by
spiritual teachings as the need to die in order for spiritual growth to
occur. (See chapter 6 and the instructions for practice when reciting
the Shema for more on this concept.)

So, from a simple reading of the Torah text, it seems that God
started to speak the Ten Commandments and then the people interrupted and told Moses to get the rest for them. This leaves the question: How much of the Ten Commandments did the Jewish people
hear before they commissioned Moses to finish? Some commentators
say they only heard the first commandment, "I am the Lord your God,
who brought you out of the land of Egypt." Others say that they heard
only the first word, *anochi* in Hebrew, or "I am" in English. Let me
share with you the way that the Jewish mystics understand what hearing that first word was like. We have already considered the idea that
it was not a normal hearing of a sound. Instead, the mystics teach that
in this moment, all two million Jews gathered at Sinai experienced a
sense of "I am" (rather than hearing anything), and there was only one
"I" having the experience. All sense of existence as separate beings
vanished. And such a moment is a holy moment. This is the meaning
of the fourth divine world, and of the phrase, "I am Holy." Of course,
an experience of no separate self proved to be a bit too much for the
people, and an instant was all they could handle. Hence, they fled the
experience and asked Moses to get the rest for them.

I can't tell you how to practice to have such an experience. It
involves grace, among many other things. I can relate some of my

experiences that I believe point in the direction of allowing such a possibility to unfold. Trying to have an experience of no self is a contradiction in terms, since it is the self who would need to "try." During deep concentration practice, many people experience a shift in viewpoint—that is, what started out as an experience of a knower knowing something that can be known, changes as the concentration deepens. Sometimes, the knower and the object known fade out of consciousness and only *knowing* is happening. Of course, without the knower being present, no one is having this experience. It is only after the fact that the knower might recall the experience, when returning to the world of "All is clear."

In my own meditation experience on retreat, I have tried to balance concentration practice with awareness practice. On one longer retreat, however, at the urging of a Buddhist meditation master from Burma, I worked exclusively with a concentration practice that focused on the breath when sitting and on the feet during walking. Along with the support of the silent environment and slowing the pace of all my movements to a crawl, I was able to slow down much of my mental experience. The teacher asked us if we were able to be aware of every single thought that arose in an hour of sitting. Being an obedient student, I tried as diligently as possible to note every single thought that arose, hour after hour. After a week or so, I would notice that in some hour-long periods I might only have four or five individual thoughts that arose. The rest of the time, my attention stayed on the physical sensations of the breath coming in and going out, or the sensations in the foot when stepping. I was using the practice of mental noting, so my mind was not empty but rather filled with thoughts such as "lifting," "moving," "tingling," "pulsing," and the like. So when I say that only four or five thoughts might arise, I mean a thought where for an instant I was thinking of something other than the sensations that arose and the internal mantra accompanying it. While I find it amazing, even to myself, that I could be so focused, I don't believe that I learned anything new in noticing the sensations. In fact, I was miserable during much of the practice, and my few thoughts were all worries about whether my next report to the teacher would be good enough.

However, about two weeks into the retreat, I had a remarkable experience. I was sitting in my room and I had stopped doing any mental noting. I sat for quite a while and had no thoughts whatsoever floating into my mind. I was aware of sensations and colors, but I didn't comment on them or label them. If my attention started to fade, I would notice that the small self was trying to come back in and reorganize itself. While these words feel inadequate to describe the experience, it seemed clear to me that the self was something that could be watched, rather than it being a separate entity doing the watching. This is the closest thing I can describe to being in *mochin de-gadlut,* and it felt like a holy experience. In that place, there was no God as "other" to be experienced.

A Guided Meditation of Peak Experience

A guided meditation based on a teaching from the Torah serves as our final example of a way to connect with God. In Jewish tradition, Moses is seen as the person who was most directly aware of the Divine Presence in the universe. In describing Moses's relationship with God, we read in Exodus 33:11, "And YHVH would speak to Moshe face to face, as a man speaks to his neighbor."[1] Of course, we know that this connection with God was not a steady state for Moses. He had periods where he displayed lack of clarity, anger, and other merely human experiences. But one of the strengths of Torah is the understanding that our ancestors and prophets were merely human as are we.

And like us, even Moses wanted his understanding to deepen. He wanted to experience the One even more clearly: "So now—if I have found favor in your eyes, pray let me know your ways, that I may (truly) know you, in order that I may find favor in your eyes" (Exod. 33:13).[2] According to Jewish tradition, Moses was the greatest prophet. He was the most advanced person in directly knowing the One, yet even he wanted something more. Here we see that even after the burning bush, the ten plagues, the Exodus, and the receiving of the first set of the Ten Commandments, Moses is still looking to know God. For each of us, the process of waking up is one that never finishes or culminates in some act of attainment. Moses says that the goal of his search is not to achieve one more rung of wisdom but rather to find favor in God's eyes, that is, to purify his heart so that nothing is left but the divine will.

God tells Moses he has found favor already: "YHVH said to Moshe: Also this word that you have spoken, I will do, for you have found favor in my eyes, and I have known you by name" (Exod. 33:17).[3] And still, Moses persists. In an act that I believe reflects the wholesome desire that we all have to know God fully, Moses says, "Pray let me see your Glory" (Exod. 33:18).[4] And God responds in a somewhat enigmatic way: "I myself will cause my Goodliness to pass in front of your face, I will call out the name of YHVH before your face: that I show favor to whom I show favor, that I show mercy to whom I show mercy. But he said: You cannot see my face for no human can see me and live!" (Exod. 33:19–20).[5]

But wait a minute. Didn't we just read in verse 11 that God and Moses spoke face-to-face? Here it says no one can see God and live. What is going on? Apparently, even though God would *speak* to Moses face-to-face, there is another layer, referred to as *seeing,* that Moses is told can't occur. Specifically, he is told that this kind of seeing can't happen for living beings if they expect to stay alive in their current incarnation. This would seem to imply that Moses is asking for a kind of seeing and knowing that fully merges into the *ayin,* or "emptiness," of God. This may be the kind of emptiness that is beyond all separateness. To reach this point might imply that the level of awareness does not fall back into the relative world of separate objects and duality once the experience is over. But this response of God's is not the end of the story. There is a way that God says he can take Moses, and each of us, to another place of knowing God—a way you can experience for yourself by using a guided contemplative meditation.

If you are able, ask a friend to lead you in the meditation by reading the extract on pages 132 and 133 for you. This friend might want to read the whole meditation through one time to get a feel for it. The words should read slowly, allowing time to pass between sentences so that you as listener have time to entertain the imagery internally.

When you are ready to begin the meditation, sit comfortably in a spot where you will not be interrupted by noise or the phone or other demands for your attention—a beautiful place outside might be nice.

Find a time to do this exercise when you can sit quietly for thirty minutes before beginning the guided imagery. If someone is reading for you, close your eyes. If you are reading the words yourself, try reading one sentence at a time, and mark the end of the sentence with your finger. Then close your eyes and imagine yourself following the imagery of the words. When you're ready, read the next sentence, continuing on to the end in this manner.

Imagine yourself at the base of a mountain with a path leading upward before you. Get in touch with that place inside that is yearning to know God, more directly and intimately then ever before. [Reader: Allow a minute or two in silence.] Feel the awe of knowing that this is a very special moment and special experience that is unfolding. You are now beginning your ascent up the mountain path. It is a clear day, with a soft breeze blowing. As you climb the path, let yourself visualize a mountain setting. At first the path is wide, allowing you to focus on the trees, the sounds of the brooks, and the animals along the way.

As you continue to climb, the path becomes steeper. The view from the mountain begins to expand. Your breath becomes more noticeable as you feel the effort of the climb. The path begins to narrow till you find yourself hugging the side of the mountain to your left, with the view out to the right. The face of the mountain has now become sheer rocks. Your climb has led you to a magnificent view of the valley below. With each step you can see farther and farther. You know with each step and with each breath that the promised moment is getting closer and closer, even as you know that this moment is already full of that same promise. Just as you get to a place where further ascent is not possible, you notice a V-shaped space in the rock wall to your left, running up and down from the path, just wide enough and tall enough for you to wedge your body into, back first. You can feel the solid pressure of the rock behind you. In front of you is open space, with a clear view as far as you have ever seen. God has promised to reveal God's self to you in this very place, and you feel this presence growing. You know that you can't see God's face, but God has promised to allow you to see God's back. With your eyes closed, you feel an alignment with the One. With God's backside to your face you are now in the position to look out at the universe through the same eyes that God uses to see the universe. This is the gift of closeness you have been granted, to see the world through God's eyes. When you open your eyes, look at the world the way God sees the world. At this most profound moment, our Torah says this is how God sees the world, so chant the following three times [if you know the melody for chanting the thirteen attributes of God, use that]:

> *Yud Hay Vav Hay,* Compassion and Tenderness. Patience Forbearance, Kindness Awareness. Bearing love From Age to Age. Lifting Guilt and Sin and Making us Free. (Exod. 34:6–7; translation by David Wolfe-Blank)

I used to think God was offering the next best thing when he offered to show his back. Now I realize he offered something better. When you see a face opposite yours, you are still in duality. In that sense, seeing God "face-to-face" is not as alive or as awake as we can be. By showing Moses the world through God's eyes, God and Moses came face-to-face in the same way that we do when we step into another person's shoes. And the Torah is clear on what the experience of seeing the world through God's eyes is like. It is total compassion and tenderness. This is what we are cultivating when we wake ourselves up.

6 Prayer and Meditation

One of the central components of a traditional Jewish practice is daily prayer. Observant Jews have three formal prayer services each day in the morning, afternoon, and evening. There is no shortage of reading materials available to help you understand the format and traditional meanings of these prayers. What I offer instead is a contemplative approach to working with the traditional prayers that stays quite close to the general meditation techniques I have presented in this book. By this, I mean that the prayers are used as the object of focus for a sustained concentration practice. Practicing in this way gives the dual benefit of further developing concentration while connecting to the values and teachings inherent in the prayers. This chapter will introduce a few additional techniques that can be used with this basic format. There are many methods for using prayer in a contemplative way—I present this method because it has proven valuable to hundreds of worshipers who have attended meditation retreats over the years.

While it is possible to use hundreds of pages of written words of prayer as an object of focus, I prefer to simplify and pare down the practice by selecting several key concepts and words that address the underlying deep structure of the service. For simplicity's sake, I will limit my description of a contemplative prayer practice to the morning service. The same approach can be used for the other two services as well, and I encourage you to do so if you wish to use this practice three times a day.

Included in this chapter is a selection of eleven lines of prayer, most of which are from the morning *(shacharit)* service, in the usual order they occur. The basic structure for the practice I describe consists of using these lines in the following way: Working with one line at a time, begin by reading the words and developing an intention based on your understanding of the words. Repeat the words over and over, chanting them out loud and with melody. Allow a period of silence after each chant, and then repeat the process for the next chant. (You will find a list of resources for learning the melodies in Appendix B.) There are many more liturgical melodies you can find on your own, or, if you are musically inclined, you can create your own melodies, which is a powerful practice in and of itself.

I will offer some thoughts about each of these prayers that you may find helpful. You will see that each teaching is intended to point you toward using these prayers in a way that has an impact on your state of mind during the prayer process. Eventually, you will want to develop your own relationship to the words and how they speak to you.

Cultivating Wholesome Mind States

Up to this point, I have been emphasizing contemplative techniques that bring your attention to the truth of what is occurring right at this very moment. This means the direct knowing of sensations as they arise, as well as knowing what moods and mind states are present. Toward that end, we explored the importance of concentration practices as a precursor to seeing with clarity the truth of each moment. Concentration practice can have the effect of quieting the mind and bringing to it some calm and openness—which are the very qualities that allow us to see more clearly. Prayer practice used to build concentration can have the same impact, but there is an important distinction as well. Rather than merely observing what mind state is present, prayer specifically cultivates wholesome mind states.

In chapter 5, I introduced the concept of paying attention to moods and mind states. All of us have different moods at different times, and these moods can sometimes impair our ability to see clearly. An example from my life illustrates this truth. For many years, I

taught meditation retreats at Elat Chayyim, where I was simultaneously the executive director. I also lived on the retreat center grounds,
which meant that in addition to being the supervisor at the center, I
was also fulfilling my role as spouse and parent. During those retreats,
I was called upon a few times per week to deliver presentations on the
theory behind our practice (much of which forms the material of this
book). These presentations usually lasted an hour and took a fair
amount of energy for me to prepare and present. These simultaneous
demands caused me to feel quite a bit of pressure.

On the days when it was my turn to make a presentation, I noticed
that I was fairly anxious about it. Because I was also meditating a few
hours per day, my sensitivity to the process was heightened. I noticed
that I was more likely on those days to be irritated or even short-
tempered with employees or with my family. Luckily, it was easy for
me to see that the problem was not their actions but my tension. In such
an anxious mind state I was more likely to see their actions in a negative light. Partly, because I was also meditating a few hours per day
during the retreat, I was usually aware enough not to let my mood
color my reactions during my practice. But, of course, this is not always
the case in life. When we are not aware of our moods, we really believe
it is other people who are acting inappropriately, never ourselves.

Conversely, there are moods that actually enhance clear seeing. As
a parent of adolescent children, I go through all the typical challenges
associated with that phase in life. Conversations with my kids do not
always go as planned, and I have experienced much frustration trying
to communicate with them. This sometimes leads me to angry
thoughts and judgments about their actions, which spill over into
judgments about their character. I recently taught two weeklong
retreats. During that time, a more accepting view of the struggles we
go through as human beings developed within me. This kinder, more
accepting viewpoint was an expanded state of mind in contrast to the
narrowness of my previous frustration, and it arose because I cultivated it with practice. Such a state of mind can be described as wholesome, because it doesn't need things to be different than they are in the
present moment in order to gratify the small sense of self. From that
expanded, more wholesome state, it was easier for me to see what was

really going on with my children. I could see their behavior in the light of their fears and needs, rather than in the light of how it affected me and my life. We see the same situations through different emotional lenses, depending on our state of mind.

Intention in Prayer versus Attachment to Results

In talking about the cultivation of wholesome mind states, it is important to distinguish between intention and results. The intention to create wholesome mind states is not done to avoid or smooth over our present difficulties; we are not trying to force change in our minds. Such states of mind cannot be created on demand. Furthermore, we can only affirm our intention that such positive states arise in us, and then try to create the conditions in our lives in which their arising is more likely. If we get attached to the outcome of our intentions, that attachment comes from the small sense of self and will likely lead to unwholesome mind states when our intention for openness isn't met with instant success. In the practices described in this chapter, we are exploring techniques and intentions that might allow wholesome mind states to arise. The very act of repeatedly setting wholesome intentions helps create the necessary conditions for seeing the truth—that is, the Divine Presence—as it presents itself to us at each moment. By consciously setting good intentions, we are planting seeds for the future arising of clear seeing.

Once when the Baal Shem Tov was with his students in their classroom, the *bet midrash,* a student asked him the following question: "It is written that 'All are judged on Rosh Hashanah (New Year's Day) and their doom is sealed (in the book of life) on the Day of Atonement (Yom Kippur).' If so, then how come it also is written in the Talmud that Rabbi Yose says, 'Man is in fact judged every day, as it says (Job 7:18), 'You inspect him every morning' (Talmud, Rosh Hashanah 16a). Which is it?" The Baal Shem Tov, ignoring the question, looked out the window and ran to the door. He opened it and called out to Yosele, the water carrier. "Yosele, come sit down in here with us for a while." Yosele's job was to go down to the river with large jugs supported by a yoke around his neck and fill the jugs and lug them back up to the village, where there was no running water. Yosele came in and the Baal Shem Tov asked him how he was doing. "Oy," he groaned. "I'm getting old. It's not so easy for this body to keep lugging these heavy jugs every day. And you think I get any help supporting the family from my two sons-in-law? They sit and study all day long. And my wife, Rachel; when I get home all tired she'll have more things for me to do. Life is not so easy." The Baal Shem Tov said some encouraging words of blessing, and Yosele went on his way.

The earlier question of the day forgotten, the students finished their studies with other matters. About a week later, they were all in class when suddenly the Baal Shem Tov saw Yosele through the window and again jumped up and went to the door and called him in. "Yosele, how are you today?" "*Baruch hashem* [praise God]," said Yosele, "I'm an old man but I still have a lot of strength in these bones. And not only that, I have two great scholars for sons-in-law. And I've been married fifty years to my wonderful wife. So everything is going really well." The student who had originally asked the question about daily versus annual judgment had his answer from Yosele's different reports. In every moment, the quality of our mind states affects how we see our lives. The situation that feels terrible today may seem perfect tomorrow, depending upon our mind state. Mind states tend to be habitual, and with awareness and practice we can learn new habits, such as cultivating more open mind states. This type of attitude is a critical component of setting positive intentions in prayer.

Starting Your Contemplative Prayer Practice

Set aside a block of time to undertake your practice. Remember to start off with reasonable expectations for yourself. It is more helpful to design a twenty- to forty-minute practice that you can perform regularly than to set your sights on two hours every morning, only to feel like a failure every time you don't meet that goal. It might be wise to set aside a shorter period on weekdays and extend the practice on Shabbat. Whatever amount of time you decide on, make sure you can devote your full attention to the practice without interruptions from family members, phone calls, or other distractions.

Before delving into the morning prayer practice, it is helpful to begin with a period of silent meditation practice. This is actually an ancient prescription that appears in the Mishnah and the Talmud: "The pious men of old used to wait an hour. On what is this based? R. Joshua b. Levi said: On the text, Happy are they that dwell in thy house" (B. Berachot 32b). The text being referred to is from Psalm 84:5, where the word *dwell, yoshvay* in Hebrew, could also be translated as "sit." This text is often cited as an example of meditation being referred to in scriptures. In my practical experience, most of my students have reported that silence before prayer deepens the prayer experience immensely.

The following practice has silence built in before and after each of the segments of prayer. As you read and take in the meaning of each verse, make an intention for what mind state you wish to cultivate. Then begin to chant the words over and over. The period of time you spend chanting is up to you and depends on the overall time you have allotted for that day's practice—you might stay with the chant for one to five minutes. As with all the concentration practices, make an intention to keep the attention of the mind on the words, melody, and meaning of the chant. If your attention wanders, gently bring it back to the chant.

When you decide you are finished with the vocalized portion of the chanting, you have a number of options. If you feel this is a day or time when your mind is really busy and active, you might decide to keep saying the words of the chant silently to yourself. This is using the words as a mantra, and has the same affect as concentration techniques, which is to bring some calm and composure to the mind. The structure created by this repetition can help lessen the arising of discursive thought and support the arising of wholesome thought patterns.

A second possibility, after you've finished the vocalized chanting, is to allow your attention to have no particular object of focus but rather simply pay attention to whatever enters your field of awareness. This technique is referred to as choiceless awareness. In daily practice, when you stop using the words of the chant as the object of focus and do not replace them with an alternative object of focus, it is quite likely that you may get lost in discursive thought. If this occurs, return to the words of the chant as soon as you stop focusing on the vocalized chant. If, however, you find that the chanting left your mind in a concentrated state, and you are able to stay present with thoughts as they arise moment to moment, then stay with the choiceless awareness. It can be a wonderful practice that allows you to be present to the truth of each moment, including the truth of what thought patterns may have the largest claim on your attention at that moment.

I mention choiceless awareness at this point for a few reasons. By now, I hope you have begun to understand the differences and the connections between concentration practices and awareness practices. I hope you have begun to use both of them to see for yourself how you can cultivate stillness in the mind for the purpose of seeing clearly. For most of us, our time budget allows for only so much formal practice each day. Using prayer as a concentration technique and following it with awareness practice provides a potent combination for a daily practice regimen.

Another variation of this technique of choiceless awareness is to see if you can greet the truth of each moment through the lens of the mind state you are attempting to cultivate. When we pay attention in everyday life, it is always through the limiting filters of our conditioned minds that make up our small sense of self. Over time we can learn to understand these filters without getting down on ourselves because they are there. These mind states are just part of what it means to be a human being. But, without denying this truth, we also don't need to think of these habituated mind states as permanent conditions. Through prayer, we can experiment with trying on new "lenses." For example, if you are trying to cultivate a sense of thankfulness and you notice a pain in your knee, instead of thinking, "Oh, dear, there's that awful pain in my knee again!" you can instead say, "Thank you for that information," or, "What a miracle that we can notice unpleasant sensations," or, "This information will help me make wise choices today about things that affect my knee." At first, this approach may feel artificial. But keep in mind that we are trying on new lenses, and the fit may not seem familiar. You may not recognize yourself.

Prayer Is a Ladder That Connects You and God

Another practice for the periods of silence following the vocalized chanting is to use the framework of the four divine worlds as discussed in chapter 5. We can understand the prayer experience as an attempt to awaken to the Divine Presence and to feel more connected to that presence as the service progresses through the four worlds. One interpreter derived this meaning for prayer from a verse in Genesis from the story of Jacob's journey from Beersheba after stealing the birthright from his brother, Esau. On the first night of the journey, Jacob went to sleep, "And he dreamt: Here a ladder was set up on the earth, and its top reaching the heavens, and here: messengers of God were going up and down on it" (Gen. 28:12).

The verse was enigmatic to careful readers, who asked why God's angels were not first coming down and then going back. The explanation given in the Zohar is that the ladder represents prayer, and it is prayer that connects heaven and earth. And it is incumbent upon us as human beings on the earth to begin the process through our prayers. Each moment of our heartfelt prayers generates angels or messengers that carry our intention to God, and God responds in kind, thereby making it a two-way connection. Put in more neutral language, as we nurture good intentions and a feeling of connectedness to the universe, we generate a real force that enters the world. It reverberates through all of existence, eventually rebounding in ways that return this good will to us as its source. If this karmic impact is too difficult to accept literally, the Rabbis have another saying that is relevant here: the reward of doing a good deed is the doing of the good deed. If you open your heart to the universe, you will feel more openhearted.

One Hasidic source took this teaching from Genesis even deeper. He looked at the last word in verse 12, the Hebrew *b'o,* which is translated above as "on it" ("it" meaning the ladder). That word has two letters, *bet* for the *B* sound and *vav* for the *O* sound. The letter *bet,* when added to a noun, can mean "in" or "on." Instead of reading the word as *bo,* which literally means "on it"—that is, the on ladder—he read it as *b'vav,* meaning "on the *vav.*" He then said that the letter *vav* refers to the spine (see the discussion in chapter 5 of the four-letter name of God as a representation of the human body). When we are aware of a sensation in the body, you might say that a "messenger" is sent up the spine to the brain, and cognition occurs. When we pray with our entire being, messengers are sent up and down the spiritual spine connecting heaven and earth, as it were.

The Prayers

In explaining each prayer, I will indicate which divine world it is a part of. For the first world, which is focused on experiencing the Divine Presence as it manifests in our bodies, place your attention during the periods of silence on the most prominent bodily sensation. In the second section of prayers, place your focus on the moods and emotional tone present. In the third world, rest your attention on how the bodily sensations and moods result in different thought patterns or mental formations. And finally, in the fourth world of prayer, open yourself up to seeing the truth and receiving intuitive wisdom from beyond the normal small mind.

There is a Jewish custom that the first thing one should do upon waking up is to recite the prayer that begins with Modeh Ahnee, which reads, "I am thankful before You, the eternal living sovereign force of the universe." The intent of this custom is to train the mind to turn to awareness of the Divine Presence as soon as normal waking consciousness returns to the body. This prayer is also the first prayer of the morning service. Since most of us usually begin the morning service some time after getting up and out of bed, I like to begin the morning practice described here with a different chant than the Modeh Ahnee and come back to those words for the second chant.

1. *Shiveetee Yud Hay Vav Hay l'negdee tamid.* (Ps. 16:8)

I equate God with the Complementing Opposite to me (creating One Whole) at every moment.

We can begin our morning prayers with the intention to cultivate our awareness of the Divine Presence throughout the entire day. The words of this psalm are often translated as, "I place God before me at all times." This translation carries with it the wonderful sense of trying to see the Divine Presence before our eyes at every moment. I believe these words can be taken to a deeper, more interactive level. *Shiveetee* comes from the same Hebrew root as the word for "equal," so I translate *shiveetee* as, "I equate." Then we have the four-letter name of God, *Yud Hay Vav Hay*. *L'negdee* is usually used to refer to something in front of yourself—in the same sense as the opposing house across the street. I use the idea of a "complementing opposite" to describe what I discussed in chapter 2 (see page 28), where I described God's first out-breath as humanity's first in-breath. Here I am suggesting that you see God as the out-breath to your in-breath, or the full to your empty. Together, these opposing forces make up the whole.

So, the intention behind chanting these words is to see the wholeness of life in each moment that comes from the integration of internal and external realities, or to borrow a term from Nobel Laureate and Buddhist teacher Thich Nhat Hanh, to see that everything interexists. (Thich Nhat Hanh believes we need a new verb in English, to *inter-be*.) Once, when I was about to lead others in this morning practice, I thought of the following example of seeing the world through this lens of interexistence. I was driving to Elat Chayyim, and it was a beautiful fall day, warm and sunny. I was appreciating the sunny skies when I realized that if it was unseasonably warm and sunny here, it was probably unseasonably cold and cloudy somewhere else. Somebody in that place was probably thinking what a lousy day it was. I had the sense that each day could be considered a perfect day with many variations in weather around the globe, and that even if it was cloudy where I was, I could still appreciate the day. So, as you chant these words, make the intention in your mind to see everything that unfolds today as part of an integrated reality that includes you and all the rest of existence in a perfect complementary unfolding.

2. *Modeh Ahnee lifah-neh-chah ruach (melech) chai v'kayam.*
I am thankful before You, living and eternal Spirit (Sovereign).

As you chant these words, let your intention be to cultivate a thankful mind state. You can begin by visualizing aspects of your life that you are thankful for—reminding yourself that these, too, exist along with whatever challenges you are currently facing. You might be thankful for the gift of being alive. Let your intention be to bring a sense of thankfulness to each moment of the coming day. Reminding ourselves to be thankful can help us cultivate an open heart that can see each moment with greater clarity. I suggest paying special attention to the physical sensations of your own body as you sit in silence after this chant. Modeh Ahnee is a part of the section of the prayers called *birkot hashachar,* or "the morning blessings," and they are dedicated to awareness of the Divine Presence in our physicality. Together with the third and fourth chant, these are prayers connected to the first world of prayer.

3. *Mah tovu o-hah-leh-chah Yah-ah-kov, Mish-k'no-teh-chah Yisrael.* (Num. 24:5)

How good are your tents Jacob, your dwelling places Israel.

These words of chant are from the famous biblical line uttered by Balaam (Num. 24:5). Balaam was a non-Hebrew prophet sent by Balak, the king of Moab, to curse the Hebrew people. Balak was afraid of the Hebrew tribes about to enter Canaan and so he enlisted Balaam as a spiritual aide. Balaam (being a true prophet) was unable to go against God's will, and these words came out instead of the desired curse. Traditionally, these words have been used upon entering a synagogue to acknowledge being in a sacred space. A close look at the words suggests a more internal intention as well. The "tent" of a person could be thought of as our very body—an idea that fits with the theme of the first section of prayers, the physical world. These words then become an affirmation of how good it is to still be in this body, and a celebration of what a great body it is. This is in marked contrast to the negative self-images many of us have about our bodies. Our contemporary culture glorifies hard-to-attain body images, which often leads to self-hatred and negativity.

There is yet a deeper layer that we can penetrate with these words of prayer. In addition to saying, "How good is your tent Jacob," we see that the prayer also refers to the "dwelling place" of Israel. In this second phrase, the name for the domicile and the name of the person have been changed. On the surface, these could just be poetic metaphors for the same place and the same person. Israel is the name that Jacob received after wrestling with a man (or an angel?) the night before he was scheduled to see his brother, Esau, for the first time since Jacob stole the birthright from him:

> And Yaakov was left alone.
> Now a man wrestled with him until the coming up dawn.
> When he saw that he could not prevail against him,
> he touched the socket of his thigh;
> the socket of Yaakov's thigh had been dislocated as he wrestled with
>   him.
> Then he said: let me go, for the dawn has come up!
> But he said: I will not let you go unless you bless me.
> He said unto him: What is your name?
> And he said Yaakov.
> Then he said: Not as Yaakov shall your name be henceforth uttered
> but rather as Yisrael for you have fought with God and men
> and have prevailed. (Gen. 32:25–29)[1]

In these verses we see that the text states this was a struggle with God as well as with a man (verse 29). The new name Jacob receives (Yisrael, or Israel) is a composite of two Hebrew words that together mean something like, "one who has striven with God." When we use the name Israel for Jacob, we are referring to his higher self, the one more in touch with the Divine. In the Modeh Ahnee, Israel's place is not referred to as a tent *(ohel)* but rather as a *mishkan,* which was the name for the portable tabernacle that traveled with the Hebrew people when they wandered in the wilderness. It was the home of the tablets on which the Ten Commandments were engraved. The *mishkan* was considered a place where the Divine Presence resided. The word *mishkan* has the same root as the word *Shekhinah,* which the mystics used to refer to the Divine Presence that dwells in everything in the created universe. So, this second half of the prayer can be taken to refer to seeing our own bodies as a dwelling place for the Divine. We are called by this prayer to see our bodies as both physical and spiritual entities.

I especially like that the words *mah tovu* (how good!) refer to both subsequent phrases, the mundane or physical level of awareness of our own bodies, as well as to the more awakened sense of our own divine nature. As you chant these words, work with the intention to cultivate a mind state of awe for your body, just as it is, while also recognizing its spiritual aspect.

4. *Elohai n'shah-mah sheh-nah-tah-tah be t'ho-rah he.*
My God, the soul that you have given me is pure.

The word *n'shah-mah,* or *neshamah,* is the focus of this prayer. *Neshamah* is a Hebrew word meaning "soul." The four divine worlds referred to in chapter 5 each have levels of soul associated with them:

World	Translation	Characteristic	Soul Level
Assiyah	Doing	Physical world	Nefesh
Yetzirah	Forming	Feeling	Ruach
Beriyah	Creating	Knowing	Neshamah
Atzilut	Nearness	Non-dualistic Being	Chayah and Yechidah

I want to focus on the first three soul levels, *nefesh, ruach,* and *neshamah.* These words are difficult to translate as distinct from each other because they have common meanings in Hebrew texts. They are all words connected to the movement of air, especially as related to the breath. And they are all used to convey a sense of spirit or soul. This link is easy to understand because we still connect being alive or having the spirit of life with whether someone is still breathing. Life and breath are deeply linked, as are the concepts of life and soul.

The Jewish mystics took these words of soul to a deeper level and said that they referred to consciousness as well. One model suggests that all inert physical objects have a consciousness that is called *nefesh.* This is true of rocks and minerals, and even of atoms and subatomic particles. If this is so, you might imagine that as particles interact and combine, they also create increasing levels of collective consciousness. Generally, we do not tend to think of the physical world as alive. This teaching of consciousness implies that everything, including the physical world, contains the divine essence, which can be conceived of as a kind of consciousness itself.

Plants are made up of physical things, yet our Sages suggested that plants contain a higher (more integrated) level of consciousness than more inert physical things. They called this higher level *ruach*. Being composed of physical matter, plants also contain *nefesh*. One way of understanding the increased level of consciousness is that the plant kingdom can utilize the physical world for its own purposes. Plants can take in water and nutrients and convert them, using their energy according to their own design. Words such as *use* and *design* imply that we assign some kind of consciousness to plants.

Next we come to the animal kingdom. Animals are able to use the physical and the plant world, and therefore possess a third level of consciousness, which the Sages called *neshamah*. When we look at these three levels from a larger perspective, the evolution of life implies an evolution of consciousness as well. As smaller units of creation find a way to come together, so their collective consciousness seems to grow. But the boundaries between the physical, plant, and animal kingdoms are not necessarily quite as rigid as this model might seem to imply. We know there are plants that make use of the animal kingdom, such as the Venus flytrap. And some recent botany studies look at how plants adapt themselves so as to get animals to eat them and spread their seeds to other places. In other words, plants figure out how to use animals for transportation.

Human beings are also a part of the animal kingdom and so we share with the rest of that kingdom the possession of the three levels of consciousness, *nefesh, ruach,* and *neshamah*. How is human consciousness different than an animal's? We can define the levels of consciousness referred to up to this point as *mochin de-katnut,* or "small mind." But in contrast to animals, the small mind of human beings is filled with discursive thinking in addition to the input coming from the five sense doorways. And yet, there is another aspect to human consciousness that allows us to rise above this small mind. We have the ability to enter into an expanded state of awareness that we can call large mind, *mochin de-gadlut*. In this state we are still integrating the consciousness available through *nefesh, ruach,* and *neshamah,* but we are also able to intuit even larger aspects of the integrated nature of all reality. These are levels of consciousness beyond *nefesh, ruach,* and *neshamah.*

The ability to enter into an expanded state of awareness is one explanation of the words of the traditional prayer from the morning liturgy, *Elohai n'shah-mah sheh-nah-tah-tah be t'ho-rah he,* or My God, the soul *(neshamah)* that you have given me is pure. The word *pure* in this sense refers to a state of consciousness that is not lost in dualistic ego. I believe it is referring to the possibility that our consciousness can, in fact, be expanded. There is a teaching that on the Sabbath day we receive a *neshamah yeterah,* an "extra soul." I think this extra soul is commonly misunderstood to refer to some outside force that comes to us on that day. A better interpretation of *neshamah yeterah* might be "more consciousness" (or expanded awareness). In this sense, we are taught that through observance of the Sabbath, a higher level of awareness is obtained. And what is the nature of Shabbat observance that brings this about? Embedded in the customs of Shabbat is the letting go of striving by the individual ego. On Shabbat we are no longer doing and making but rather trying to live in a world of being. The Jewish mystics understood that the deep meaning of Shabbat was to see through duality and thereby give each of us a sense of union with the One.

Many Shabbat customs are reflections of this desire for union. The mystics imbued Shabbat practice with the metaphor of a wedding, which is followed by intercourse where the two come together as one. Many people wear white on Shabbat as one might to their own wedding. Shabbat begins with the lighting of candles. The multiple candles have multiple flames. At the end of Shabbat, the ceremony of separation called *havdalah* uses a braided candle with multiple wicks yet only one flame. The symbolism of the candles reminds us to enter Shabbat with the intention of allowing our Shabbat practice to shift our perspective from seeing ourselves as individual beings, to the knowledge that we are all part of the oneness of being.

As human beings, we can take in the consciousness that arises out of our physicality *(nefesh)* and our cellular nature *(ruach),* thereby giving us a *neshamah.* But we also are able to incorporate wisdom from even more integrated levels of awareness, known as *chayah* and *yechidah. Chayah* is a term referring to the life force of the universe. *Yechidah,* on the other hand, is a level of radical oneness in which no universe can be said to exist on an absolute scale. In the space afforded us through contemplative practice, we do occasionally get a glimpse of this greater wisdom. Through repeated practice and the growth that practice causes in us, it is possible to live more selflessly, dedicated to continued growth and to serving the world we live in. The levels implied in the terms *chayah* and *yechidah* reflect this kind of wholesome striving. While *chayah* and *yechidah* are discussed by Jewish mystics, they embody levels of awareness in which words and concepts fail us. They can be experienced, but not fully described.

Finally, this prayer uses a play on words. The word *neshamah* is closely related to the Hebrew word *n'shee-mah,* which shares a root with *neshamah* and means "breath." When we rest our attention on the arising and passing of each breath, we can do so with a sense that each breath is a pure gift from the Divine. At the same time, the very fact that we can be aware of the breath indicates that we are capable of expanded awareness. Both the breath and awareness are implied in the word *neshamah.* As you sit quietly after this chant, try to allow appreciation for the miracle of breath, and at the same time, pray that you might see all of this world through the eyes of *neshamah yeterah,* or "expanded awareness."

5. *Halleluyah.*

Praise Yah.

With these words we begin the transition to the second world of prayer, the world of the heart and emotions. *Halleluyah* is a compound of two Hebrew words: *hallelu* and *Yah*. *Hallelu* is a verb in the command form meaning "you shall praise," and Yah is a name for God. This section of the prayers is called *p'seukei d'zimra,* which means "verses of song." Keep in mind that as we move up the ladder of prayer, we are not leaving earlier worlds behind but rather including them in our expanding awareness. You may recall that this world of heart and emotions is characterized by the Hebrew letter *vav,* which means "and." So, in this world of prayer, we begin to focus on connecting. In addition to being aware of our own bodies, we add consciousness of the world around us. This section of the prayers is the traditional place for using Psalms as the liturgical vehicle. One way to view the book of Psalms is as a collection of individual sacred poems that describe times when the authors experienced and felt connected to the Divine Presence in the world around them: "I lift my eyes unto the mountains from where my help (God) comes"; "The heavens tell of God's glory"; "If I descend into the depths of Sheol (abode of the dead), You are there." In each psalm, we see a description of what it was like when the connection to the Divine was alive.

At moments when we move out of existential loneliness and feel connected to the Divine Presence, our natural response is to say, "*Halleluyah,*" "Praise Yah." Perhaps the transcendent nature of such moments is hinted at in the choice of the God name Yah. According to the mystics, Yah is the God name that refers to wisdom, or *chochmah.* In the Jewish mystical understanding, this is the name connected to the first act of creation, even before relative duality came into existence. Yah is the source of the intuitive wisdom that arises when we move out of small mind. By using this particular God name as we start the second world of prayer, we make an intention to feel heartfelt connections to others and all the world, knowing that these connections will eventually allow us to access the wisdom that is beyond time and space, and yet real. Beginning this section of the morning prayers with the chant *Halleluyah* moves us into the second world, while pointing out the worlds yet to come.

On days when you have sufficient time to extend your prayer practice, the silent space following this chant is a great time to take your practice outside into the natural setting of a park or forest. Practice walking meditation. Try feeling your whole body. (A more formal set of instructions for walking practices appears in chapter 8.) At this point in the prayer service, the emphasis is on connecting the internal experience of our lives with what we encounter externally in the world. Notice the trees and bushes, the ants and flies, the sun and sky, and see if you can greet each of these elements with a *Halleluyah.*

6. *Kol haneshamah t'hallel Yah, Halleluyah.*
The entire awareness will praise Yah, Praise Yah.

This chant is the last line of the last psalm in the Bible. It is a natural summary of all that has come before, and the last chant connected to the second world of prayer. The first two words, *kol haneshamah,* can mean "every soul," "each soul," "the entire soul," or, as we have been translating *neshamah,* "the entire consciousness itself." To feel truly connected and see clearly the natural response of the unencumbered heart is to say, *"Halleluyah."* As you chant these words, let your intention be to make each moment of the coming day such a moment of praise and connection.

7. *Yotzer or u-vo-ray choshech o-she shalom u-vo-ray et ha-kol.* (Adapted from Isa. 45:7)
Forming light, creating darkness, making peace, creating everything.

With this chant, the third world of prayer begins. In this world, we pray for the Divine Presence to shine through more clearly in every moment and every experience. References to the light of day coming after the darkness of night are more than just a description of the returning of the sun. They are a metaphor for Divine Presence, the shining light, and Divine Wisdom, the light that brings clarity and understanding.

At this point in the prayers it is helpful to pay attention to the light of day that has returned. There is a deep message that the Sages wanted to impress upon us in blessing the new day and the return of light—more than just that we should be happy that night has ended. In the evening prayers, we say a blessing welcoming the evening. And in both prayer services, the evening and the morning service, we acknowledge both the dark and the light. Hence, in the chant above we say, "Forming light, creating darkness." In the evening prayers, the words used are "rolling the light away from before the darkness, and the darkness from before the light." The profound teaching here is that we need to understand that the nature of the universe is to flow back and forth between polar opposites, light and dark, empty and full, pleasure and pain, good fortune and bad. To bless God is to recognize that the Divine is in both sides of these turnings and is in the process of turning and returning itself.

The wisdom of this world of prayer comes from recognizing the impermanent nature of all things. As we learn to be open to the turning, we can let go of the desire to hold on to anything. The more we let go, the more we can learn from whatever comes to us. The teaching is that the dark times are as holy as the light times. The Rabbis who crystallized this part of the liturgy chose to adapt the words from their original source in Isaiah 45:7. In Isaiah's version, the phrase ends with *"u-vo-ray rah,"* which means "creating evil." The Sages chose to say, "creating everything," and left out the word *evil*. Perhaps they were worried that it is too difficult to say that God creates evil, and that we might get stuck, unable to complete our prayers. Nevertheless, "everything" includes evil. The aim in this section of the prayers is to develop the ability to see all of creation as interconnected and part of the One. This theme occurs again later in this practice, when we chant the Shema (listen), perhaps the best-known line of Jewish prayer. In order to really experience oneness, the present chant aims us toward the deep reality of impermanence and the wisdom that can flow out of accepting the cyclical nature of life.

8. *Kadosh, kadosh, kadosh Yah (YHVH) Tz'vah-oat M'lo kall hah-ahretz K'vodo.* (Isa. 6:3)

Holy, Holy, Holy is Yah of Hosts; the whole world is filled with God's glory.

These are the words of prayer uttered by the seraphim in Isaiah's vision. In Jewish mystical parlance, the seraphim are a class of angels that reside in *Beriyah*, the third world, where we find this prayer. It is possible to explore many esoteric levels in the teachings about angels. For the purpose of this prayer practice, I will try to explain a simple intention and allow you to explore these concepts through your own prayer and study if you are so moved. In repeating the words of the seraphim, we take on the intent to serve the same function that they serve. Angels can be seen as the messengers or the carrier wave for the Divine Wisdom to reach our consciousness. The seraphim, the beings of this level, bring the wisdom from the fourth realm, the realm of no separation, of nonduality. At this point in our prayers, we are still in the world of separate things but are reaching for the consciousness that sees these separate things as interconnected in one vast pattern of form and flow. The threefold repetition of the word *Holy* in this chant can be seen as another reference to the levels of consciousness in the three "upper" worlds. The last part of this chant, "the whole world is filled with God's glory," is the movement of that consciousness into this physical world of ours.

The chanting practice for these words can include a choreographed set of bodily motions. Jewish practice has a less-developed use of movement meditation compared to practices such as tai chi or yoga. Contemporary Jewish teachers are filling these gaps by creating Jewish forms of these movement practices (you can find a list of some Jewish movement practice resources in Appendix B). Here I'll offer one version of a movement meditation.

Stand and place your feet together. In some versions of angel anatomy, angels are seen as having only one leg. The image of having only one leg to stand on is a way of expressing that angels do not live in duality. Another way to say this is that angels do not have free will—they are only messengers. So, with your feet together, place your hands at head level, shoulder width apart, with your palms facing backwards. Chant the word *kadosh* for the first time. The hand placement indicates that we are starting out this prayer in the world of knowing (traditionally associated with the head), the world where seraphim reside and the place to which our prayers have progressed thus far. As you chant the word *kadosh* a second time, raise your hands as high as they can go, allowing the palms to turn and face each other and the hands to get closer together. Continue this motion until you feel yourself stretching and rising onto your tiptoes. The intention is to cultivate a sense of reaching for a deeper (or "higher") connection to the One. As you chant the word *kadosh* a third time, allow your hands to come down toward your head, parting to descend alongside the head and continuing until they are facing each other in front of your heart.

As you chant *"Yah (YHVH) Tz'vah-oat,"* or "Yah of Hosts," place your hands on top of your heart, with the right hand on top of the left. This motion is a metaphor for channeling the wisdom you have obtained "down" to the heart level, feeling the emotion of praise. The "Hosts" referenced here are the heavenly hosts—that is, the stars—which are traditionally deemed to be a part of the second world, *Yetzirah*.

As you chant *"M'lo kall hah-ahretz K'vodo,"* or "The whole world is filled with God's Glory," stretch your hands forward, palms up, and turn to the right from your waist, as far as you can, and then turn to the left with your eyes open, looking at the whole world as the manifestation of divine glory.

Repeat the whole process of this chant three times. I suggest alternating between Hebrew and English, unless you are very comfortable with the meaning of the Hebrew words. In the silence following your chant, let your intention be to cultivate a mind state that is able to see the connections and flow between body, feelings, thoughts, and presence.

9. *Or chah-dahsh al tzion tair.*
May a new light shine on Zion.

The words of this prayer invoke the possibility of receiving some new insight. They are part of the third world of prayer, where wisdom is cultivated. If we have done our prayers in a focused manner and with clear intentions, it is quite possible that we will have created a more expansive state of mind. It is into such a mind that wisdom sometimes presents itself. In preparing for this chant, it is good to make an intention of being open to seeing the truth of this moment. If you wish, you can be specific and ask for insight into a particular situation in your life. Language such as, "May I receive the deepest truth possible and the wisdom of how to respond in a kind way in this situation," puts forward a gentle hope that the light of the new insight will shine. Try to make your intention without being attached to the results of whether any insight arises. Ask that "it be so" from a nongrasping heart. Allow enough silence for insight to arise. You can always have gratitude for the silence if the insight doesn't arise in the "allotted" few minutes. Keep in mind that the insight may arise later in the day as you move through your normal life with more awakened awareness.

10. *El melech neh-eh-mahn, Shekhinah Malka neh-eh-mahnah.*
God is a faithful king, the Shekhinah is a faithful queen.

I am including this chant primarily because it is traditionally one of the few lines that we recite when praying alone; it is not usually used in the synagogue. I also wanted to take the opportunity to reflect on the traditional male references to the Divine that were the norm in Judaism until this generation. The traditional version of this prayer had only the first three words.

We recite this prayer before the Shema, which requires some existing faith in order to be recited with meaning. That faith is expressed in the words of this chant. This phrase uses a reflexive verb form that implies a sense that God is the type of king that we can have faith in or trust. As I have explained previously, God as king is not my favorite metaphor in a post–Baal Shem Tov theology. The particular words used here can have another meaning, however. In using the God name El, we reference a particular quality of the Divine. According to Jewish mystics, El is the God name associated with the divine quality of lovingkindness or *chesed*. Lovingkindness is that unbounded sense of total loving acceptance. It is the quality mentioned in the guided meditation on the mountain in chapter 5, when we see the world through God's eyes. God sees everything that exists with infinite lovingkindness. If that is the kind of king we mean when we say God is king, then I could affirm faith in such a king. So, as a preparation for the Shema, cultivate a mind state that sees the world through those eyes.

The second set of words, *Shekhinah Malka neh-eh-mahnah,* were added by my friend and frequent coteacher, Shoshana Cooper. They are words in the feminine gender of Hebrew and address the fact that all the traditional names and references to God are in the male gender of Hebrew, except for the Shekhinah. As I already explained, the Shekhinah is the indwelling Divine Presence as developed by the Zohar. By adding these words to the prayer, we intentionally commit to cultivating a mind state that can recognize the Divine Presence as being beyond gender.

11. *Shema Yisrael YHVH Elohaynu, YHVH Echad.* (Deut. 6:4)
Listen, You who wrestles with knowing God, All Being is our God, All Being is the Interconnected Oneness Of All.

These are the words called out to the nation of Israel by Moses as he stood on Mount Sinai. These words are the centerpiece of the third world of prayer. They are an expression of the mind that can see the interconnected oneness of all being. Once we have reached this place in the service, we metaphorically leave behind the worlds of separation and are ready to enter into an experience of oneness that is characterized by the silent Amidah, the standing prayer of the fourth world. This is indicated by the last word of the Shema, the word *Echad,* or "One." Because of the importance of this prayer, a more lengthy discussion follows, and I'll offer a few ways of using these words in prayer. In your own practice, you can decide which practices to use on any particular day.

In their most literal sense, the words seem to be a call by Moses to the people of Israel to be faithful to YHVH. At this point in the book of Deuteronomy, Moses is recapping the laws and practices to the nation of Israel. Deuteronomy chapter 5 begins with the words, "And Moses called unto all of Israel." The word *Israel* is here used as the collective name for the descendants of Jacob, whose name was changed to Israel after he wrestled with the angel. And in the same verse, after calling the people together, Moses tells them to listen to what he is about to say: " Hear, O Israel, the statutes and the ordinances which I speak in your ears this day." Likewise, in Deuteronomy 6:4, Moses addresses the whole nation of Israel. As you work with this verse, using whatever meaning all six words have for you, remember that the first words, "Hear O Israel," or, "Hearken O Israel," are meant to include you as the person who should be paying attention to the words that follow. Whether you are a part of the people called Israel or someone who wants to work with these teachings, make an intention to become the one who needs to pay attention to these words.

In preparation for reciting the Shema, the following vocalized chant, based on the letters of the word *Shema,* is helpful. You will chant each of the three letters of the word. Sound each letter for the length of an entire out-breath, in a somewhat extended fashion. It is not necessary to force every last ounce of breath out, but neither should the sounds be rushed.

The first letter is *shin,* which has the sound *shh.* It is chanted out loud without any vowel sound and without using the vocal chords. It is the sound you make when you want to tell someone to be quiet, which is what your intention should be when you chant this sound. You are telling yourself to be quiet, to listen and pay close attention to what is coming in the prayer or to the deep truth of this very moment. By extension, you are setting your intention to closely pay attention to each moment of the coming day by quieting your discursive mind. This is a very powerful sound. Across different cultures and languages it is universally known as the sound for being quiet and paying attention. The sound is also a kind of white noise in scientific language. White noise has the power to mask other particular sounds. So saying "shh" is a way of blocking out distracting sounds—that is, any other message than the one being conveyed in these words.

The second sound comes from the letter *mem,* which has the sound *mmm.* This sound comes from the vocal chords, and you can't produce it without vocalizing. Perhaps because it is the first sound of speech that a child intentionally forms other than cooing and crying, this sound has become connected to the person of the mother, not just in English, but in almost every language. When put together with the first sound, you might say you are calling attention to the mother, or source of all that is, that which gave birth to the universe.

When vocalized alone without being part of a word, the sound *mmm* is like listening to a pure vibration. Vibrations underlie everything that exists. Every atom is in constant vibration. Vibrations can be represented in two dimensions by drawing a sine curve—a curve that looks like a wave, with peaks and troughs. Once again this basic pattern is represented by the divine name YHVH, which, as I explained in chapter 2, is connected to the phases of the breath: empty, in, full, and out. By calling our attention to the underlying structure of all that exists, the chant of Shema points us toward the origin, the mother, and the building blocks upon which all else is based.

Finally, we chant the third letter in the word *Shema,* the *ayin.* In modern Hebrew, *ayin* has become a consonant that is not vocalized, and so it possesses only whatever accompanying vowel sound is assigned to it. But in its origin, *ayin* was a guttural stop. The very back of the tongue closes off the windpipe, and the sound is made deep in the throat through the force of the air pressure that builds up and is then released in a small explosion of sound. It is this explosion that can remind us of the mother *mem* giving birth to the universe in the big bang. Make the sound of the guttural with just an instant of vocalization, and then allow the rest of the out-breath to have the sound *ahh* without vocalizing. This sounding of *ahh* takes the energy from the mother *mem* through the bang *ayin,* and then allows it to go out into the universe.

When time allows, I like to repeat this sequence of the three letters four times. It allows for a marshalling of attention before reciting the whole line of the Shema. Repeating the sequence four times is another way to connecting with the four worlds and the four letters in YHVH. It can be a signal that we are coming to the end of the third world of prayer and about to enter the fourth world, where there is only oneness and no separation. As much as possible, try to sustain your attention on each sound and the intention behind it as you do this chant.

The Shema itself follows immediately on the next out-breath after the final *ayin* in the preparation chant. Take as focused an in-breath as possible after that *ayin.* When you chant the Shema in this fashion, give each word a full out-breath. On the in-breath, reconnect with the meaning of, or intention behind, the word about to be vocalized. Before uttering the word *Shema,* remind yourself, once again, to pay attention. Before speaking the word *Yisrael,* try to remember that *you* are the one who should hear these words, not someone else, and that you are also part of the collective group of those who "wrestle with God." Before speaking *YHVH,* remind yourself that the impermanent flow of arising and passing is the divine process of the universe. Sometimes, rather than make any sound at all on that out-breath, I allow the out-breath itself to be the container for all possible names of God. Remind yourself that this unfolding process is Elohaynu our God, the sum of all that collectively is. And once again, note with the next in-breath this sense of the impermanent flow of arising and passing and breathe out *YHVH* for the second time. Finally, before speaking *Echad,* take in the sense that this arising and passing is not two separate things but rather only one.

There is another way to chant the Shema that I learned from Reb Zalman. He called it preparation for the Shema on the deathbed, referring to a Jewish tradition that these words are the last ones to be spoken with your dying breath. When I first learned of this custom, I thought of it as a final profession of faith or as pledging loyalty to the Jewish God in case you had not lived that way. I now see it in a different light. I think the intention is to bring your consciousness at the last moment of life to the realization that you are returning to the oneness from which you came, and from which you were never really separate.

In order to be *fully* present for the moment of death, it is important to start practicing now. Reb Zalman developed a liturgical form for practicing for this moment. In this form, you recite or chant the full Shema four times. You can use the melody that you know. Use the practice of chanting each word for a full breath each time, except on the third round—I'll explain that in a moment. The second time you chant, change the word *Yisrael* to your own name. For example, I would chant, *"Shema Jeff YHVH Elohaynu YHVH Echad."* If you are a woman, you might change the first word to *shim-ee,* which is the feminine of the command form in Hebrew. Treat the third round as the rehearsal for the last recitation at the time of your death. Go back to the original words, but chant them much more softly. Speak the whole Shema with one breath, timing it so that you literally run out of breath as you say the word *Echad*. Pause for a moment and note the sensations in your body, which is temporarily out of breath. Then, breathe in and do the fourth recitation as you did the first. While Reb Zalman taught this practice as a preparation for the final recitation in your life, it is clear that it is also a helpful practice right now. Part of learning to be present to each moment is to let go of what is past. The more we can "die into" each present moment, the more we can be fully awake for it.

12. *Baruch shem kavod, malchuto l'olam va-ed.* (Pesachim 56a)
Blessed is this glorious name (YHVH)—its reality eternally pervades existence.

Following the Shema is the tradition of silently saying these words, which come from later Jewish tradition, not directly from the text of the Torah. There are a number of beautiful legends about the origins of these words. According to one midrash (legend), the patriarch Jacob spoke these words on his deathbed, when he gave all of his sons a final blessing. After Jacob finished those blessings, his sons responded to him by saying the words of the Shema. Since Yisrael was Jacob's divine name, they were, in effect, telling him that he could trust that they, too, acknowledged the sovereignty of YHVH. In his weak, almost-dying breath, Jacob responded to them with the words, *"baruch shem kavod malchuto l'olam va-ed."* At this point in the prayers, we, too, have given our final blessings for the morning and are about to enter the silent prayer section of the fourth world. Hence, we say these words softly to this day.

13. The Amidah

The final section of the morning prayers is called the Amidah, or "standing prayer." This corresponds to the fourth world, *Atzilut,* in which there is no separation from God, only unity. This prayer is traditionally done silently and while standing. The standing relates to the traditional root metaphor of God as king. If we were to come before the Divine Presence, we would rise, as we might do if a king entered the room. The prayer has that imagery. The silence is an acknowledgment that the words are not really the connection we seek but a replacement for it. You can imagine that God is now speaking through whatever comes into your awareness. Traditionally there are fixed words associated with this prayer. The Amidah contains a set of benedictions with variations for weekdays, the Sabbath, and holidays. These words were created to help enter this final arena of prayer.

I would like to share an alternative practice that you might use at this point in your prayers. It was developed by Reb Nachman of Breslov, a noted Hasidic rabbi and a great-grandson of the Baal Shem Tov. He suggested that each day you go out into the fields and have a conversation directly with God, out loud, in essence, speaking both parts. He stipulated that for this process to work, you must talk non-stop. You simply begin telling God what's on your mind, and you keep the words flowing the entire time. You can gripe, ask questions, make suggestions, or whatever you decide is appropriate in that moment. If you try the practice for the first time and realize that you are not sure who or what you think God is, start by saying, "I don't know why I am out here talking to myself when I don't believe in You." The non-stop aspect of the practice is the key, as is a commitment to honesty. Since you are responsible for both parts of the dialogue, at some point in the process, the line blurs between whether the words are yours or God's. It is the exhaustion of your own planned thoughts that allows something unplanned to manifest. Inevitably, when I teach this practice on a meditation retreat that features all the other intense practices I have described in this book, a number of people will tell me that this was the most profound experience of the week. You can do this practice any time, not only in place of the Amidah.

There are many other ways to bring contemplative practices to prayer. The one I use most frequently and that works with any prayer is to slow down the speed of prayer to one word per breath. I first learned a related idea from Reb Zalman. He pointed out that there are texts suggesting that the traditional words used during the Amidah should be recited for an hour. He figured out that this meant one word every seven seconds. He built a little gadget with electronics that beeped every seven seconds and directed us to do the Amidah at that speed. As I later developed my meditation practice, I began praying at the pace of one word per breath, which is close to seven seconds when you slow down in meditation. When you try this technique, use the entire length of the in-breath to stay focused on the meaning of the word you are about to utter. In the next chapter, I will present still another method of using prayer and blessing to cultivate the awakened heart.

7 A Blessing Practice

I have been blessed in my life to encounter the practices I have shared with you in this book. I have also had the good fortune of having taught these practices to hundreds of participants on numerous retreats. But of all the techniques I've practiced and taught, the meditation technique I am about to share, which I call the blessing practice, is a favorite of my students, many of whom have told me that they have gotten so much out of it that they practice it every day. It is a technique that has firm roots in two traditions, Jewish prayer and the Buddhist divine abode practice. Practicing this meditation effectively cultivates the kind of openheartedness I referred to in the guided meditation on the thirteen attributes of the Divine at the end of chapter 5. As I was told by one student with a long history of serious depression, it was his use of this technique that opened up his heart and gave him a container of safety in which to do all the awareness practices described in this book.

Escaping from Egypt

Most of the awareness practices described in this book aim at cultivating a calm and open attitude to the truth of each moment's experience. It is this mindful attention to the truth of each moment that leads to wisdom and, ultimately, to kindness and compassion. Yet sometimes it is hard to be mindful when we are trapped by feelings such as despair, anger, or compulsive desire. Sylvia Boorstein compares these difficult mind states to being stuck in slavery in Egypt. In Hebrew, the word for "Egypt," *mitzrayim,* also means "a narrow, constricting place." Trying to escape from these enslaving mind states, from our personal Egypt, takes a lot of effort. The direct approach is to notice when our minds are trapped and to shine the light of awareness on this situation. In that approach, we try feeling the constriction itself in the body and the mind. But sometimes, when we are faced with painful mind states that drain our mental resources and make it difficult, if not impossible, to stay aware and balanced in the present moment, such direct attention is too much for us. If the mind begins to wilt in the effort, it can actually increase our suffering.

Another way of dealing with something like a flood of compulsive or aversive thoughts is to actively engage the mind in an alternative activity with a more constructive purpose. This can be understood as cultivating wholesome mind states, as I mentioned in chapter 6. One way of accomplishing this is the technique of continuously repeating phrases of blessing in the mind. This is a very rich practice and is a core part of my contemplative routine.

By cultivating positive mental states, we give ourselves much-needed breathing room in the face of our emotional challenges. When our state of mind becomes more stabilized and positive, we can return to the bare knowing of these difficult mind states with more spaciousness and composure. Another way the blessing practice is useful is that by occupying our minds with repeated blessings, we temporarily evict our habitual patterns of thinking, and in a sense recondition the mind to be more positive.

Cultivating a Heart Full of Peace

The blessing practice consists of a series of phrases that are repeated over and over, silently, in the mind. These phrases are derived primarily from a particular prayer that is part of the daily Jewish liturgy, referred to as Sim Shalom, or "grant peace." These words come at the end of the morning version of the Amidah, or "standing prayer," which is traditionally recited silently. In the Amidah, we see a variety of types of prayer. These include the invocation of blessing in the world, praise, contrition, petition, and thanks. As we finish the prayer, its all-encompassing sentiment is summarized in an invocation of peace for the world and all its beings. As I will describe later in this chapter, the prayer for peace is central to Judaism and also a central pillar of all spiritual life.

The words of Sim Shalom begin thus: "Grant peace, goodness and blessing, graciousness, lovingkindness and compassion upon us and all Your people Israel." Theologian Arthur Waskow translates the Hebrew name *Israel* as "God-wrestlers," the name given to Jacob, as previously mentioned, after he wrestled with the angel (see Gen. 32:25–29). When we awaken to the fact that we are in an interconnected web with all being, we see that our every move causes the universe to shift in response. Every other vibration that occurs in this universe also moves us. The Hebrew word for "people" or "nation" is *ahm,* spelled with the letters *ayin* and *mem.* The word is derived from a sense of connectedness, which underlies the idea of a nation or tribe of people. More broadly, it could also mean that all being is connected. "Your people" refers to every being that belongs to this web of God. The use of these words means to me that this prayer is invoking the six qualities it mentions for all people and for all beings.

In turning this prayer into a usable contemplative practice, I wanted to create a set of repeatable phrases. This form of practice is modeled after a technique I learned from Sylvia Boorstein, and I have practiced it on a number of retreats over the last nine years. I have used the phrases in daily formal practice, during other daily activities, and sometimes for extended periods of as long as nine days. I have also taught hundreds of people these phrases and a way to use them. The phrases are:

> May I be blessed with peace.
>
> May I be blessed with joy.
>
> May I be blessed with lovingkindness.
>
> May I be blessed with compassion.

(Note: You can find a Hebrew version of these phrases at the end of this chapter, along with some comments on doing the practice in Hebrew versus in English.)

As you can see, I used four of the six qualities mentioned in the Sim Shalom prayer. I added the quality of joy because I felt it to be an important and necessary ingredient for daily prayer. Joy (or *simcha* in Hebrew) is cited by many Jewish Sages as an indispensable spiritual practice in the path of service. As King David says in Psalm 100:2, "Serve God in joy." One shift I made from the structure of the Sim Shalom prayer was to move the quality of blessing to the beginning of the phrase. In Sim Shalom, we pray that the universe might feel blessed. By placing the invoking of blessing as the action or verb function of each phrase in the blessing practice, I hoped to draw focus on the possibility that people can bless themselves, and they can bless others. This is a way of making prayer an empowering function.

When I began working with Reb Zalman, one of the things that appealed to me was his ability to open up the gates of prayer. My growing involvement in Jewish life had been nourished by what was and still is called the *havurah* movement, which grew out of the counterculture of the late sixties and emphasized a nonhierarchical approach to religion. *Havurot* (small groups of equal friends) were initially a do-it-yourself form of Judaism that emphasized learning and seeing the meaning in Jewish texts and ritual. Leadership is shared among the members rather than coming from the top down. When I would participate in *havurah* (singular of *havurot*) services, the Torah discussions were deeply inspirational, as was the general learning component. These were intellectual riches that I treasured. The singing component of prayer services was also emotionally moving. Perhaps the strongest feature was the fellowship or communal nature that developed among the members of our intentional practice group. I will discuss the importance of community in spiritual practice more extensively in chapter 8.

What was missing for me in my early *havurah* experience was the seeming lack of meaning in the act of praying and in the prayers themselves. Reb Zalman used to say, "The prayer book is like freeze-dried soup. If you open a package of freeze-dried soup and try pouring it in your mouth, yuck! You have to add the hot water." Reb Zalman taught us how to supply the "hot water." It can only come from each individual who participates in the prayer process.

Experience the Power of Giving Blessings

Of the many things Reb Zalman showed us, one of the most exciting was how to give and receive blessings. There was actually very little to teach except to demonstrate the act of blessing someone and then blessing each other. If you haven't tried it yourself, you can begin by thinking of the concept of giving a toast to a friend. The idea of wishing someone well is not a foreign one. Imagine saying to a friend, "I hope you get that job you are interviewing for tomorrow." Then compare that to saying, "I want to bless you that you get the job tomorrow." The difference is immense. Using the word *bless,* for most people, seems to establish a feeling of connection to the divine nature of the universe.

In one of my first forays as a student rabbi, I led services for a small group of people on Long Island, New York, who met in each other's houses. Like me, the people in this community had not often experienced prayer in a meaningful way. I was one of Reb Zalman's students at the time, and I liked to try out many of the approaches to prayer I had learned from him. It was a somewhat conservative community, and many of the innovations in prayer techniques were a bit of a stretch for the group. However, the practice that they most easily picked up and valued was the practice of giving blessings to each other. They loved doing it. Before you continue with the practice I am teaching here, try giving someone you know a blessing. It may be a blessing for healing or a blessing that their struggles with their child should be all for the good in the long run. Try tailoring the blessing to what you know the person really needs. Practicing in this way will make your use of these phrases much more real if you have never tried blessing someone before. It might also make you, and the person you bless, feel wonderful.

In the blessing practice, you repeat the four phrases—"May I be blessed with peace; may I be blessed with joy; may I be blessed with lovingkindness; may I be blessed with compassion"—silently over and over, in the order suggested. While variations are useful and will be discussed shortly, begin by saying each of the four phrases one time, and go back to the first phrase and keep the cycle going.

You'll notice that each phrase begins with the words *may I.* Try saying the following two sentences and see if they feel different:

I want to be happy.

May I be happy.

The phrase, "May it be" has a softness to it compared to the phrase, "I want." It expresses a heartfelt wish for something without the whining of the ego for things we feel we must have in order to be happy.

Be a Source of Blessing for All Beings

As I indicated earlier, in the Sim Shalom prayer, the invocation of blessing is made not only for ourselves, but also for all beings. So instead of saying, "May I be blessed with …" I can offer blessings to my partner by saying, "May Joanna be blessed with peace; may Joanna be blessed with joy; may Joanna be blessed with lovingkindness; may Joanna be blessed with compassion." As you work with this practice, challenge yourself to focus the blessings on the seven different categories of recipients:

1. Ourselves
2. Our benefactors
3. Our closest loved ones and family
4. Our friends and acquaintances
5. Neutral people
6. Annoying/difficult people
7. All beings

The purpose of this practice is for you to develop a quality of openheartedness toward yourself and all other beings—a quality that is quite naturally present in us when the obstructions created by our grasping are removed. In this practice, results are secondary to intention. This is a crucial point. When I say, "May you be blessed with peace," I am expressing the hope that you experience a sense of peace. I may really mean it when I wish you peace, but whether you actually experience peace is secondary to the primary intention of inclining my heart to open toward you. Most likely, you will wish deeply that this outcome should manifest in the person or being you are blessing. However, the practice is about our own state of heart/mind and the cultivation of lovingkindness. This state of mind acts as an antidote to the grasping quality of mind and allows us to see the world more clearly and with more kindness. It also fosters in us a desire to act more compassionately from moment to moment.

There has been much speculation about the efficacy of prayer. If practicing the blessing meditation allows us to develop an open heart, then everyone we touch through our lives will directly benefit from our openheartedness. This is the efficacy of this form of prayer. Attachment to the outcome of our heartfelt blessings that peace or joy should manifest tends to close the heart, especially if that outcome does not seem to occur. It is the attachment to outcomes, not the wholesome wish for peace, that causes this closing. In the blessing practice, we hope to keep our hearts open even when what we pray for does not manifest.

Using the Blessing Practice

The basic technique for saying the phrases of the blessing practice is somewhat involved, for reasons that serve to strengthen the technique. There are also many ways to vary the practice. For example, I suggest that you coordinate the phrases of the blessing with your breath, while some people decide to forgo any connection whatsoever to the breath. Some people use only one or two of the phrases, especially when first learning the technique. Some people change the wording or add different qualities than the four I am using. But please consider the following before beginning to improvise with this or any other contemplative practice: it is good to work extensively with a practice for a significant amount of time before changing it. It takes time to understand the impact of a practice. It is also helpful to see how a practice works as our lives go through various cycles. Often, the desire to change a practice comes from the same mind states we are seeking to transform. We might be bored with the "same old thing," or we might be seeking something more exciting. We may be projecting difficult feelings that arise during a session of practice to the technique of that practice, rather than owning those feelings. On the other hand, sometimes you do need to make changes to keep your practice engaged and alive. It is extremely useful to discuss your practice with friends and teachers. They can provide an extra level of objectivity, as well as practical knowledge from having walked the same roads you are traversing.

As I mentioned, I suggest you begin your blessing practice by linking the phrases to your breath. This will allow you to stay connected to another core practice discussed in this book—breath awareness—and the important aspect of that practice, noticing the Divine Presence at all times. Linking the phrases with your breath serves to keep the phrases moving without getting lost in one particular phrase or a train of thought that arises from it. I find that my mind wanders less from the person I am blessing when the next breath, joined to the next phrase, is already upon me. It also grounds the practice in the present moment of experience and in the body, since the breath is happening at this moment, in this body.

The linking works as follows: On the in-breath, say the words, "May I be blessed with." On the out-breath, say the quality you wish to cultivate. So one cycle of phrases would be spoken as:

> May I be blessed with (in-breath)
>
> peace; (out-breath)
>
> May I be blessed with (in-breath)
>
> joy; (out-breath)
>
> May I be blessed with (in-breath)
>
> lovingkindness; (out-breath)
>
> May I be blessed with (in-breath)
>
> compassion. (out-breath)

Say each phrase one time and then begin again with the first phrase and continue on through the next three phrases.

In addition to connecting the phrases to the breath, the following instructions will help you make the most of your blessing practice. During the in-breath, as you say, "May I be blessed with," visualize yourself, or whoever it is you are directing the blessing toward. For example, I might say, "May Joanna be blessed with," in which case I will visualize my wife, Joanna. Some people find it difficult to visualize someone or something with their eyes closed. If that's the case for you, close your eyes for a moment and try to visualize yourself. Now, for comparison's sake, try to visualize someone else. You may find it easier or more difficult to visualize someone else. When doing this in connection to the phrases, the goal is to bring to mind as strong a sense of that person as possible. Try feeling their presence beside or inside you. Remembering the sound of a person's voice—or even laugh—can often connect you to that person's presence more easily than visualizing him or her. So, if visualizing is hard for you, you may try "audioizing" them. This is an example of how you might customize the practice for yourself.

In addition to saying the word for the quality you wish to cultivate in your mind, try experiencing a bodily knowing of that quality. The blessing that you invoke for ourselves and others is an expression of the hope that they will feel the quality in their body/being at the same time as you feel it. This idea may be somewhat foreign to you, if you haven't worked with paying deep attention to your own bodily sensations. In chapter 3, I discussed the practice of knowing the body and the emotions and sensations that arise in the body. Undertaking the blessing practice might help you learn to know your body, but rather than waiting for bodily sensations to arise and be noticed, the blessing practice asks you to cultivate particular emotions. Before beginning to work with the phrases on your own, I suggest trying the following guided meditations, which focus on each of the qualities we will be cultivating. Do these guided meditations as often as you like and at your own pace. Hopefully you will be able to experience these qualities as a felt bodily sense.

A Guided Meditation for Experiencing Peace (Shalom)

Let's start with the quality of peace or, in Hebrew, shalom. *Peace* is a rich term in Jewish life. The term *shalom* carries with it the meaning of completeness. Peace can be a state of acceptance, not wanting, calmness, serenity, fulfillment, satisfaction, or equanimity. Reflecting on these qualities deliberately in the mind, imagine what your body would feel like if you were feeling very peaceful right at this moment.

If you can bring to your body that feeling of peacefulness, see how long you can hold its presence. Sometimes it is helpful to recall a time or situation in your life when you felt very peaceful. Maybe it was a time on vacation, away from the trials of daily life. Many people think of the beach or mountains. Some of these moments may call forth joyful or loving feelings as well. If you can, try to distinguish peace from these other wonderful feelings. If you can get a sense of peacefulness, you might experience it as a mind state. If you pay careful attention, you will also feel peace as a bodily sensation. Don't worry if you can't immediately cultivate a sense of peacefulness. After all, at this particular moment you may not be feeling peaceful at all, and that's okay. Peace is not the predominant reality during most of the moments of our lives. Over time, in the context of living and practicing wisely, we can cultivate a feeling of peacefulness in our lives. While it is helpful not to be attached to the idea of peace becoming a permanent reality, peace can, over time, replace the feeling of anxiety as our default response to life.

A Guided Meditation for Experiencing Joy (Simcha)

Try doing a similar meditation for the experience of joy. In Hebrew, the term is *simcha*. Joy needs less explaining than peace, even if it is not necessarily experienced frequently. Joy is not to be confused with ecstasy. The desire for ecstatic experience can often be tinged with ego gratification. We are not looking to cultivate the most ecstatic state we ever felt, but a more simple sense of happiness. In this case, when you imagine a time you were happy or felt joy, don't pick your most peak experience of joy. For example, rather than visualizing the birth of my children, which was an ecstatic experience, I would be better served remembering what it felt like to see them asleep in their cribs.

See if you can experience joy with your eyes closed. Pay attention to the way joy manifests as a felt physical sense. With practice, you might be able to recognize the feeling of joy as a bodily pattern of sensations. Once again, recall scenes from your life when you were joyful. It is important in these exercises to get a sense of the bodily knowing of these qualities. As you try to learn what joy feels like when it is present, you might try consciously putting a half-smile on your face. Many people can feel the shift in their bodies when a smile forms. Later, when you are doing the actual blessing practice, you won't have time to do these visualizations all in the space of one breath, but if you have a bodily memory of what joy feels like, you will find it easier to reexperience it during the practice.

A Guided Meditation for Experiencing Lovingkindness (Chesed)

Lovingkindness is a good composite term for the Hebrew word *chesed*. As I mentioned in the discussion of the *sephirot* in chapter 3, *chesed* represents the quality of unbounded lovingkindness. Borrowing from psychological language, we might say it refers to unconditional positive regard. It is the quality of feeling held in a loving embrace. Acting kindly and with unbounded love is a feeling that comes not from ego or wanting anything in return. Sometimes, parents can understand this term when relating to their children (sometimes—but not always). Generally, it is the response evoked in us when looking at a newborn. Of course, that may not be the feeling you have if you are sleep deprived and need to get up at 3:00 a.m. to hold that same crying child!

As you imagine times in your life when you felt that kind of unconditional love flowing outward, once again see if you can experience that quality as a bodily sensation. You can work with this feeling either as the giver or recipient of lovingkindness. Try it both ways.

A Guided Meditation for Experiencing Compassion (Rahamim)

Finally, try experiencing the quality of compassion, or *rahamim* in Hebrew. Compassion is a very heart-centered, balanced feeling. It is useful to think of compassion as the quivering of the heart in response to seeing suffering, whether our own or someone else's. In your visualization, you might remember a time someone you know was suffering. It is helpful to imagine someone other than yourself in this visualization because the feeling you are looking to cultivate is not suffering itself but your response to seeing suffering. If we are feeling compassionate, then recognizing suffering is not demoralizing. When compassion is present, we are able to keep paying attention to the suffering, and out of its recognition, we are motivated to act to ease it. The heart quivers but does not flinch or turn away. When we need to turn away, we have already entered the experience of suffering ourselves. It is our desire to avoid pain that is behind our unwillingness to face the suffering of others. Compassion has a spirit of generosity behind it, even as our hearts quiver. Try imagining situations where you are aware that someone is suffering and you can feel for them in a spirit of wanting to be helpful. Once again, try experiencing the feeling as it manifests in bodily sensations.

If you feel your heart closing down while doing this exercise, try imagining a situation that is perhaps less tragic than your original visualization. For example, if I imagine someone starving to death, it is possible that my sense of helplessness, or perhaps guilt for not doing enough, will be so painful that it will become hard to manifest compassion. On the other hand, if I imagine a little girl I know whose balloon has just popped, I can feel her sense of loss without being overwhelmed by her suffering.

Another visualization I actually have used is to visualize a therapist I used to see. I can still remember how compassionately he would look at me when I was describing something painful in my life. He looked exactly like what I imagine compassion feels like, and just remembering him looking that way evokes the feeling of compassion in me. Remember when doing this blessing practice to focus on the feeling of being the one offering compassion, not the recipient.

Blessing All Beings

As I mentioned earlier, we direct the phrases of the blessing practice toward different categories of recipients. Common sense might dictate that we start with ourselves. Most of us intuitively know that it is hard to feel open to another person if we are not open to ourselves. But for many people, directing these blessings toward themselves turns out to be very difficult. Many of us have complicated and self-deprecating feelings about ourselves. For that reason, I suggest staring out by saying the phrases for a benefactor.

A benefactor is someone who inspires you, who has supported and helped you, and who looks out for your best interests. It should be someone about whom you have few, if any, negative feelings, and who is not looking for you to be or act a certain way in order to get his or her approval. Many people pick an important teacher or a mentor. Chances are, when you think of your benefactor, your heart naturally opens. Since we are trying to cultivate openheartedness in this practice, the benefactor is a natural starting place.

As with any new practice, you will first need to become familiar with its form. You may even want to make this the focus of your daily practice for a week. If you were to join me on a weeklong retreat and wanted to learn this practice, I might instruct you to do these phrases for a full day, repeating the phrases of blessing focused on the benefactor, before moving on to working with yourself. I recently taught this practice to a group of rabbis over a four-day period. We devoted one hour per day to meditation practice. We spent an hour of the first day using phrases focused on the benefactor. On the second day, we blessed ourselves, and by the third day, we worked with blessing a difficult person. On the fourth day of the retreat, we blessed all beings. As you can see, the amount of time to devote to this practice depends entirely on the circumstances in which you intend to practice it. Since you will likely be beginning this practice on your own, I would suggest that you spend twenty to thirty minutes of your daily practice focused on the benefactor for a week or two before switching to direct the phrases toward yourself. One teacher I have suggests using this practice for the first few minutes of any sitting period, even when doing mindfulness practice, as a way of coming to your practice with an open heart.

When you feel ready to move on from the benefactor, you can start to say phrases of blessing for yourself. On the in-breath, as you say, "May I be blessed with," visualize yourself in a few different ways. Sometimes when I do this practice, I imagine seeing myself in a full-length mirror, so that I see my whole person. Other times I see myself from the chest down, since that is all I can see of myself when I am not in front of a mirror. Most of the time, rather than visualizing myself, I do a quick scan of my body and try feeling the totality of the physical experience I call "me."

Sometimes when I am doing the practice for myself, I find myself wondering if directing blessings at myself is a good idea, since I am already so self-preoccupied. After all, much of my meditation practice is devoted to softening my addiction to "me." Yet I do know that when my heart is closed, it is because the small sense of self, *mochin de-katnut,* is manifesting in a strong way. In that case, these phrases can help soften my heart, especially if I keep setting an intention to see myself through kindly rather than judgmental eyes. I also know that while the concept of there being no separate self is true in the absolute sense, in the relative sense, I identify with the "little me" and therefore need to practice with him.

Here are some additional pointers that will apply no matter who is the focus of the blessing. The first time you do the practice, be patient with yourself. There are many parts to remember. Eventually you will be familiar with all the phrases, and with adding visualizations while connecting it all to the in-breath and out-breath. If all four phrases seem to be too confusing, try starting out by using only one or two phrases—then add in the other phrases as you get comfortable.

As you work to coordinate the phrases with the breath, it will be helpful to intentionally slow down your breathing. When I gave instructions for breath awareness, I suggested that you allow your breath to come and go at whatever was its natural pace. This meant not deliberately speeding up or slowing down. In the blessing practice, however, it is helpful to slow down the breath. It takes a moment to try visualizing someone. It is helpful to have a slight amount of additional time to see if a feeling is cultivated in the body and to be able to experience it in the body. Since an open heart is generally a calm heart, this slowing down is usually helpful in and of itself.

The use of the word *blessing* in the phrases deserves some further discussion at this point. While I refer to this meditation as the blessing practice, I also call it an experience in prayer. Offering blessings is one type of prayer experience. As such, it is helpful to think of this practice as a prayer session as well as a meditation session. You might even want to consider your time spent doing this practice as sacred time. Of course, as I have emphasized in this book, all awareness practice is about paying attention to the Divine Presence unfolding in each moment.

There are not any changes in the basic instructions as you move on from the self to close family and friends. It is helpful to decide on frequency and order if you are going to work with more than one person in any given practice session. In other words, you might bless your spouse or one friend for a whole session. But it is also possible to bless your entire family in one session. In that case, you could bless each person separately for five minutes, or you might decide to bless each person with one round of four phrases and then start over again. Usually, when I bless my family, I speak all four phrases for Joanna, and the same four each for my children, Esther, Jesse, and Suri. I then start over again with Joanna.

As you use this practice of cultivating an awakened heart, you can begin to see that this too is an awareness practice. The intensity of keeping your attention on the set of phrases, the accompanying visualizations, and the attention to your body make this a powerful concentration practice. As with other practices, when your attention wanders away from the phrases, gently bring yourself back to focusing on them. This is the concentration aspect of this practice. But there is also an awareness side of the blessing practice: it allows you to see more clearly the state of your own heart. You can begin to really know the difference in how your heart feels when it is open as compared to when it is closed. You also can become aware of *where* the particular relationships in your life stand. For example, as you try sending blessings to your immediate family, you may notice resistance you might have toward those you love. This can come in the form of more distractions, or as stories of unresolved hurts that seem to pull your attention away from the phrases. Discovering these truths is just as important as cultivating openheartedness and gives you insights into aspects of your life to which you can bring more awareness by using the other tools described in this book.

Eventually, your blessing practice will include people outside of the familiar sphere of family and friends. You can begin to send blessings to colleagues, neighbors, and casual acquaintances. This is an important step in the expansion of your openheartedness. The practice of opening the heart is also the practice of beginning to see more clearly that we are not the center of the universe. The web of being has no center. I remember having a strong experience of this insight in connection to the next stage of the blessing practice, the neutral person.

For this part of the practice, I suggest picking a person that you regularly come across but toward whom you have no strong feelings one way or the other. It may be difficult at first to find such a person, because such people don't easily register in our consciousness. This is somewhat similar to working with bodily sensations that are neither pleasant nor unpleasant. In that case, you will remember, the tendency of the mind is to ignore a neutral sensation, even though it is quite knowable. In order to find a neutral person, you may need to think about the flow of your day and attempt to visualize the people you routinely come across but have never particularly noticed. Perhaps it will be a clerk in a convenience store, or even someone at your workplace with whom you have limited contact.

On one weeklong retreat, I had the group use the blessing practice exclusively for the entire week. When we came to the neutral person phase, I picked a man who was sitting very close to me that I had never noticed before. I spent the entire day blessing him with peace, joy, lovingkindness, and compassion. It was an amazing experience for me because by the end of the day, I realized that I had spent most of my time in thoughts that were not self-referencing. This was even truer than on the day I spent blessing my best friend. He is *my* friend after all—but with the neutral person, it didn't seem like I was doing this practice for my benefit, but rather for his benefit.

Sending Blessings to Difficult People

When you feel ready, move on to extending blessings to difficult people. You may hear that term as a substitute for the word *enemy,* but I think the term *difficult person* is more appropriate in framing what this phase of the practice is about. We can have difficulties with many people who aren't, strictly speaking, enemies. A difficult person is someone who bothers you in some way. It may be someone you have a feud with or someone who once insulted you. Or it may be someone you just don't like. If you are holding a grudge against someone, this is the time to work with it. Remember the reason for doing the blessing practice: you are trying to cultivate an opening in your heart. It is not about fixing people or correcting their behavior. When you hold a grudge, the person who is most hurt is you.

Initially in doing this practice, it is not a good idea to pick the *most* difficult person you can imagine. As in the earlier phases of the practice, keep in mind that you don't want to evaluate the practice by the results. You may or may not be able to cultivate an open heart at any time, but the very intention to try opening your heart, made over and over again, has an impact on your attitudes and helps to recondition the heart. When you think of "your" difficult person, you may notice your chest tightening, your heart closing down. If you find it very difficult to continue the practice, you can always go back to an easier person and allow your heart to open, then come back to the difficult person and try again. If you find yourself thinking that this person doesn't deserve your blessings, you can practice kindness to yourself, noting the arising of anger, while also acknowledging honestly that this anger arises out of your own sense of hurt. Remember who it hurts when you feel angry. At the very least, if people we disliked really did feel loved and blessed, they probably wouldn't be as difficult for us. Blessing the difficult person is really the active pursuit of peace. I imagine you will find many insights as you take on this practice. Good luck.

Finally, I invite you to send blessings to all beings. Since it is hard to visualize all beings at once, you can do this by imagining classes of beings. You might spend a few rounds blessing all birds, then all creeping things, then all insects, and on and on. You might think of the people in refugee camps or the starving people of the world. I find this to be a particularly appropriate activity for Shabbat afternoon, when the rhythm of Sabbath practice calls for imagining a time of peace on Earth. When I do this practice outdoors, I once again bless whatever being I see. On a walk, I will bless the tree I see, and then the driver who next passes by, and then the weeds—whatever catches my eye.

A Note on Keeping the Heart Open

Remember that this is a heart-opening practice. Because there are many mental components to it, from visualizing to saying the phrases, there can be a tendency to experience this meditation as occurring in the region of the head. It is advisable to imagine instead that this practice is being done in the chest area rather than in the head. As a reminder, when I use the word *mind,* I am not talking about the region of the head. The mind, as discussed in this book, does not exist in an isolated place in the body. Rather, the mind is the aggregate of a series of processes that take place in the entire body, and perhaps in realms not physically based at all. When saying the phrases, it is possible to feel yourself making those intentions in the middle of the chest, in the heart center. This may be difficult to understand if it is not your experience. Perhaps if I suggest that you say each phrase of blessing in a heartfelt way, you can at least understand the sentiment I am discussing. As you work with this practice, try feeling the phrases originating from your heart.

Finally, as you move through the different categories of people as described above, remember that the main focus of this practice is the cultivation of your own heart of compassion. You may find that your heart opens when blessing your benefactor, but that it closes when you move on to yourself or to the annoying or difficult person. If this happens, feel free to go back to the benefactor. You don't have to force yourself to push through your closed heart by persisting with the phrases where you are blocked. This principle applies to each of the people you wish to bless. You can always go back to a set of phrases that open your heart, and when your heart feels open again, try moving on to the phrases where your heart felt blocked.

Trying Not to Waste Any Blessings

It is important to keep another deep intention when undertaking the blessing practice. There is a Jewish teaching that we should not recite a blessing in vain, a *brachah l'vahtelah.* For example, when kindling the Sabbath candles we say that we bless the Holy One (wholly one), the sovereign of the universe, who commanded us to kindle the

Sabbath lights. If we were to say that blessing formula and not light the candles, that would be a blessing in vain. Or, if we said the blessing twice before lighting the candles, some would consider the second recitation in vain since you had already fulfilled the obligation to say the blessing.

We are not "commanded" to do the practice I am describing here, at least not according to a traditional halakhic point of view. There is no limit on saying new blessings, so there is no problem with repeating the blessings in this practice. However, the principle, as I see it in this concept, is that a blessing should not be wasted. If I say to someone, "I bless you with happiness," I want to really mean it. If I don't mean it, or at least really intend to mean it, then it feels like I am wasting a blessing. Blessings are too special to be wasted. For me, there is an inherent difference between saying to someone, "I hope you are happy," and saying, "I want to bless you with happiness." For me, using the word *blessing* invokes God as a partner in the enterprise and raises the ante. In this way, when I do the blessing practice, I want to make each phrase really count. This framework helps me to stay more present to the practice and allows me to sustain my focus, leading to deeper concentration. This focus on blessing and on God as a partner in the practice is one of the aspects of this practice I find most powerful. It is also what makes it feel like a Jewish practice for me. I hope it works that way for you as well.

Blessings on the Subway and at the Airport

One of the good things about the blessing practice is that you can do it any time and in any place. You can do it while driving, or on the subway, or walking on a sidewalk. I remember doing it in an airport one time. I was in the middle of a phase of compulsive eating. When this happens to me, I find that I spend a good portion of my day planning my next snack or meal. It can become the most persistent thought pattern of the day. On this day at the airport, I decided to practice the phrases instead of planning which food stand I'd go to on my layover in Chicago. I felt it was a better use of my time to be repeating phrases of blessing than to be thinking about food all day. I started by blessing myself and then, as I continued, I began to bless people at the airport. In such a setting there is no need to visualize. You can take someone in with your eyes during your in-breath, and bless him or her with joy while trying to feel joy in your body on the out-breath. When you do this, you get in touch with feelings of joy and compassion. This practice works well to deflect your mind's attention from the compulsive thought pattern, whatever it is.

A Special Note

When you notice that your heart is wide open and you feel the love that you have been trying to cultivate, it is fine to drop all the words and techniques. At such times, you can just look out at the world and allow these feelings of lovingkindness to flow outward to everything you see, hear, feel, taste, smell, and know.

In finishing this chapter, I want to offer blessings to you, the reader. Please try hearing these words as the recipient—not the giver:

> May you be blessed with peace.
>
> May you be blessed with joy.
>
> May you be blessed with lovingkindness.
>
> May you be blessed with compassion.

For those of you who are actively pursuing a Jewish spiritual life and who have an affinity for Hebrew, especially as the language of prayer, I offer a version of the phrases in Hebrew. Generally, it is helpful to work with the language you know best for the phrases to sink in deeply. But whether Hebrew is your native language or not, the Hebrew may strengthen the practice for you. You may want to try it both ways and see what works best for you. I have noticed that I have to work harder to really feel the Hebrew sinking in. For that reason, I usually practice in English, but if I notice my attention waning, I might switch to Hebrew precisely because I do give it more effort.

T'hee ahl-eye birkat shalom.

T'hee ahl-eye birkat simcha.

T'hee ahl-eye birkat chesed.

T'hee ahl-eye birkat rahamim.

For another person, the phrase becomes: "*T'hee ahl* [insert name]."
For example, "*T'hee ahl David.*" For all beings, I say, "*T'hee ahl kall chai.*"

8

L'chayyim— Into Life

When Franz Rosenzweig, a noted Jewish philosopher of the early twentieth century, finished his major work *The Star of Redemption,* his last words were: *"L'chayyim*—into life." After exploring the relationship between the Jewish people and the Divine in his book, he wrote those words to emphasize the need to take this relationship to the Divine into the arena of everyday life. Both Rosenzweig and Martin Buber were proponents of bringing spirituality "into the marketplace." After finishing his book, Rosenzweig decided to leave the world of academia and the writing of scholarly books and to focus on interacting with regular people.

The critique most commonly heard about meditation is that it is self-involved and distances the practitioner from the world. But the practices in this book are meant to be taken into the world of our everyday existence, so that the wisdom, kindness, and compassion we have been cultivating can become interwoven into all aspects of our lives.

The Benefits of Regular Meditation Retreats

Before describing the methods by which you can take these practices into your life, I want to share some thoughts about the value of going on extended retreats. As you have noticed, many of the vignettes I have shared come from insights that arose while I was a participant on such retreats. I highly recommend participating in such retreats at least once a year, for they provide us with the kind of intensive training that can open our hearts and minds and change our lives for the better. Meditation retreats can be of various lengths, but I suggest doing a weeklong retreat. A week is a long enough time to sustain your daily practice for the rest of the year. This can be augmented by daylong practice periods from time to time, as well as weekend retreats. Occasionally, an even longer retreat period of two weeks or perhaps a month can be of radically profound value.

A meditation retreat is a chance to remove yourself from the day-to-day grind of routine that shapes your habitual way of seeing and doing things. On retreat, it is possible to cultivate levels of concentration that most people do not experience in daily formal practice. Such a retreat is usually held in silence, which means there is no conversation between participants. Silence is observed during sitting and walking practice, as well as during meals or when back in rooms for sleeping. The practice of observing silence supports the deepening of concentration, as we continually pay attention to what is occurring in the present moment. Each moment of awakened attention cultivates the possibility of being awake in the next moment and deepens concentration. The silent space and the group presence are generally supportive to each person in attempting to do this.

Being in silence for a prolonged period is a novel experience to most people. While anticipating the practice of silence may cause some anxiety, most people find that, after some initial awkwardness, being in silence is a precious gift. All the normal preoccupations with making a good social impression on those around us become extraneous and it then becomes possible to see more clearly just how profoundly influenced we are by social norms, allowing great insight into what is normally just our background social conditioning. Being in silence and doing formal concentration practices also allows the level of discursive thought in the mind to slow down beyond what is likely in daily practice.

Most people find that the settling-in process on a retreat takes about three days. On the last day of a retreat, the mind tends to refocus on all the normal worldly matters that are the usual business of our lives. On a weeklong retreat, this leaves a few precious days in the middle where it is possible to be present, with fewer obscurations, to the "truth" of each moment. As I have said in previous chapters, this experience of the "truth" is really a more direct experience of the Divine Presence. It is this experience, rather than any intellectual understanding, that is the source of the profound insight that you carry into your life outside of the retreat.

A retreat provides both a booster for living with an awakened heart and a means of deepening that awakening. The effects of a retreat last long after it has ended. But, like every transient state of mind, even these effects will fade over time, which is why regular retreats are so valuable. I have noticed that my own practice suffered during years I didn't manage to go on a retreat. For me, taking such retreat time is a priority in my overall spiritual practice.

Using the Sabbath as a Day of Deep Practice

Returning to the theme of taking these practices into the fabric of our everyday lives, one Jewish practice in particular serves as a bridge into our daily rhythms. I am referring to the practice of observing the Sabbath. The Jewish spiritual life is built around the observance of one day out of every seven as a period for enhancing the very values we have been addressing in this book. The Sabbath is Judaism's recognition that in order to stay awake in this life, human beings need to devote themselves regularly to practices that take us out of our everyday or "weekday" mind—a mind that is so often focused on getting what we need for ourselves.

It is beyond the scope of this book to explore in detail how central some kind of Sabbath observance is to the Jewish spiritual path. Many books have been written and will continue to be written about how to work with the Sabbath. Here, suffice it to say that, in order to nourish and maintain an awakened heart, it would be wise to spend extended time at least one day per week on the experience of "being" rather than "doing." This is one of the essences of the Sabbath experience and has been a central theme in this book. Focusing a day of your week on "being" rather than "doing" stresses the central holiness inherent in "being." It is also the anchor for living in the world of "doing" without losing that sense of holiness. The Jewish practice of the Sabbath is intrinsically linked to fostering a holy life during the other six days of the week.

Creating a Well-Rounded Spiritual Life

At this point, it may be helpful to summarize what needs to be included in a comprehensive Jewish practice. A teaching from a classic source in the wisdom tradition, *Pirkei Avot* (Principle Ethics), provides such a framework: "The World Rests on Three Things: On *Torah,* on *Avodah,* and on *Gemilut Hasadim,*" or to put this in English terms, on acquiring wisdom, on the service of cultivating an open heart, and on committing deeds of lovingkindness (*Pirkei Avot* 1:2). These three realms can be seen as legs of a three-legged stool. Without any one leg, the stool cannot stand. Each leg implies an active process—acquiring, cultivating, and committing. Having an awakened heart means functioning in a balanced way in these three areas. The word *awakened* refers to the wisdom component. It means that the heart or heart/mind is seeing clearly and that it is balanced, opened, and in an ongoing process of purifying itself. When this is true, harmful actions are dropped and loving ones naturally occur. Each pillar influences the other.

Torah—Recognizing the Truth as the Path to Acquiring Wisdom

As Jonathon Slater, a Conservative rabbi and meditation teacher, points out in his book *Mindful Jewish Living,* "If we wish to know that which signifies God's presence in the world and in our lives, we must seek to know the truth."[1] He cites the Talmudic text: "Rabbi Hanina taught: Truth is the Seal of the Holy One" (Shabbat 55a). Wherever and whenever we recognize the truth of things in this world, we see the divine process in action. Knowing the truth of our own experience is a direct realization of the Divine Presence. Seeing this truth depends on an awakened heart. Without an awakened heart, we are just lost in our normal conditioned ways of misinterpreting the world that is characteristic of the small mind.

Practice Awareness All the Time

Having learned the formal tools of meditative practice is just the starting point in living a meaningful, holy life. The purpose of learning how to keep the heart/mind open is to look at the entirety of our lives through minds that have acquired a more clarified lens. As we bring this awakened attention to what we experience moment-by-moment, we gain in wisdom while at the same time further polishing the lens. The wisdom we need comes from keeping our hearts open to the whole range of life's experiences. This is much more challenging than the simpler practice of staying present when we sit silently in a quiet place for formal practice.

> And these words, which I have commanded you this day, shall be upon your heart. And you shall teach them to your children and shall speak of them when you sit in your house, when you walk by the way, when you lie down and when you rise up. (Deut. 6:5)

In these words we see an injunction to honor and share the teachings of the Torah in every possible physical position—sitting, lying, or erect while walking, and in the transitions between these postures. That is the Torah's poetic way of saying "all the time." Likewise, the awareness of the awakened heart is to be cultivated in each moment. As I have said before, this desire for awakening in each moment is a way of orienting your intention but not something to which you should become attached. You will be missing the point if you get exasperated that you haven't reached this goal of constant wakefulness. Such attachment to the outcome is driven by the small mind's mistaken need for perfection. What is possible, however, is that setting such an intention can help you see more clearly more of the time.

The things you can learn from your own life are exactly the things you need to learn. Take the practice of paying attention to your relationships as lover, partner, parent, child, boss, worker, colleague, and friend. Notice what your experience is in each of the four divine worlds when you eat, when you are angry, when you are tired, and when compulsive patterns are playing out. Over time you will come to learn what your own patterns are after you act, while you are acting, and before you act. This learning is relevant whether the action is a skillful one or an unskillful one. As you begin to see clearly the pain and sorrow that is generated by unskillful actions, you will naturally become more able to respond to life's challenges with greater kindness and compassion. This is a direct result of the wisdom you acquire in knowing how you feel inside, and in seeing the causes and conditions from which both skillful and unskillful action arise.

Practicing Eating Meditation

I would like to share some instructions in eating meditation as an example of a formal practice you can use on a regular basis in your life. If you can, try doing the practice now. You can skip over it if you are not home at the moment.

Select three small food items that you will eat as a part of the practice. A good item to use is a raisin. You can also use chocolate chips, nuts, dried fruit, or anything else you desire that is bite-size. As you follow these instructions try to continually monitor your inner experience. Eating meditation began as soon as you read the words *eating meditation* in the first sentence of this section. You can already monitor what happens at the suggestion to be awake and attentive as you eat. Perhaps you are already looking forward to eating. You can watch your mind create stories about the future in anticipation of a pleasant experience. Perhaps your mind is already planning what food items you'll eat. How do you decide which items to take? Are you taking three different items or did you choose three of the same item that you really like? Perhaps you can already get an inkling of how much can be learned about yourself in this form of meditation.

When you have the three items, sit down and choose one of them to begin the next step. How do you choose the order of use for these items? If you have a favorite in the items you selected, did you pick it to eat first or are you saving it for last? Try feeling your body for any physical experience of preferences. Take the item in your hand and look at it. Allowing time for visual contact with the food may seem different than usual. This difference is good. It encourages you to be more present with the experience. Often we can eat a meal and pay no attention at all to the food or to the experience of eating. As you look at the item, use your imagination to get in touch with the wonder of everything that had to happen in the universe for this food item to be in your hand at this moment. There had to be a big bang. Stars had to form, and out of them came all the elements larger than hydrogen or helium that eventually became the planet Earth. The sun needed to continue to shine on the planet in just the right way for plant life to grow. Farmers had to grow the crops that eventually became this morsel. Truckers, accountants, and store clerks all had to add their labor for you to be able to eat this morsel. Seeing all this into each bite, try getting in touch with a sense of gratitude for the act of eating. In keeping with Jewish practice, offer a blessing of appreciation to the divine process that manifested in this food. Then go ahead and eat it. (Formal blessings for each kind of food item can be found in Jewish prayer books.)

Now choose the second item to eat. Roll it around your fingers and get a tactile sense of the item as you also explore it visually. Bring it up to your nose and smell it. After a few moments, place it on your tongue but don't begin to chew yet. Notice the process of salivation, if that occurs. Concentrate now on the taste of the item without yet chewing. Roll the item around different areas of the tongue and explore the changing taste sensations. The sensors in the tongue pick up different flavors in different areas. Where do you notice sweetness? Where do you notice saltiness? Keeping your attention on the taste of the item, begin chewing and continue to track the changing taste sensations. Finish this piece with swallowing. Wait a moment to see how the sensation of taste changes after you have swallowed the item.

Choosing the third item, repeat the earlier steps. This time as you chew, pay attention to the processes involved in swallowing. Where does the sensation to swallow arise from? Can you feel it as a desire in the body? As you finish this piece of food, notice if you have a desire to eat more. As you take this practice into entire meals, try watching the connection between eating and desire. If you eat slowly, you can do many of the steps of this practice repeatedly. See if you can establish the difference between the desire that we call hunger and the desire for pleasant sensations. How do you decide when to stop eating or how big a portion to take in the first place? How do you decide to have seconds, and when do you choose not to? Eating meditation can be a very rich practice. For so many of us, eating is a complicated activity that has large social and health ramifications. Eating meditation allows the possibility of cultivating greater wisdom in all these areas, potentially giving us greater freedom to make wise choices.

Many people feel they do not have time to do formal practice in their busy lives. This practice of eating meditation, in addition to bringing tremendous insight into a central aspect of our lives, is useful because it can fit into your existing schedule. Everyone makes time to eat, usually more than once a day. While you may not choose to make every meal a silent meal focusing on the act of eating, you might experiment with trying this once a day or a few times a week.

As You Walketh by the Way

Walking is another daily activity that lends itself to meditation practice in our lives. If you can, spend some time each day paying attention as you walk. I don't necessarily mean a formal walk in a park, but simply when you are moving from place to place. For example, walking from the parking lot into a store or from the subway station to a job are times when you can practice walking meditation.

Walking meditation can become another opportunity to leave behind the rush of a planning or judging mind and simply return to the present moment of experience in your body. There are a number of ways you might do this kind of practice. It might be for a specific minute or two on the spur of the moment, or it might be based on your daily routine—for example, each morning on your way to work.

As you begin walking, start by bringing your awareness to the bottom of your feet and notice the changing sensations as each foot lifts off the ground, moves, and is placed back down. For learning purposes, begin by standing up and, when ready, closing your eyes for about one minute to see what it is like to let your attention rest in the sensations in the bottom of your feet while you are standing still. Can you feel the sensations in your feet? As with the other practices mentioned in this book, when your attention wanders away from noticing the sensations in your feet, gently bring the attention back. You might repeat this period of awareness a few times before moving on to the next step.

When you're ready, close your eyes, pick one of your feet, and rest the attention on the sensations in the bottom of that foot. Slowly, shift your weight so that most, but not all, of your weight is on that foot. You can leave the other foot on the ground so that you aren't trying to balance on one foot. As you shift your weight, notice the changing sensations in the foot that is receiving the extra weight. Most likely you will be able to track the changing pressure as you apply more weight to that foot. The pressure on the outside edge of the foot increases and less pressure is on the ball of the foot. As you finish shifting weight to that foot, allow your attention to shift to the foot now carrying less weight. Now begin to shift your weight back so that more weight is on the other foot. Notice the sensations in the bottom of the other foot as you begin to return weight to it. Do this back and forth a few times to get the experience of tracking changing sensations in each foot as you shift your weight.

Now, when you are ready and with your eyes open, pick one foot and slowly lift it and begin moving it forward. Try tracking the changing sensations as the foot becomes free of any weight, lifts, moves forward, and is placed down. When it is fully down, shift your attention to the back foot and begin to notice the sensations as the heel and then the rest of that foot lifts and moves forward till it becomes planted. For practice, do this for about ten steps, and then turn around and return over the same ten paces. You might try doing this back and forth for ten or twenty minutes to get the sense of it. Try various speeds when learning this practice or when using it in a daily way. Sometimes moving too slowly can lead to more discursive thought. See what speed allows you to be most present to the physical sensations.

This kind of formal walking meditation is an excellent practice to couple with sitting meditation if you want to do some formal practice periods that help develop extended concentration. In this chapter, I introduce the technique so that you can begin to use it in daily life. By having some practices that you can do for even a few minutes in the middle of a busy day, you give yourself the opportunity to wake up and become present throughout your day. In those few moments you can get in touch with how you feel right at this moment in your body, in your heart, in what moods are present, and in what your intentions are for the next few moments of your life. Paying attention as you walk into your place of work can bring you into this moment and can also let you become aware of tensions that are present or judgmental thoughts or perhaps the excitement you feel upon coming to work. All these added sensations and emotions that you notice are the benefits of the wisdom that comes with simply paying attention.

It Is Very Hard to Do This Work Alone

Learning to pay attention to your life in all of its different facets is a direct path to acquiring wisdom. It is supported by learning from others who have followed or are following this same path of awakening. Toward this end, it is very useful to cultivate relationships with teachers and spiritual friends. My practice has been deeply influenced and inspired by wonderful teachers. You were lucky to meet them in this book, whether by name or by their wisdom that I shared with you. I want to bless you that you find such teachers who speak to your heart. I tend to look for people whose real lives are a model for what they teach. You don't necessarily need to meet these teachers directly. I highly recommend reading books and listening to recorded lectures as a real practice in acquiring wisdom, especially in conjunction with the direct path I share in this book. Some suggestions for further reading and listening are included in Appendix B.

Friends are an equally important part of this practice, for this is a path that cannot be walked alone. Find like-minded souls to be your main fiends. One of the deep truths we see about ourselves is that we are social beings who are highly influenced by the behavior and thoughts of those around us. Try to find a practice group where you can meditate. If there isn't one in your area that you are comfortable with, start one. Nothing supports regular practice more than sharing it with others. Make a commitment to find and nurture relationships with some special friends with whom you can share your insights, experiences, feelings, and the wisdom you find in the books and tapes you use. All of these things will help you in making your whole life a practice from which you acquire wisdom.

Working with Pain

It would not be fair to offer ideas and practices to keep the heart open without talking about how to work with pain—both physical and emotional. The key step in the practice of dealing with pain is to turn your attention toward the experience rather than turning away from it. This does not necessarily mean looking for extra opportunities to experience pain. Without trying, each of us will be offered all the opportunities for pain that we need in the course of a life. It is impossible to be born into a body and not experience physical pain, whether through sickness, illness, or simply sitting still in one position for too long. It is the intense effort spent trying to avoid pain that causes us so much grief and usually makes the situation worse. As Sylvia Boorstein says, "In this life, pain is mandatory, suffering is optional."

In regular life, as I have said, we will be offered all the opportunities we need to practice bringing mindful attention to painful situations. In order to be able to meet those situations without adding additional suffering, it can be helpful to work with some formal practices in meditation. I was once on a meditation retreat led by Sayadaw U-Janaka, a Burmese master of mindfulness meditation who worked with physical pain in meditation as one of his primary teaching tools. "Pain is the friend of the meditator," he told us. "Do not evade it. It can lead you to *nibbana*.... It may not disappear, but if it does, you may cry over it, for your friend has gone away."[2]

After about one week on this retreat, one of Sayadaw U-Janaka's assistants, U Wansa, asked me in an interview how I dealt with physical pain during meditation. I sit in a chair when doing sitting meditation rather than on cushions on the floor. I already had some knee problems when I learned to meditate and never put the effort into learning to sit cross-legged on a cushion. I have also been fortunate (or not, according to U-Janaka) in my life not to have had significant issues with chronic pain. So when U-Wansa asked me how I dealt with pain while meditating, I told him that I didn't have much pain when sitting. On that retreat, the practice was to do one-hour sitting periods followed by one-hour walking periods. When U-Wansa heard my answer, he told me that Sayadaw U-Janaka would most likely tell me to sit for two hours at a time.

Sure enough, two days later, in my next interview with the Sayadaw, he asked me the same question. In response to my reply of having little pain when sitting, he told me to begin sitting for two-hour periods. I left the interview and promptly began to follow the instructions I had received. And of course, at about the sixty-one-minute mark, I began to feel a painful burning sensation at the base of my spine where my sit-bones made contact with the chair. This pain began to steadily increase over the next fifty-nine minutes. Having anticipated this situation, I began to work with being present to the experience of physical pain. As with the core practices I introduced earlier in this book, the basic way of working with physical pain that is strong is to make the painful sensations the primary object of focus.

Using pain as an object of focus can be a powerful tool in developing strong concentration. This is one of the reasons Sayadaw U-Janaka says that pain is a meditator's friend. As an object of focus, the breath often fades from prominence in the mind, and this can make it more challenging to sustain the attention. Sustained attention is one of the keys to developing deeper levels of concentration. When the body is in significant pain, it is difficult to ignore, as I am sure you already know. The pain, then, can be a powerful object on which to rest your attention. Sustaining attention on something that is unpleasant runs counter to our normal way of being, but if you reflect on this idea for a moment, the truth becomes clear: learning how to be with pain and difficulty while we meditate trains us to be present with the suffering and challenges in the rest of our lives.

When working with physical pain in formal meditation practice, the first step is to bring attention to the painful sensations themselves. It is useful to note the quality of the sensations rather than merely noting the fact that you are in pain. What is the pain like? Is it burning or tearing or stabbing or tingling? Is it hard, soft, warm, shallow, or deep? It will most likely be the case that the mind will want to go into discursive thought as it plans how to get rid of the unpleasant sensation. When this happens, simply notice this and bring your attention back to the physical sensations. Spiritual teacher Ken Wilbur, noted author, spiritual philosopher, and integral theorist, points out a helpful reframing that applies to working with pain. Often the thought arises that, "I am in pain." This carries with it the image of "poor me caught in a big pool of pain!" Wilbur suggests trying to reverse the image to "pain is in me," which is closer to the truth of the situation. Stated this way, you become bigger and the pain becomes smaller, being merely a subset of your total experience.

As I mentioned, the experience of pain usually causes constriction in the mind, which leads to the experience of pain as a large problem, beyond what we can handle. By bringing attention to the direct experience of the painful sensations, a number of transformations are possible. First, each moment of paying attention brings with it the realization that it is, in fact, possible to be present to pain without "dying." Often the fear of experiencing pain is worse than the actual experience itself. Second, if you can sustain your attention on the pain, it is possible to develop a very deep concentration, as Sayadaw U-Janaka suggested. The experience of deep concentration has an expansive effect on the mind. It tends to bring with it calm and ease and openness. When this occurs, the experience of the painful sensations radically changes in nature. To the expansive mind (*mochin degadlut,* or "big mind") the pain stops being a problem. Sometimes this means that the pain stops altogether. Other times the sense of unpleasant sensation remains, but without it being a problem that has to be "fixed." In fact, in that open-mind state, the genesis of the pain itself may even become more apparent. The pain may continue, but may have little impact on the happy state that comes along with the concentrated mind.

When this occurs, your relationship to pain changes. Pain can then become the real attention getter it is meant to be. Pain represents real information that the body is trying to communicate, and it is helpful to be able to listen. It is also empowering to know that you can meet your pain without flinching. With the added confidence that pain can be managed, you will hopefully find yourself more able to look deeply into the painful situations that arise in life, including your emotional pains. These pains are also manageable, and the wisdom gained by staying present rather than avoiding them is the key to sustaining an awakened heart. I remember thinking during the retreat with Sayadaw U-Janaka that it might be possible for me to face a painful experience at the end of life without needing drugs that would cloud my mind. I felt grateful to have received this training.

Avodah—Cultivating an Open Heart

The natural state of the disencumbered heart is one of expansiveness, joy, and compassion. But as I have tried to point out in this book, many of the regular things that occur in life, when left unexamined, can cause our hearts to shut down. It takes a regular and sustained spiritual practice to allow the heart to stay open. A daily period of sitting meditation is especially valuable in this regard. People always ask how long the daily practice period should be. There is no one-size-fits-all answer; it is wiser to commit yourself to a short period of meditation that you can successfully fit into your daily schedule than it is to insist on sitting for forty-five minutes each day, only to feel badly when you don't do it. If five minutes is what you can do successfully, then five minutes it is. Thirty or forty-five minutes does allow for more settling in and for more concentration to develop, but many people find it hard to commit that much time in their lives. Practicing for longer periods often develops organically over the years as you see the value of meditation and are drawn to make it happen. And don't forget, some periods in your life allow more space for formal meditation practice than others. Whatever the schedule of your life looks like, you can still practice being awake whenever possible, moment by moment, as best you can, every day of your life.

Most people find that having a regular time in the day for formal practice is helpful. The time that most often lends itself to regular practice seems to be first thing in the morning (after the toilet), before you begin serious interactions with the world. A morning meditation gets the day started with more awareness, and it can help you reconnect with that awareness in more moments throughout your day. Most people also find it helpful to have a regular place in their house for formal practice. It can help to have an altar of some type nearby, with whatever items are holy to you. In terms of the daily practice itself, I suggest that you split up whatever time you have committed in the following way: Use the first half, or even the first two-thirds, of the allotted time for concentration practice. Use whichever concentration tool works the best for you, unless you are working to develop a particular kind of concentration, such as on a word or the breath. Use the remaining time to open up the attention to whatever is arising (open awareness) in the moment. This might include body sensations, but pay particular attention to feelings and mind states that arise as you prepare to enter your day. In my life, I find that regular periods of meditation do, in fact, reopen my heart and rekindle the flames of love.

Depending on your available time, prayer is a valuable tool in your morning practice. As you may recall from chapter 6, one of prayer's effects can be the cultivation of wholesome states of heart and mind. Making prayer a regular part of your daily practice is another support to maintaining an open heart as you move through your day. Some people find it helpful to do their meditation first and then pray, as I mentioned in chapter 6. Or you might combine prayer and sitting meditation by using your prayer practice and chanting as the concentration side of a daily morning practice, and then using the Amidah (see chapter 6) portion of the practice to work on open awareness.

As you work on trying to keep your heart open in daily life, remember the blessing practice. It is an invaluable tool for cultivating an open heart, especially when you feel overwhelmed with difficult emotions such as sadness, fear, or anger. When your heart is contracting and shutting down, the blessing practice can soften the identifications that cause us distress and allow our natural capacity for love and compassion to shine once more.

Cultivating Generosity

Generosity is also an important practice. It serves both the recipient and the giver. When we act in generous ways, we benefit because our heart opens in the act of giving, and the separation we feel between ourselves and others begins to break down. Once again, much has been written on this topic. Here I want to offer some simple prescriptions so that you will make generosity an integral part of your daily practice.

First, I offer a story about how generosity can work. Rabbi Schneur Zalman, the founder of the Chabad/Lubavitch movement of Hasidic Jews, was once on a mission to raise ransom money in order to free some Jewish prisoners. In his time, non-Jewish officials of various towns would imprison innocent Jews specifically to raise money. He came to a town where a very rich Jewish man who was known as a complete miser lived. He asked two of the local rabbis to come with him to visit this man and ask for his help. They tried dissuading Schneur Zalman from making this visit, informing him that the miser never offered anyone more than a rusty penny. He was insistent, however, and convinced them to come along.

Before he entered the house of the miser, he asked the other two rabbis to make no comments while inside. Once inside, Schneur Zalman explained the situation to the man and asked for his help. The miser left the room and returned moments later with a small velvet purse. He told the rabbis that this was indeed a tragic situation for the captive Jewish widows and orphans and took out an old rusty penny and offered it to Reb Schneur Zalman.

To the surprise of both the man and the other two rabbis, Schneur Zalman took the penny looking very pleased. He invoked God's blessing on the miser and turned to his associates and said it was time to go on to the next house. As they were walking away from the house, the two rabbis turned to Schneur Zalman and asked him how he could accept the penny and not be affronted by the wealthy man's stinginess. Before he could respond, the door of the house opened and the miser ran out, calling the rabbis back. He inquired how much money they needed to free the captives. Schneur Zalman told him they needed to raise five thousand rubles. The man said that he would give them a thousand rubles. Schneur Zalman blessed him profusely, as he had done the first time. The rabbis once again took their leave. The two rabbis turned to Schneur Zalman and exclaimed that a miracle had occurred. He asked them to be quiet once again, and the door reopened.

Calling the rabbis back for a third round, the wealthy man (no longer a miser) promptly told them he had decided to give them the entire sum needed. After they once again left, the rabbis asked Schneur Zalman how he had gotten the miser to give them the funds.

Schneur Zalman explained that he was not truly a miser—no one is. No one had ever accepted a penny from this man before now, seeing it as a sign of insult. The man had simply never experienced what it was like to feel generous. When Schneur Zalman took his gift with gratitude, the man's heart began to crack open.

In just the same way, generosity can work for each of us, opening our hearts and softening the distinction between ourselves and others. Here is another way to hear the lesson: It is told of Rebbe Avraham Yithak of the Toldot Aharon Yeshiva in Jerusalem that, when he was a young man in Karoli, he often went around collecting money for *tzedakah* (charity). Someone whom he approached for a contribution once asked him, "For whom are you collecting?" He answered, "For myself and for you. The money is going to a third person."

When a voice inside wants to hold back your generosity, experiment with ignoring that voice, paying careful attention to your feelings both before and after you decide to act. Try working with the practice instruction to always give when asked. Working with such a practice does not necessarily mean that you always do give when asked—rather, it is held out as a model that you can use to shine light on your heart, accepting the truth of who you are in each moment without harsh judgment. I try giving something to each person I encounter on city streets who asks. I make it a practice to help condition my heart. When I remember, I also try to make eye contact and offer a blessing. If the blessing is all you can offer, that is also generosity. Another practice instruction is to trust your own inclination whenever you have a generous thought. Even when you have second thoughts or doubts about whether to give, experiment with trusting your generous inclination.

The Result of Practice: Deeds of Lovingkindness— *Gemilut Hasadim*

As I have stated throughout this book, it is not sufficient for me if the practices I am describing result in my happiness but have no positive impact on the world around me. I believe that the wisdom and open-heartedness acquired by following these practices naturally leads us to act in the world in helpful and compassionate ways. You may have heard the joke that asks, "What did the Zen priest say to the hot dog vendor?" The answer, "Make me one with everything," reflects the awareness that all things are interconnected. When we see this interconnection directly, we recognize that the suffering of the world is our own suffering as well. There is no separation between the two. And when we see the universality of this suffering that connects us all, our hearts naturally open with compassion for others, and we can't bear the idea of contributing more pain to the world and its inhabitants. This is the supreme motivating force that encourages us to stop acting cruelly to others. Not adding to the suffering of the world is in itself an act of lovingkindness.

It is also important to act in the world in ways that help alleviate suffering, both our own and the suffering of others. An open heart propels us to speak kindly rather than harshly, with patience and understanding rather than with anger. It impels us to act through generosity rather than with greed. I have no doubt that if any one of us were to come across a starving person in our regular, day-to-day lives, we would know instantly what to do and would do it. We would feed them. But because of our fear of the pain we feel in being present to this kind of suffering, we generally live in "antiseptic" conditions that help us avoid seeing that pain. The awakened heart does not fear this kind of pain and is able to meet it, knowing how to respond wisely. While we may not have perfect wisdom and certainty about how to respond, actually seeing the suffering changes everything.

I can't say exactly how you will act out the compassion you will touch. Too many specifics can just become another list of "shoulds" that won't be of great help—or may be a hindrance. I can testify that, with an awakened heart, you will be a better partner, parent, child, colleague, boss, worker, organizer, and friend.

No End, Just a Journey

As this book winds to its conclusion, I want to share some thoughts to help you keep a healthy perspective on the task of living with an awakened heart. I believe we are all on a journey that we take when we incarnate as a human being. The journey is why we are here. A cartoon in the *New Yorker* showed a Bedouin family traveling on camels, with the parents up front followed by three children. The youngest child in the rear is yelling to the head of the family, "Are we almost there?" The head turns around and shouts back, "We are nomads, for crying out loud!" We are all nomads, and the journey is the real story. It is wise not to become attached to reaching any particular destination. When our small mind says we should be doing better already, this causes a tightening of the heart. We have a wonderful example of these principles in the Torah itself. The five books of the Torah describe the journey of the Jewish people, through slavery in Egypt, liberation, and wandering in the wilderness, to the promised land. The five books end before that reentry takes place. I believe this is a message emphasizing the spiritual journey rather than the "happy ending." Life is such a journey, and we are all on it.

I'll remind you of the teaching in *Pirkei Avot* (Principle Ethics) that parallels this profound wisdom:

> Rabbi Tarfon says: The day is short, the task is abundant, the laborers are lazy, the reward is great and the Master of the house is insistent. He used to say: You are not required to complete the task, yet you are not free to desist from it. (*Pirkei Avot* 2:20–21)

Here Rabbi Tarfon begins by pointing out what you most likely have already realized: the work of purifying the heart so that you can stay open and balanced is a full-time task. At times it seems that there is more to do than we can accomplish. We can easily fall into a sense of doom that might make us feel unequal to the task, a sense that we are too lazy. Yet we know that the reward of an open heart is great because we have experienced it from time to time. And we see that life is insistent that we continue our journey. When we stop traveling the path of spiritual growth, we feel stagnant and disheartened. So while Rabbi Tarfon encourages us to never give up, he gives the sage advice that "you are not required to complete the task." It is only in holding the narrow view that we should be farther along or already finished that we lose heart. But when we realize that we need only continue the journey but not complete it, we can then open our hearts to ourselves and continue our journey with ease.

May we all be blessed to accept the journey that we are on, in all its particularity. May we all see that we are traveling this path with each other. And may our hearts stay open and awake as we travel the path in joy.

APPENDIX A

Psalm 145

An Interpretive Translation by Moshe Ben Asher

I exalt You God and guide. I bless Your name for all time.
Daily I'll declare Your fame, till the very end of my life.

I freely praise Your majesty, whose depths I cannot fathom.
It was so for Abraham and Sarah, and all who came after them.

Each generation knows the awe of witnessing Your wonders.
I, too, hushed by creation, davven Your mitzvoth and universe.

We are all struck mute by the length of Your reach,
Surprised to find Your mark in every cell and cosmic space.

Our image of You the highest good, we live in Your righteous law.
You rule with compassion and grace, Your kindness quick, Your
    anger slow.

You're held high in every land, creator of our forgiving world.
We weep in Your compassionate face, yet bless You with faith untold.

In Your grant we give and get, sage and fool both know Your hold.
Even those who say You're not, live as if you mind the world.

We know and trust Your holiness, a sacred imprint on all we see.
Empowering our lifelong struggle to find through You what we need.

Hopeful eyes look beyond Your name to the goodness we make
    together.
Yet all things are in Your hands, from our food to the smallest favor.

O God, You're righteous in every way, the most gracious Divine ruler.
We ask too that You dwell in our hearts, a path of goodness in all we
    live for.

Living in God we have no wants, our spirits are at peace.
We are shepherded and prepared for the challenges we face.

Count me as one who praises God, a blessing for every woman and
    man.
In God lies true and certain good.

Appendix B

Resources for Further Learning

Audio Recording Sources

www.awakenedheartproject.org/podcasts/morning-chants.

Sources of Jewish Movement Practices

Torah Yoga, see http://www.torahyoga.com/.

Ottiyot Chayyot, Living Letters, http://www.otiyot.com/.

Audio files

For talks by the author, Sylvia Boorstein, Norman Fischer, and rabbis Joanna Katz, Alan Lew, and Sheila Weinberg, go to http://www.awakenedheartproject.org/podcasts.

Books

Boorstein, Sylvia. *Happiness Is an Inside Job: Practicing for a Joyful Life*. New York: Ballantine Books, 2008.

———. *That's Funny, You Don't Look Buddhist: On Being a Faithful Jew and a Passionate Buddhist*. New York: HarperOne, 1998.

Buber, Martin. *I and Thou*. London: Hesperides Press, 2008.

Cooper, David A. *God Is a Verb: Kabbalah and the Practice of Mystical Judaism*. New York: Riverhead Books, 1998.

———. *The Handbook of Jewish Meditation Practices: A Guide for Enriching the Sabbath and Others Days of Your Life*. Woodstock, VT: Jewish Lights, 2000.

Davis, Avram, ed. *Meditation from the Heart of Judaism: Today's Teachers Share Their Practices, Techniques, and Faith*. Woodstock, VT: Jewish Lights, 1999.

Eckstein, Menachem. *Visions of a Compassionate World: Guided Imagery for Spiritual Growth and Social Transformation*. Jerusalem: Urim Publications, 2001.

Fischer, Norman. *Opening to You: Zen-Inspired Translations of the Psalms*. New York: Penguin, 2003.

———. *Taking Our Places: The Buddhist Path to Truly Growing Up*. New York: HarperOne, 2004.

Gefen, Nan Fink. *Discovering Jewish Meditation: Instruction & Guidance for Learning an Ancient Spiritual Practice*. Woodstock, VT: Jewish Lights, 1999.

Lew, Alan. *Be Still and Get Going: A Jewish Meditation Practice for Real Life*. Boston: Little, Brown, 2005.

———. *This Is Real and You Are Completely Unprepared: The Days of Awe as a Journey of Transformation*. Boston: Little, Brown, 2003.

——— with Sherril Jaffe. *One God Clapping: The Spiritual Path of a Zen Rabbi*. Woodstock, VT: Jewish Lights, 2001.

Schachter-Shalomi, Zalman. *First Steps to a New Jewish Spirit: Reb Zalman's Guide to Recapturing the Intimacy and Ecstasy in Your Relationship with God*. Woodstock, VT: Jewish Lights, 2003.

———. *Gate to the Heart: An Evolving Process*. Philadelphia, PA: ALEPH, 1993.

Shapira, Kalonymus Kalman. *Conscious Community: A Guide to Inner Work*. Lanham, MD: Jason Aronson, 1996.

Slater, Jonathan. *Mindful Jewish Living: Compassionate Practice*. New York: Aviv Press, 2007.

Notes

Chapter 3: The Nature of Mind

1. Pupul Jayakar, *Krishnamurti: A Biography* (San Francisco: Harper and Row, 1986), 48.
2. Ibid., 68.

Chapter 4: Making the Darkness Conscious

1. Aryeh Kaplan, *Inner Space: Introduction to Kabbalah, Meditation and Prophecy* (New York: Moznaim Publishing Corporation, 1990), 26.
2. Everett Fox, *The Five Books of Moses: Genesis, Exodus, Leviticus, Numbers, Deuteronomy: A New Translation with Introductions, Commentary, and Notes* (New York: Schocken Books, 1983), 15.
3. Ibid., 19.
4. Ibid.
5. Ibid., 33.
6. Ibid., 42.
7. Bereshit Rabbah 9:7.
8. Fox, *The Five Books of Moses,* 20.

Chapter 5: Embracing the Divine

1. Fox, *The Five Books of Moses,* 451.
2. Ibid.
3. Ibid., 452.
4. Ibid.
5. Ibid.

Chapter 6: Prayer and Meditation

1. Fox, *The Five Books of Moses,* 155.

Chapter 8: *L'chayyim*—Into Life

1. Jonathan P. Slater, *Mindful Jewish Living: Compassionate Practice* (New York: Aviv Press, 2004), 26.
2. Sayadaw Ashin Janakabhivamsa (U-Janaka), *Vipassana Meditation Guidelines* (Yangon, Myanmar: Chanmyay Chanmyay Yeiktha Meditation Centre, 1999), 7–8.

Meditation

The Handbook of Jewish Meditation Practices
A Guide for Enriching the Sabbath and Other Days of Your Life
By Rabbi David A. Cooper
Easy-to-learn meditation techniques.
6 x 9, 208 pp, Quality PB, 978-1-58023-102-2 **$16.95**

Discovering Jewish Meditation
Instruction & Guidance for Learning an Ancient Spiritual Practice
By Nan Fink Gefen
6 x 9, 208 pp, Quality PB, 978-1-58023-067-4 **$16.95**

A Heart of Stillness: A Complete Guide to Learning the Art of Meditation
By David A. Cooper 5½ x 8½, 272 pp, Quality PB, 978-1-893361-03-4 **$16.95**
(A book from SkyLight Paths, Jewish Lights' sister imprint)

Meditation from the Heart of Judaism
Today's Teachers Share Their Practices, Techniques, and Faith
Edited by Avram Davis
6 x 9, 256 pp, Quality PB, 978-1-58023-049-0 **$16.95**

Silence, Simplicity & Solitude: A Complete Guide to Spiritual Retreat at Home
By David A. Cooper 5½ x 8½, 336 pp, Quality PB, 978-1-893361-04-1 **$16.95**
(A book from SkyLight Paths, Jewish Lights' sister imprint)

Ritual/Sacred Practice

The Jewish Dream Book
The Key to Opening the Inner Meaning of Your Dreams
By Vanessa L. Ochs with Elizabeth Ochs; Full-color illus. by Kristina Swarner
Instructions for how modern people can perform ancient Jewish dream practices
and dream interpretations drawn from the Jewish wisdom tradition.
8 x 8, 128 pp, Full-color illus., Deluxe PB w/flaps, 978-1-58023-132-9 **$16.95**

God in Your Body
Kabbalah, Mindfulness and Embodied Spiritual Practice
By Jay Michaelson
The first comprehensive treatment of the body in Jewish spiritual practice and an
essential guide to the sacred.
6 x 9, 288 pp, Quality PB, 978-1-58023-304-0 **$18.99**

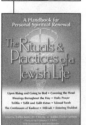

The Book of Jewish Sacred Practices
CLAL's Guide to Everyday & Holiday Rituals & Blessings
Edited by Rabbi Irwin Kula and Vanessa L. Ochs, PhD
6 x 9, 368 pp, Quality PB, 978-1-58023-152-7 **$18.95**

Jewish Ritual: A Brief Introduction for Christians
By Rabbi Kerry M. Olitzky and Rabbi Daniel Judson
5½ x 8½, 144 pp, Quality PB, 978-1-58023-210-4 **$14.99**

The Rituals & Practices of a Jewish Life
A Handbook for Personal Spiritual Renewal
Edited by Rabbi Kerry M. Olitzky and Rabbi Daniel Judson
6 x 9, 272 pp, illus., Quality PB, 978-1-58023-169-5 **$18.95**

The Sacred Art of Lovingkindness: Preparing to Practice
By Rabbi Rami Shapiro 5½ x 8½, 176 pp, Quality PB, 978-1-59473-151-8 **$16.99**
(A book from SkyLight Paths, Jewish Lights' sister imprint)

Or phone, fax, mail or e-mail to: JEWISH LIGHTS Publishing
Sunset Farm Offices, Route 4 • P.O. Box 237 • Woodstock, Vermont 05091
Tel: (802) 457-4000 • Fax: (802) 457-4004 • www.jewishlights.com
Credit card orders: (800) 962-4544 (8:30AM–5:30PM ET Monday–Friday)
Generous discounts on quantity orders. SATISFACTION GUARANTEED. Prices subject to change.

Theology/Philosophy/The Way Into... Series

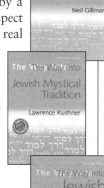

The Way Into... series offers an accessible and highly usable "guided tour" of the Jewish faith, people, history and beliefs—in total, an introduction to Judaism that will enable you to understand and interact with the sacred texts of the Jewish tradition. Each volume is written by a leading contemporary scholar and teacher, and explores one key aspect of Judaism. *The Way Into...* series enables all readers to achieve a real sense of Jewish cultural literacy through guided study.

The Way Into Encountering God in Judaism
By Rabbi Neil Gillman, PhD
For everyone who wants to understand how Jews have encountered God throughout history and today.
6 x 9, 240 pp, Quality PB, 978-1-58023-199-2 **$18.99**; HC, 978-1-58023-025-4 **$21.95**
Also Available: **The Jewish Approach to God:** A Brief Introduction for Christians
By Rabbi Neil Gillman, PhD
5½ x 8¼, 192 pp, Quality PB, 978-1-58023-190-9 **$16.95**

The Way Into Jewish Mystical Tradition
By Rabbi Lawrence Kushner
Allows readers to interact directly with the sacred mystical text of the Jewish tradition. An accessible introduction to the concepts of Jewish mysticism, their religious and spiritual significance and how they relate to life today.
6 x 9, 224 pp, Quality PB, 978-1-58023-200-5 **$18.99**; HC, 978-1-58023-029-2 **$21.95**

The Way Into Jewish Prayer
By Rabbi Lawrence A. Hoffman, PhD
Opens the door to 3,000 years of Jewish prayer, making available all anyone needs to feel at home in the Jewish way of communicating with God.
6 x 9, 208 pp, Quality PB, 978 1 58023 201 2 **$18.99**

Also Available: **The Way Into Jewish Prayer Teacher's Guide**
By Rabbi Jennifer Ossakow Goldsmith
8½ x 11, 42 pp, Quality PB, 978-1-58023-345-3 **$8.99**
Visit our website to download a free copy.

The Way Into Judaism and the Environment
By Jeremy Benstein, PhD
Explores the ways in which Judaism contributes to contemporary social-environmental issues, the extent to which Judaism is part of the problem and how it can be part of the solution.
6 x 9, 288 pp, Quality PB, 978-1-58023-368-2 **$18.99**; HC, 978-1-58023-268-5 **$24.99**

The Way Into *Tikkun Olam* (Repairing the World)
By Rabbi Elliot N. Dorff, PhD
An accessible introduction to the Jewish concept of the individual's responsibility to care for others and repair the world.
6 x 9, 304 pp, Quality PB, 978-1-58023-328-6 **$18.99**; 320 pp, HC, 978-1-58023-269-2 **$24.99**

The Way Into Torah
By Rabbi Norman J. Cohen, PhD
Helps guide in the exploration of the origins and development of Torah, explains why it should be studied and how to do it.
6 x 9, 176 pp, Quality PB, 978-1-58023-198-5 **$16.99**

The Way Into the Varieties of Jewishness
By Sylvia Barack Fishman, PhD
Explores the religious and historical understanding of what it has meant to be Jewish from ancient times to the present controversy over "Who is a Jew?"
6 x 9, 288 pp, Quality PB, 978-1-58023-367-5 **$18.99**; HC, 978-1-58023-030-8 **$24.99**

Spirituality/Lawrence Kushner

Filling Words with Light: Hasidic and Mystical Reflections on Jewish Prayer
By Lawrence Kushner and Nehemia Polen
5½ x 8½, 176 pp, Quality PB, 978-1-58023-238-8 **$16.99**; HC, 978-1-58023-216-6 **$21.99**

The Book of Letters: A Mystical Hebrew Alphabet
Popular HC Edition, 6 x 9, 80 pp, 2-color text, 978-1-879045-00-2 **$24.95**
Collector's Limited Edition, 9 x 12, 80 pp, gold foil embossed pages, w/limited edition silkscreened print, 978-1-879045-04-0 **$349.00**

The Book of Miracles: A Young Person's Guide to Jewish Spiritual Awareness
6 x 9, 96 pp, 2-color illus., HC, 978-1-879045-78-1 **$16.95** *For ages 9 and up*

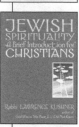

The Book of Words: Talking Spiritual Life, Living Spiritual Talk
6 x 9, 160 pp, Quality PB, 978-1-58023-020-9 **$16.95**

Eyes Remade for Wonder: A Lawrence Kushner Reader *Introduction by Thomas Moore*
6 x 9, 240 pp, Quality PB, 978-1-58023-042-1 **$18.95**

God Was in This Place & I, i Did Not Know: Finding Self, Spirituality and
Ultimate Meaning 6 x 9, 192 pp, Quality PB, 978-1-879045-33-0 **$16.95**

Honey from the Rock: An Introduction to Jewish Mysticism
6 x 9, 176 pp, Quality PB, 978-1-58023-073-5 **$16.95**

Invisible Lines of Connection: Sacred Stories of the Ordinary
5½ x 8½, 160 pp, Quality PB, 978-1-879045-98-9 **$15.95**

Jewish Spirituality—A Brief Introduction for Christians
5½ x 8½, 112 pp, Quality PB, 978-1-58023-150-3 **$12.95**

The River of Light: Jewish Mystical Awareness
6 x 9, 192 pp, Quality PB, 978-1-58023-096-4 **$16.95**

The Way Into Jewish Mystical Tradition
6 x 9, 224 pp, Quality PB, 978-1-58023-200-5 **$18.99**; HC, 978-1-58023-029-2 **$21.95**

Spirituality/Prayer

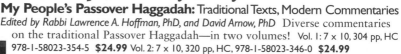

My People's Passover Haggadah: Traditional Texts, Modern Commentaries
Edited by Rabbi Lawrence A. Hoffman, PhD, and David Arnow, PhD Diverse commentaries
on the traditional Passover Haggadah—in two volumes! Vol. 1: 7 x 10, 304 pp, HC
978-1-58023-354-5 **$24.99** Vol. 2: 7 x 10, 320 pp, HC, 978-1-58023-346-0 **$24.99**

Witnesses to the One: The Spiritual History of the *Sh'ma* By Rabbi Joseph B.
Meszler; Foreword by Rabbi Elyse Goldstein 6 x 9, 176 pp, HC, 978-1-58023-309-5 **$19.99**

My People's Prayer Book Series

Traditional Prayers, Modern Commentaries *Edited by Rabbi Lawrence A. Hoffman*
Provides diverse and exciting commentary to the traditional liturgy, helping modern
men and women find new wisdom in Jewish prayer, and bring liturgy into their lives.
Each book includes Hebrew text, modern translation, and commentaries from all
perspectives of the Jewish world.

Vol. 1—The *Sh'ma* and Its Blessings
7 x 10, 168 pp, HC, 978-1-879045-79-8 **$24.99**
Vol. 2—The *Amidah*
7 x 10, 240 pp, HC, 978-1-879045-80-4 **$24.95**
Vol. 3—*P'sukei D'zimrah* (Morning Psalms)
7 x 10, 240 pp, HC, 978-1-879045-81-1 **$24.95**
Vol. 4—*Seder K'riat Hatorah* (The Torah Service)
7 x 10, 264 pp, HC, 978-1-879045-82-8 **$23.95**
Vol. 5—*Birkhot Hashachar* (Morning Blessings)
7 x 10, 240 pp, HC, 978-1-879045-83-5 **$24.95**
Vol. 6—*Tachanun* and Concluding Prayers
7 x 10, 240 pp, HC, 978-1-879045-84-2 **$24.95**
Vol. 7—Shabbat at Home
7 x 10, 240 pp, HC, 978-1-879045-85-9 **$24.95**
Vol. 8—*Kabbalat Shabbat* (Welcoming Shabbat in the Synagogue)
7 x 10, 240 pp, HC, 978-1-58023-121-3 **$24.99**
Vol. 9—Welcoming the Night: *Minchah* and *Ma'ariv* (Afternoon and
Evening Prayer) 7 x 10, 272 pp, HC, 978-1-58023-262-3 **$24.99**
Vol. 10—Shabbat Morning: *Shacharit* and *Musaf* (Morning and
Additional Services) 7 x 10, 240 pp, HC, 978-1-58023-240-1 **$24.99**

Inspiration

Happiness and the Human Spirit: The Spirituality of Becoming the Best You Can Be *By Abraham J. Twerski, MD*
Shows you that true happiness is attainable once you stop looking outside yourself for the source.
6 x 9, 176 pp, Quality PB, 978-1-58023-404-7 **$16.99**; HC, 978-1-58023-343-9 **$19.99**

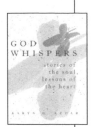

The Bridge to Forgiveness: Stories and Prayers for Finding God and Restoring Wholeness *By Rabbi Karyn D. Kedar*
Examines how forgiveness can be the bridge that connects us to wholeness and peace.
6 x 9, 176 pp, HC, 978-1-58023-324-8 **$19.99**

God's To-Do List: 103 Ways to Be an Angel and Do God's Work on Earth
By Dr. Ron Wolfson 6 x 9, 150 pp, Quality PB, 978-1-58023-301-9 **$16.99**

God in All Moments: Mystical & Practical Spiritual Wisdom from Hasidic Masters
Edited and translated by Or N. Rose with Ebn D. Leader
5½ x 8½, 192 pp, Quality PB, 978-1-58023-186-2 **$16.95**

Our Dance with God: Finding Prayer, Perspective and Meaning in the Stories of Our Lives *By Karyn D. Kedar* 6 x 9, 176 pp, Quality PB, 978-1-58023-202-9 **$16.99**
Also Available: **The Dance of the Dolphin** (HC edition of *Our Dance with God*)
6 x 9, 176 pp, HC, 978-1-58023-154-1 **$19.95**

The Empty Chair: Finding Hope and Joy—Timeless Wisdom from a Hasidic Master, Rebbe Nachman of Breslov *Adapted by Moshe Mykoff and the Breslov Research Institute*
4 x 6, 128 pp, 2-color text, Deluxe PB w/flaps, 978-1-879045-67-5 **$9.99**

The Gentle Weapon: Prayers for Everyday and Not-So-Everyday Moments—Timeless Wisdom from the Teachings of the Hasidic Master, Rebbe Nachman of Breslov *Adapted by Moshe Mykoff and S. C. Mizrahi, together with the Breslov Research Institute*
4 x 6, 144 pp, 2-color text, Deluxe PB w/flaps, 978-1-58023-022-3 **$9.99**

God Whispers: Stories of the Soul, Lessons of the Heart *By Karyn D. Kedar*
6 x 9, 176 pp, Quality PB, 978-1-58023-088-9 **$15.95**

Restful Reflections: Nighttime Inspiration to Calm the Soul, Based on Jewish Wisdom
By Rabbi Kerry M. Olitzky & Rabbi Lori Forman 4½ x 6½, 448 pp, Quality PB, 978-1-58023-091-9 **$15.95**

Sacred Intentions: Daily Inspiration to Strengthen the Spirit, Based on Jewish Wisdom
By Rabbi Kerry M. Olitzky and Rabbi Lori Forman 4½ x 6½, 448 pp, Quality PB, 978-1-58023-061-2 **$15.95**

Kabbalah/Mysticism

Awakening to Kabbalah: The Guiding Light of Spiritual Fulfillment
By Rav Michael Laitman, PhD 6 x 9, 192 pp, HC, 978-1-58023-264-7 **$21.99**

Seek My Face: A Jewish Mystical Theology *By Arthur Green*
6 x 9, 304 pp, Quality PB, 978-1-58023-130-5 **$19.95**

Zohar: Annotated & Explained *Translation and annotation by Daniel C. Matt; Foreword by Andrew Harvey* 5½ x 8½, 176 pp, Quality PB, 978-1-893361-51-5 **$15.99**
(A book from SkyLight Paths, Jewish Lights' sister imprint)

Ehyeh: A Kabbalah for Tomorrow
By Arthur Green 6 x 9, 224 pp, Quality PB, 978-1-58023-213-5 **$16.99**

The Flame of the Heart: Prayers of a Chasidic Mystic *By Reb Noson of Breslov. Translated by David Sears with the Breslov Research Institute* 5 x 7¼, 160 pp, Quality PB, 978-1-58023-246-3 **$15.99**

The Gift of Kabbalah: Discovering the Secrets of Heaven, Renewing Your Life on Earth
By Tamar Frankiel, PhD 6 x 9, 256 pp, Quality PB, 978-1-58023-141-1 **$16.95**
HC, 978-1-58023-108-4 **$21.95**

Kabbalah: A Brief Introduction for Christians
By Tamar Frankiel, PhD 5½ x 8½, 208 pp, Quality PB, 978-1-58023-303-3 **$16.99**

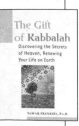

The Lost Princess and Other Kabbalistic Tales of Rebbe Nachman of Breslov
The Seven Beggars and Other Kabbalistic Tales of Rebbe Nachman of Breslov
Translated by Rabbi Aryeh Kaplan; Preface by Rabbi Chaim Kramer
Lost Princess: 6 x 9, 400 pp, Quality PB, 978-1-58023-217-3 **$18.99**
Seven Beggars: 6 x 9, 192 pp, Quality PB, 978-1-58023-250-0 **$16.99**

See also *The Way Into Jewish Mystical Tradition* in Spirituality / The Way Into... Series

About Jewish Lights

People of all faiths and backgrounds yearn for books that attract, engage, educate, and spiritually inspire.

Our principal goal is to stimulate thought and help all people learn about who the Jewish People are, where they come from, and what the future can be made to hold. While people of our diverse Jewish heritage are the primary audience, our books speak to people in the Christian world as well and will broaden their understanding of Judaism and the roots of their own faith.

We bring to you authors who are at the forefront of spiritual thought and experience. While each has something different to say, they all say it in a voice that you can hear.

Our books are designed to welcome you and then to engage, stimulate, and inspire. We judge our success not only by whether or not our books are beautiful and commercially successful, but by whether or not they make a difference in your life.

For your information and convenience, at the back of this book we have provided a list of other Jewish Lights books you might find interesting and useful. They cover all the categories of your life:

Bar/Bat Mitzvah	Life Cycle
Bible Study / Midrash	Meditation
Children's Books	Parenting
Congregation Resources	Prayer
Current Events / History	Ritual / Sacred Practice
Ecology / Environment	Spirituality
Fiction: Mystery, Science Fiction	Theology / Philosophy
Grief / Healing	Travel
Holidays / Holy Days	12-Step
Inspiration	Women's Interest
Kabbalah / Mysticism / Enneagram	

Stuart M. Matlins, Publisher